THE COMING OF FRENCH ABSOLUTISM

THE STRUGGLE FOR TAX REFORM IN THE PROVINCE OF DAUPHINÉ 1540–1640

The introduction of absolutism in France has conventionally been seen as a process of centralization imposed from the top down. The Crown, the chancellor, the principal ministers, and the secretaries of state are all supposed to have worked in concert to break the power of the nobles and governors, abolish local Estates, and even intervene in the selection of municipal councillors. The fiscal and institutional development of the province of Dauphiné, however, suggests a very different absolutist dynamic. While it is clear that the Crown wanted to standardize and, when possible, centralize the institutions of the province, it is equally clear that, from the 1540s on, certain groups anxious for provincial tax reform actively encouraged royal intervention.

Daniel Hickey analyses the individuals and groups that directed each stage of the struggle for tax reform: rural villagers, the élite of the ten major cities, lawyers and legal groups, and new and old nobles. Each group expressed itself through the means available to it: peasant revolt, courtroom hearings, local village meetings, or lobbying at court.

The social alliances made during the struggle were temporary in nature and often united groups that would normally have been opposed to each other. But they were effective. Hickey identifies two major results of this social movement: the Crown was able to take major steps towards integrating Dauphiné into the kingdom, and the province's fiscal structure underwent a major reform.

DANIEL HICKEY is chairman of the Département d'histoire-géographie, Université de Moncton.

DANIEL HICKEY

The Coming of
French Absolutism:
The Struggle for Tax Reform in
the Province of Dauphiné
1540–1640

UNIVERSITY OF TORONTO PRESS
Toronto Buffalo London

© University of Toronto Press 1986
Toronto Buffalo London
Printed in Canada

ISBN 0-8020-5676-8

Printed on acid-free paper

Canadian Cataloguing in Publication Data

Hickey, Daniel
The coming of French absolutism

Bibliography: p.
Includes index.
ISBN 0-8020-5676-8

1. Taxation – France – Dauphiné – History.
2. Dauphiné (France) – History. 3. Dauphiné (France) –
Economic conditions. 4. Despotism. I. Title.

HJ2669.D3H53 1986   336.2'05'094496   C86-093639-2

Cover illustration French Gate, Grenoble, part of the right-bank fortifications built by Lieutenant-Governor Lesdiguières in 1620. The engraving was executed towards the middle of the seventeenth century by Israel Silvestre, le jeune, and Gabriel Perelle.
Source: Bibliothèque municipale de Grenoble, Pd 4.73

This book has been published with the help of grants from the Social Science Federation of Canada, using funds provided by the Social Sciences and Humanities Research Council of Canada, and from the Faculty of Arts, Université de Moncton.

FOR HÉLÈNE, CHANTAL,
ERIC, AND JEAN-PIERRE

Contents

Illustrations

Preface

The writing of this book began twelve years ago with the presentation of my doctoral thesis on the socio-economic structures of the Valentinois-Diois region of Dauphiné during the French Wars of Religion. The thesis was submitted and defended before the History Department of McGill University in 1973. During the ten years from 1973 to 1983 I totally reworked the manuscript, enlarging its scope to cover the whole province of Dauphiné and, more importantly, integrating the structural socio-economic analysis more fully into the chronological and narrative history of the province. The integration of the thematic and narrative approaches presented numerous problems, for long-term social and economic evolutions are difficult to place within a fixed, relatively short-term chronological framework. The emergence of French absolutism in Dauphiné and the struggle for tax reform became the vehicles for integrating the two approaches. These two important aspects of the history of Dauphiné converge during the period 1540–1640, and they provide a time-frame and a variety of types of confrontation within which numerous long-term thematic problems can be treated, issues such as town-village relations, the evolution of the urban elite, the difficulties confronting the provincial tax system, and the political problems of Crown intervention.

Each of the different steps involved in the production of this book entailed revisions, reworking of hypotheses, a return to old data, and the collecting of new evidence. At each of these stages I received considerable aid from numerous colleagues, students, and friends, to all of whom I owe a debt of gratitude. Two scholars deserve special mention, for they had a considerable influence on my work. The first was the director of my PH D thesis, Pierre Boulle. Throughout the four years of

research and writing of the thesis as well as during the subsequent revisions, he posed questions and problems that often reoriented my research or led me to seek further material to support my hypotheses. He
also insisted upon the rewritings with which I became so familiar in the
later stages of manuscript preparation. The second person who has
constantly stimulated me through his suggestions and friendly criticism
is L. Scott Van Doren of Boston College. An expert in the history
and institutional complexities of sixteenth-century Dauphiné, Scott Van
Doren gave me access to his large collection of transcripts of the sessions
of the Dauphiné Estates. During a very agreeable three-week period that
I spent in Boston in 1977, he helped me to understand the functioning
of the military and civil institutions of the province. Since that time he
has continued to provide me with advice on the manuscript.

My research in the archives of the province was aided constantly by
the advice of Vital Chomel, *directeur* of the Archives départementales de
l'Isère. One of the most knowledgeable specialists in the history of early
modern Dauphiné as well as in the difficult paleography of the sixteenth
century, Chomel introduced me to manuscript-finding aids, record series, and documents that were invaluable to my research. When I left
France, he and Janine Roger-Lucet, *documentaliste*, continued to provide
me with references, photocopies, or microfilms from their holdings.
Pierre-Yves Playoust, Danielle Robert-Lebis, Gérard Ermisse, and Gérard
Vidal were among the other archivists who expedited my work. Back in
Canada the staff of the Bibliothèque Champlain at the Université de
Moncton relentlessly searched out interlibrary loans for me.

In the succession of manuscript revisions I was aided by my good
friend Dominic Martini and by my colleague Serge Morin. They read
and commented in detail upon stylistic, historical, and logical problems
that showed up in the manuscript. Susan Kent of University of Toronto
Press provided me with invaluable editing advice.

These last twelve years of research, writing, and revision have been
funded by numerous sources. First and foremost is the Social Sciences
and Humanities Research Council of Canada, which provided me with
a two-year research grant from 1979 to 1981. The Conseil de recherche
of the Université de Moncton also contributed to my research in 1975
and 1977. Finally, the Social Science Federation of Canada and the
Faculty of Arts of the Université de Moncton accorded me grants for
the publication of the manuscript. The present volume could not have
been produced without the aid of these institutions.

THE COMING OF FRENCH ABSOLUTISM

Introduction

The introduction of absolutist government[1] into France has generated much discussion and debate. Historians have disputed the chronology of absolutist interventions, their philosophical and juridical origins, and the roles of the men and ministers who used them as vehicles for imposing royal power upon provincial and local governing structures. Most of these historians have treated the leaders of local and provincial spheres of government only in terms of their resistance to each new attempt at centralization. The object of this book is to demonstrate that such local leaders were far from being a homogeneous social group with the clear goal of resisting new royal initiatives in their fields of jurisdiction. The book will approach the significance of the roles these local leaders played by focusing on the problems that confronted them in the province of Dauphiné, the first major French province into which the new absolutist institutions were introduced. The period under study extends from the middle of the sixteenth century, when the king was trying with great difficulty to reduce the independence of the governor of the province, up to the 1630s, when Crown financial districts (*élections financières*) were imposed, intendants were sent in, and the provincial Estates was suspended. The central issue confronting local leaders in Dauphiné during this period was the attempt by the third estate to reform the provincial taxation system, and the implications of this issue eventually dictated the position of the province on the long series of hesitant efforts at centralization initiated by the Crown or its agents.

The debate over the initiatives to introduce absolutist structures in France has been dominated by three major historiographical movements, the institutionalists, the socio-economic historians, and the school of *les Annales*. The underlying contention of the first group has been that absolutism was an essential step in the building of the modern French state. J.H. Mariéjol, in the monumental Lavisse *Histoire de France*, spoke of the 'restoration' of government under Sully and Richelieu. He organized his treatment of the reigns of Henry IV and Louis XIII around the refunding of the national debt, the financial operations aimed at stabilizing government accounts, and the 'grand design' of Sully, all of which Mariéjol saw as leading up to the 'new spirit' of government under Cardinal Richelieu.[2] To carry out such fundamental reforms, according to Mariéjol, the cardinal 'stripped' the old intermediary authorities of a part of their power and replaced them with a new, 'more dependent and docile personnel.'[3] Richelieu moved against the 'excessive powers' of the old nobles, the *parlementaires*, the provincial Estates, and the municipal governments. And yet, in Mariéjol's opinion, even with the initiatives of Sully and Richelieu there remained a great deal more to be done before the absolute power of the French Crown could be established. Though the monarchy appeared to be absolutist, he argued, the privileges granted to the different classes, to the provinces, and to the king's own officials still constituted 'obstacles' to the proper functioning of the system.[4]

If the Mariéjol approach reflects too clearly the nineteenth-century view of the merits of the progress of state building, institutionalists have more recently placed greater emphasis upon the slow, evolutionary nature of the building up of royal power. These historians have noted the important role of several new or revitalized institutions that became key elements in the march towards increasingly centralized government. The Conseil du roi was one of them. Georges Pagès, Roger Doucet, Noël Valois, and Roland Mousnier have all shown that from the end of the sixteenth century there was a decisive movement within the Conseil du roi to divide up responsibilities among the principal ministers of the Crown. The Conseil des affaires, Conseil d'état, Conseil des finances, and Conseil privé, the four traditional sections of royal household government, were given increasing independence, and the areas under their jurisdiction became greater and better defined.[5]

This bureaucratization of the principal source of power in the kingdom was often accomplished by increasing the responsibilities of the principal Crown officials. Doucet argues that it was the chancellor whose authority increased the most rapidly in the course of the sixteenth century. The position was filled by important jurists and legal experts such as Michel de l'Hôpital and Antoine DuPrat, both of whom were important advisers to the king. At the same time the number of secretaries of state who worked under the chancellor was increased and their functions were defined more clearly. This centralization of power in the chancellery even continued during the Wars of Religion, and it permitted the Crown to communicate with every corner of the kingdom.[6]

Institutional historians have also noted that during the late sixteenth century the monarchy began to create instruments by which it could intervene to enforce its edicts and to inform the central government of local problems. Important among these were the Crown commissions that were sent out into the different provinces from time to time under Henry II. The personnel for these assignments was drawn alternatively from the Parlement of Paris and the *maîtres de requête* of the Hôtel du roi. The recruitment, mandates, and missions given to these commissioners bore a close resemblance to those established a century later under Richelieu when he named intendants of justice and of the army.[7]

The increase of Crown powers at the expense of the sovereign courts, the Estates, provincial institutions, and municipal councils created tensions. With the notable exception of J.R. Major, who has done considerable work on the organization and structure of local governments, institutional historians tend to limit their examination of these tensions to the debates of the royal councils. Georges Pagès and Gaston Zeller have both described the running controversy in the Conseil du roi between the traditionalist ministers who felt that the Crown should try to collaborate with existing provincial and local institutions and the centralists who felt that it was necessary to impose royal officials and central controls upon all lower levels of government. Both Sully and Richelieu are obviously placed within the latter group.[8] According to most of the institutionalists, the views of Sully and Richelieu prevailed during each crisis situation. In his article on the 1603 effort to impose financial elections upon Guyenne, J.R. Major argues that by the early 1600s the royal government had already established a clear plan to impose elections in all of the remaining *pays d'état* in the south of France.[9]

In partial reply to the emphasis of these theses on the bureaucratic origins of absolutism came the remarkable study by Orest Ranum of the Richelieu administration. It showed that under Richelieu the real exercise of power passed not through ministeries of Crown agencies but through lines of patronage, through 'clients' and 'creatures.'[10] The dependence upon family and kinship links has been demonstrated further by Richard Bonney in his study of the intendants created in France under Richelieu and Mazarin.[11] However, well before the discussion of kinship and patronage as limitations upon the bureaucratic development

of the seventeenth-century state, a second major historiographical movement was already concentrating upon social and economic change in
order to unravel another side of the institutional role of absolutism. By
examining long-term serial data in the social, economic, and judicial
fields, this school of historians demonstrated that the absolutist process
was constantly hindered by structural *blocages*.

One of the first to look specifically at the limits of the absolutist state
was Roland Mousnier. In his monumental study of the practice of office
selling in France under Henry IV and Louis XIII, Mousnier showed that
this new practice was characterized by a certain institutional advancement
when compared to feudal traditions, but also by serious limitations when
compared to modern bureaucratic government. The sale of offices had
the advantage of providing the king with immediate and important financial resources. After 1604, when the *paulette* was introduced, officeholders who wished to assure the right to bequeath their offices to their
descendants paid an additional annual tax. Mousnier argues that, besides
providing revenues, this system also broke with the feudal concept that
offices should be distributed according to the power of the officeholder
within the feudal structure. During the fourteenth and fifteenth centuries nobles or non-nobles had been awarded offices because they represented an important power base within the kingdom or within different
regions. Further, most major officials in the kingdom presided over a
series of minor positions, and this permitted them to distribute patronage
appointments to their followers and relatives. Since the structure was
based upon such pyramid relationships, it became very difficult to revoke
major appointments or to choose successors outside the family of the
officeholder without creating considerable friction.[12]

For Mousnier the sale of offices, which had become a current practice
by the end of the sixteenth century, placed the bureaucratic organization
of the kingdom upon a new footing. Offices became the private property
of those who had the means to acquire them and to pay the annual tax.
They no longer constituted a feudal power-base for their holders. While
the *paulette* did not assure a competent modern civil service, it did eliminate the previous tendency of the great nobles to build up a clientele
within Crown jurisdictions. According to Mousnier the nobles generally
did not have the capital necessary to acquire the new positions. The
bourgeois who did buy them were more easily manipulated by the Crown,
at least at the beginning. Richelieu further tried to confirm and extend
royal primacy over officeholders through edicts removing positions from
individuals and groups who resisted royal policies. Through such means

the Crown tried to 'depoliticize' officeholders, rendering them more obedient and submissive to its authority. This policy, however, encountered regular resistance from officials, resistance that culminated in the Fronde.[13]

In his pioneering work Mousnier concentrated on who and what social categories had acquired the newly created offices. His analysis of the purchases of offices in Normandy demonstrated that the immediate social origins of the new officials were to be found far less among the merchant and commercial bourgeoisie than historians have often presumed. In fact the new positions were most often acquired by men who were already Crown officials, tax farmers, or negotiators. There were, of course, purchases by minor nobles who had realized profits from their estates and by the legal milieu of *procureurs* (solicitors), *avocats* (lawyers), and the like.[14] Mousnier maintained that rather than increasing the number of sons and direct descendants of merchants who became Crown officials, sale of offices served frequently to concentrate the new positions in the hands of an official bourgeois class:

The purchasers of offices are generally men enriched through service to the king, through tax farms and special duties: or men who lived nobly on their fiefs and their domains and who built up their fortunes by collecting feudal and seigneurial dues, by granting loans to peasants, and by different forms of placements, often peasants, managers of domain lands, and usurers; and naturally the men of the law, jurists, solicitors, lawyers. All of them could retrace their fortunes to usury and not to productive activities. They had been socially whitewashed [*decrassés*] before obtaining their offices by services to the king, directly through financial services, or indirectly through fiefs and seigniories.[15]

This model of advancement argues that the bourgeoisie through its financial and social dealings was solely responsible for its social and economic rise and that the members of the official bourgeoisie were eventually able to concentrate considerable political power in their own hands and to negotiate their future directly with the Crown. It was precisely this notion of the 'whitewashed' newcomers' imposition of their own bourgeois values upon the state that became the subject of a polemic between Mousnier and the Russian historian Boris Porchnev. To develop his thesis Porchnev turned away from the discussions of Crown policy, the evolution of royal institutions, and the concept of state building. In a major work first published in the Soviet Union in 1948 he analysed the long series of popular revolts that decimated France between 1623 and 1648.[16] Porchnev underscored the repressive fiscal yoke that lay behind the 'spontaneous' uprisings in both the towns and the country-side. He went further. The 'revolutionary situation' in that period cre-ated an underlying class conflict in which the bourgeois groups, after momentarily siding with the masses, were attracted eventually towards the feudal-absolutist system because of the basic desire to protect their economic situation and because of their vested interests in the favours that the Crown was ready to bestow upon them, such as ennoblement and offices. Mousnier saw them buying into the public power and im-posing their bourgeois values upon royal policy, but Porchnev considered them to have been already committed to the existing feudal power struc-ture before they obtained their offices. For him their committment to the existing government structure was evident because they bought up rural holdings, sought titles, and became integrated into the existing mode of agricultural production.[17] Rather than the bourgeois transfor-mation of royal structures argued by Mousnier, Porchnev proposed that a rehabilitated feudal system had absorbed the new officeholders and become the new social basis for exercising absolutist power.

Numerous historians have fuelled the Mousnier-Porchnev debate.[18] Most have limited themselves to interpreting the causes of the popular disturbances. Yves-Marie Bercé, one of Mousnier's former students, has demonstrated that there was a multitude of reasons for the popular eruptions in the southwest of France. Though most of them were gen-erated in a direct or indirect way by fiscal questions, other factors did provoke popular response. Passing troops and the insecurity of wartime, harvest failures, reductions of traditional peasant access to the forest, hunting rights, the introduction of any new tax, be it of seigneurial, clerical, or Crown origin, and the arrival of any new officials in the community were all among the many reasons for these revolts.[19] In a similar study of revolts in Provence, René Pillorget, like Bercé, empha-sizes the role of the towns or rural communities in the face of any new outside initiative, and further explores the social bases of local protest movements. To Pillorget revolts in Provence were not simply sponta-neous reactions of the peasants and the *menu peuple* of the towns to outside initiatives but were frequently manifestations of local social prob-lems. Jealousy between competing family clans or between local groups divided over fiscal and social issues could easily spark outbreaks, but at the same time such jealousies created irreparable divisions in the com-munity. In Provence none of the risings against absolutist initiatives attained the dimensions of those in Normandy or the southwest because, according to Pillorget, local social conflicts made it difficult for communities to present united opposition to the new Crown policies.[20]

Going beyond the problem of the disturbances, another Russian historian, A.D. Lublinskaya, has returned to some of the hypotheses of the Porchnev-Mousnier debate. Concerning the Porchnev premise of a class conflict, she refuses to concede that France in the first half of the seventeenth century constituted a truly revolutionary situation, because capitalism was not developed sufficiently to confront the feudal system. For her the popular revolts only represent reactions against structural *blocages* and short-term 'crises.'[21] Further, she provides an important conceptual framework for an understanding of the role of the bourgeoisie. She contends that there were, in fact, two bourgeoisies: the 'official' bourgeoisie and the 'commercial' bourgeoisie. Mousnier and Porchnev concentrated their debate on the official class because they saw this group on its way to constituting the nobility of the robe and sharing in the public power of the kingdom. Lublinskaya, however, distinguishes a second group, which was drawn from the merchants, traders, and artisans. She agrees with Porchnev that the official bourgeoisie was on its way to becoming integrated into the feudal-absolutist system through its acquisition of landholdings and titles, but she maintains that the commercial bourgeoisie through its involvements in trade and commerce retained its distinctive identity. She emphasizes that, in the course of the repetitive financial crises that affected late sixteenth- and early seventeenth-century governments, advocates of French absolutism sought to establish close links with the commercial bourgeoisie. The Crown often sought to aid this group through protectionist economic policies in return for its support of Crown efforts to implant and stabilize the new initiatives against the great nobles, the Huguenots, and the forces of provincial autonomy.[22]

The problem with the Mousnier-Porchnev discussion, just as with the discussions of the institutionalists, is that they have seen all policy initiatives as emanating from above. All of these historians focus upon the introduction of new and powerful men into the major offices of the royal government, men who had family and financial connections that tied them solidly to the most mobile social groups and linked them to the new Crown policies. These policies produced regular royal interventions in provincial and village life, generating the local resistance and revolts that punctuated early seventeenth-century French history. In the works of most of these historians the discussions of the popular revolts constitute the only treatments of the situation in the provinces of the regions.

And for most of them these revolts were mere reactions to the policies that had been imposed from above.

In contrast to these views, the third of the major historiographical groups, the school of *les Annales*, has produced some of the most important studies of absolutism by analysing its development 'from below.' The Annalistes concentrate their work upon economic tendencies and the repercussions of those tendencies upon the other components of society. They have very rarely discussed institutional structures, and they have reinterpreted what others have seen as absolutism, characterizing it instead as a process of state building in which economic, social, and political forces interact continually. In a recent essay Pierre Chaunu argues that progressively 'the state acquired supreme power to command, order, force, and dictate the law and to impose durable structures upon the society.'[23] The power of a monarchy at any given moment, he contends, is determined by its population, its fiscal resources, the extent of its bureaucracy, and the size of its military. But, he adds, none of these criteria is as important as financial resources.[24]

As this structuralist approach defines them, the financial resources of a state depend upon its land surface, demographic evolution, agricultural production, distribution network, and fiscal and social organization.[25] The study of these factors has allowed the Annales school to demonstrate that the state-building process at the beginning of the seventeenth century was characterized far more by structural *blocages* than by progressive advances. The fiscal structures were still marked by the fundamental division between *pays de taille réelle* and *pays de taille personnelle*; the great majority of the French revenues still remained with the seigneur or the *curé*; agriculture was depressed; and the demographic structures were stagnating. Further, important sectors of the French economy were still dominated by Italian capital. Very rarely at the grass-roots level of the kingdom do we see reflections of the bureaucratization that has so preoccupied the institutional historians.

In recent studies Pierre Goubert and Denis Richet have made remarkable attempts to apply the Annales methodology to French institutions. Both of them have challenged the continual upward spiral of the state-building thesis that underlies both the institutionalist position and the Mousnier approach. Denis Richet has demonstrated that there were periods during which royal institutions advanced at the expense of parlements, provincial institutions, local governments, and social orders, but there were other periods when local resistance halted and in some cases reversed the Crown initiatives. Though royal institutions advanced noticeably between 1492 and 1559, new initiatives brought uneven results between 1559 and 1653. The Wars of Religion, the regency of Marie de Médicis, and the Fronde slowed down or compromised attempts to extend royal authority.[26] Goubert has gone even further and shown how royal institutions were limited throughout the *ancien régime* because their powers were shared with hundreds of local levels of government. The state itself was limited by the participation of the nobles and the local Estates in the legislative field. Judicial power was limited not just by the parlements but by the local and regional courts of the *bailliages*, *élections*, *maîtres des eaux et forêts*, *présidiaux*, by the provincial financial structures of the *chambres des comptes*, *cours des aides*, *cours des monnaies*, or by the jurisdictions of towns and villages. Goubert sees no real breakthrough in the social and economic structure of the kingdom until after 1750, and only after 1789 a renewal of the institutional framework.[27]

It is very significant that many of the more recent historical works on absolutism have underlined the difficulties of changing or suppressing local and provincial institutions. Up to now there have been few efforts made to clarify the causal relationships between events outside the royal court and the installation of absolutist government in the different provinces of France. Within this perspective the province of Dauphiné constitutes an important case study. In the seventeenth century Dauphiné was the first major *pays d'état*, or province with its own representative assembly (Estates) and legal and fiscal structures, in which the Crown succeeded in imposing *élections financières*. In these fiscal districts Crown officials were made responsible for levying all the taxes, or *tailles*, requested by the king.[28] This procedure removed the traditional right of provincial Estates to debate royal requests for funds, to vote the imposition of all or part of the requested levy, and to petition the Crown concerning their grievances. The installation of *élections* was followed by the suppression of the Dauphiné Estates and by the organization of a reduced representative mechanism that had no financial powers.

Six years after the *élections* were imposed, the fiscal system of Dauphiné was also altered by the Crown. All of the lands in the province were ordered to be entered in *cadastres*, or land registers, and classified either as noble holdings on which *tailles* were not to be imposed or as *roturiers*, tax-paying possessions. The privileged social groups of the province thereby lost exemptions for their recent and all their future acquisitions of *roturier* land. The province was transferred from the status of a region where elements of a *taille réelle* structure cohabited with elements of the *taille personnelle* system. It became explicitly a *pays de taille réelle*, provoking a change that Vital Chomel has described as 'a fiscal revolution probably without precedent in the annals of the *ancien régime*.'[29]

How did this change come about? How was the French monarchy able to carry out two such fundamental transformations in the institutional structure of one of the most independent of the French provinces?[30] One of the important keys to answering this question lies in the *taille* controversy, a long-term challenge to the fiscal system employed in the province. This controversy broke out in the 1540s and lasted until well after the taxation system was altered in 1639. It was not a challenge directed towards a single policy or even spearheaded by a single group. At different periods different aspects of the *taille* system were objects of attack. Different social groups directed each stage of the movement, and even the methods of contestation differed. Cahiers of grievance addressed to the king alternated with bitter exchanges in the provincial Estates. A full-scale popular revolt demanded changes in the *taille* system in 1579, while a series of courtroom debates before the Conseil d'état marked the period between 1599 and 1602. Finally, the *taille* question became the rationale for sending royal commissioners into the province during long periods in the early 1600s.

This book will concentrate upon the links between local movements to reform the provincial tax structure and Crown initiatives to impose absolutist government in Dauphiné. Within this context it will consider the relevance to Dauphiné of each of the models proposed by the different historiographical movements to explain the coming of absolutism. It will approach the role of political institutions by linking the different royal initiatives to the evolution of power relations within the province, in order to determine the extent to which the new institutions were unilaterally imposed upon Dauphiné. The social structure of the province will be studied, using the conclusions produced in studies of other regions of France concerning the different groups that supported and benefited from absolutism. Finally, the fiscal structure of Dauphiné will be analysed for the critical period during and after the Wars of Religion, especially in the light of the attempts of the Crown to increase its tax revenues through numerous ad hoc initiatives and eventually through the royal decisions to install *élections financières* and to transform Dauphiné into a *pays de taille réelle*.

These aspects of the three major historiographical theses concerning absolutism will be developed within the framework of the different stages of the *taille* or tax controversy. The aim of this approach is to test the extent to which the *taille* conflict modified the long-term institutional and socio-economic evolution of Dauphiné as compared to that of the other French provinces. Were the same institutional and socio-economic influences at work in Dauphiné as elsewhere? In the final analysis, what made Dauphiné the first major *pays d'état* to lose its independent institutions and to be integrated into the new absolutist state during the seventeenth century?

The sources for such research in Dauphiné are plentiful. On the institutional side, the archives in Dauphiné and in Paris contain documentary sources that shed light on the internal quarrels that marked the period: deliberations of the provincial Estates, correspondence, pamphlets, and legal pleas concerning the *taille* dispute, letters exchanged between the royal chancellery and the commissioners and intendants sent into the province, and a multitude of royal edicts. At the same time a wide variety of serial sources can be used to test the theses of the social and economic historians: landholding records, *taille* rolls, registers of ennoblement, and the sales of offices. These records permit an evaluation of the degree of social or economic mobility that was possible. They also help to identify eventual obstacles to such mobility, providing keys to the actions of the different groups that confronted each other over the *taille* question. The existence of such rich material for the province of Dauphiné provides a useful opportunity to evaluate the three principal historiographical explanations for the introduction of absolutism in the provinces. It permits the adoption of a critical approach to the rigid explanations proposed both by the institutionalists and by the socio-economic historians. Even more important, it allows for the testing of new explanations of and hypotheses concerning the beginnings of absolutism in France.

1

Prelude to the *Taille* Affair

Towards the middle of the sixteenth century the first signs of the *taille* controversy coincided with the attempt by the Crown to reduce the independent status of Dauphiné while the provincial elite struggled to maintain its institutions. Dauphiné, a *pays d'état*, had been acquired by France in 1349 as a result of the bankruptcy of the dauphin Humbert II. Complete control of the province had been assured during the centuries that followed by the acquisition of the counties of Valentinois and Diois in 1404 from the dauphin's vassal, Louis de Poitiers, and by the addition of a number of feudal enclaves, such as Montélimar and Tallard, during the late fifteenth and early sixteenth centuries.[1]

The 1349 transfer of Dauphiné to the French Crown, or the *transport*, as it was officially called, had been marked by the negotiation of a special status for the province. In the text of the *transport*, the French Crown accepted the Statut delphinal, a document issued by Humbert II two weeks before the *transport*. The *statut* confirmed the 'liberties' of the people of Dauphiné as well as the territorial integrity of the province. More importantly, the *statut* guaranteed the maintenance of existing provincial institutions: Estates, Conseil delphinal, and Chambre des comptes. In the finest feudal tradition, the *statut* granted the nobles the right not only to build and maintain fortresses but also to fight private wars and to limit their military service to the Crown. Equally important, the document assured the *roturiers* of the province that the dauphin would continue to respect their immunity from all regular direct taxation.[2]

In spite of the liberties guaranteed in 1349, the following two centuries were marked by continual tension as the Valois monarchs tried to reinterpret or ignore major provisions of the *statut*. Their efforts were char-

acterized by contradictory actions. Though they established new hierarchical links by imposing more effective bureaucratic institutions upon
the province, they carried out strategic retreats when the wrath of the
nobles, the parlement, or the king's own advantage warranted. Both of
these tendencies were most evident during two reigns, that of Louis xi,
particularly in his years as Dauphin Louis ii, and under Francis i.

The institutional reforms of Louis ii centred upon the judicial and
financial elements of provincial administration. In the judicial sphere he
transformed the Conseil delphinal from an advisory body of eminent
nobles into the parlement, or supreme court of the province. Competent
jurists such as Mathieu Thomassin and Guy Pape were attracted to the
new provincial parlement, and a chancery office was organized to write
and dispatch their directives to the *baillis* and *sénéchaux*, the judges of
the district courts who had been the local representatives of the old
Conseil delphinal. The districts of these regional judges, the *bailliages*
and *sénéchaussées*, were reduced from eight to three, and each court
therefore became more important within the juridical hierarchy of the
province (see Map 1).[3] Below them Louis organized the courts of the
châtelains, who were also royal appointees and to whom seigniorial ver-
dicts could be appealed. In the financial sphere, the existing Chambre
des comptes was retained as the pre-eminent fiscal court of the province,
and its powers were extended to include the right to examine local
accounts. There was some erosion of its responsibilities, however, in that
the accounts of the *trésorier général* of Dauphiné were made subject to
re-examination by the Paris Chambre des comptes for all 'extraordinary'
income, such as *tailles*, or grants accorded to the Crown by the Estates.[4]

The changes carried out by Louis ii were concerned principally with
strengthening central institutions in the province at the expense of the
nobles and local privileged groups. During the reign of Francis i, however, it became clear that the French Crown had decided to reduce the
independent status of the province itself. Against the advice of the provincial Estates, the Edict of Abbeville was issued in 1539. It declared that
Dauphiné was to be ruled and governed by the same 'laws and statutes
as the other parts of the kingdom.'[5] As a consequence of this edict the
Crown moved into established provincial jurisdictions. It set the salaries
of members of the parlement and the tariffs for judicial proceedings. It
regulated the length of lawyers' pleas and the quota of notaries authorized for the province. It required the use of French in all official documents. More important, the powers of the parlement of Dauphiné were

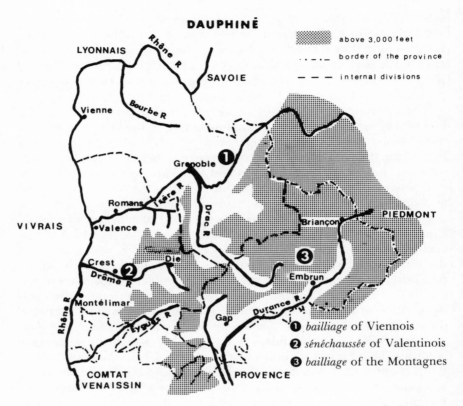

Map 1 The province of Dauphiné in 1601, showing relief, the three principal administrative divisions, and the ten recognized cities

reduced and those of seigniorial courts even more so.[6] On the financial side the province progressively lost control of its right to coin money; a long series of royal edicts beginning in 1530 and ending in 1553 turned this right over to the *trésorier général* of France.[7] All these changes demonstrated a clear erosion of the feudal, local, and individual liberties that had been guaranteed to the inhabitants of the province at the time of the *transport*.

The attempts to centralize the bureaucracy and to render it more efficient were accompanied by tactical retreats. The Crown resorted to feudal methods of patronage, established 'client' networks, and granted local rights whenever it became expedient. This tendency can be seen in Louis's nominations of *châtelains*. Rather than auctioning off leases to the Crown châteaux, as had been prevailing practice, he awarded them to his most trusted men for specific periods of time. One of the dauphin's closest aides, Jean d'Armagnac, held simultaneously the posts of *maréchal* of Dauphiné, *sénéchal* of the Valentinois, and *châtelain* of Crest.[8] The possession of key châteaux throughout most of the province permitted the dauphin to exercise considerable control over the judicial apparatus, over the implementation of edicts registered in the parlement, and over the decisions rendered by the seigniorial courts.

Local rights were also strengthened when it suited the designs of the monarch. In 1447, when Louis II acquired the key city of Montélimar from the pope and the Adhémar family, he was determined to show its inhabitants and its municipal council all the advantages that they had acquired through the transaction. To do this Louis lavished favours upon the city, designating it as a judicial seat of the *sénéchaussée* of Valentinois, creating two additional fairs in May and November, and re-establishing it as a salt depot.[9] Louis also adhered to his promise to respect the traditional liberties of the city, including the commitment not to levy *tailles*. In 1452 he intervened to invalidate the demand of the Estates and the Chambre des comptes, which had ordered the municipal council to pay its share of the *taille* levy. In 1462 the courts reaffirmed the Montélimar exemptions. In a 1467 edict Louis confirmed that Montélimar had at the time of its annexation been promised exemption from *tailles* because it was located in the county of Venisse of the principality of Orange, an area that had always been exempt from *tailles*.[10] The opportunistic Louis II, known as the 'Spider King' after he acceded to the French throne as Louis XI, had no qualms about stating that he would respect the *taille* immunity promised to Montélimar at the same time that he was violating it for the rest of the province.

During the reign of Francis I, strategic retreats were no less evident. The Edict of Abbeville was followed by a long series of temporary arrangements that conceded the right of the parlement to set legal fees and enlarge the number of towns where the *baillis* could hear cases.[11] Francis also maintained traditional exemptions for Montélimar, Gap, and Crest, all the while increasing the amounts and the regularity of *tailles* levied upon other towns of the province.

In the midst of this see-saw struggle between central and provincial institutions, the *taille* controversy broke out. The costs of the prolonged Italian wars increased the weight of provincial impositions and placed considerable strain upon the antiquated and unjust fiscal structures of Dauphiné, a province that had been promised exemption from all regular tax levies. Despite the Statut delphinal guarantee, Charles VI and Charles VII had attempted almost immediately to impose *tailles* upon the province. Their attempts had always been contested, and only in 1447 did the dauphin Louis II address himself directly to the contradictory problem of levying *tailles* upon a province that had been guaranteed exemption. Louis recognized that the *statut* prohibited the imposition of regular *taille* levies in the province, but he argued that subsidies and *dons gratuits* were not regular levies. He held that the Dauphiné Estates should accord these impositions in cases of need. On the question of the complaints of the third estate against the numerous privileges and exemptions built into the system, Louis promised that in the future all but nobles 'living nobly' and clerics 'living clerically' would be expected to pay the impositions.[12]

The subsequent regularity of the demands for subsidies and *dons gratuits* demonstrated that they were merely *taille* levies in disguise. By 1484 even the Estates accepted to pay an annual levy of twenty thousand *livres*. This represented a compromise, since the Crown had demanded annual payments of more than twenty thousand *livres* on several occasions. The levy agreed upon was not excessive, and until the Italian wars of Francis I and the integration of new extraordinary levies into the regular *taille*, these taxes aroused little protest.[13] A similar gap became evident between Louis's promises to limit the exaggerated exemptions permitted by the tax system and continuing taxation practices. Traditionally, nobles, their legitimate heirs, and clerics were exempted from *taille* levies. The legal decisions of the fifteenth-century jurist Guy Pape make it clear, however, that as a result of numerous privileges and precedents accepted in the past, exemptions could be claimed legally by other groups; these included officials of the parlement and Chambre des comptes, medical doctors, university regents and professors, *avocats consistoriaux*, officials of the provincial mints, town and village consuls, and non-nobles who had purchased or leased a noble holding and occupied it for at least twenty years.[14]

Even more numerous were the cases where powerful individuals used their social and economic positions to force illegal claims to tax exemptions upon local town councils. Immigrants who claimed to possess noble status at their places of origin, the illegitimate children of nobles and clerics, and the sons of officials who had been ennobled because of their positions but whose titles were not hereditary were among those who held self-declared exemptions. Perhaps the most important exemption of all, however, was the claim of well-to-do townspeople that taxes could be imposed upon them only at their place of residence and not in each village where they held property.[15]

The *taille* assessment system as it was applied to Dauphiné definitely discriminated against the villages. In contrast to the towns, the great majority of villages did not possess written assessment rolls (*cadastres* or *compoix*). The absence of such registers stemmed from the fact that the legal system of most of the province followed the Germanic tradition of customary law. Accordingly, tax assessments and exemptions were based upon the social status of each property owner at the time the *taille* was levied; a *roturier* paid the *taille*, while a noble, a cleric, or an owner benefiting from an exemption was not subject to *taille* levies. Everything depended upon the personal status of the owner, and the system resembled the *taille personnelle* imposed in northern France. This individually oriented method of assessment differed from that of Provence, Languedoc, and the *bailliage* of the Montagnes in Dauphiné.[16] These areas applied the *taille réelle* system, which was derived from written codes based upon Roman law. Under the *taille réelle* all village property was listed in a register (*cadastre*) at a given date and classified as being owned by nobles or *roturiers*. Thereafter the property was exempt or taxed on the basis of its initial classification, regardless of any later change in the social status of its owner.

Village residents did not enjoy a stable taxation system. Their contributions to each provincial levy represented a fixed proportion calculated according to the *feux* enumerations that had been carried out in the middle of the fifteenth century. The *feux* for each community had been assigned on the basis of the number of inhabitants and the amount and quality of taxable landholdings. However, the key to taxation instability was the acquisition of taxable holdings by exempted or privileged groups who escaped *tailles*. Since village quotas remained fixed, tax rates on individual *roturiers* increased proportionately whenever any part of the village holdings became exempt. In the event that nobles or beneficiaries of tax-exempt status acquired large amounts of *roturier* land in a certain village, that land was excluded from the tax roll, and the remaining taxpayers were required to make up the difference.

Even though the townspeople, unlike the nobles, were clearly subject to the *taille*, their purchases of land in the villages had a similar effect upon village taxes. It was claimed traditionally that one could not be taxed more than once. Townspeople insisted that the rural property they acquired should be taxed at their principal place of residence. Their rural holdings were, therefore, listed in special supplements to the town *cadastres*, called *forains*. This method had two advantages for townspeople: first, there was always the possibility of concealing rural purchases from city assessors and paying no taxes on one's rural property; second, even if the property was listed and taxed, it constituted an addition to the town's fiscal resources that had not been calculated in the *feux*. It widened the tax base of the town without increasing its assessment and therefore lowered the *taille* rate for each unit of town property value. For the villages, the purchases of land by townspeople had the inverse effect: their acquisitions were subtracted from rural *cadastres* just as were those of the nobles and exempted groups. As a result of this whole process, village assessments on the same piece of *roturier* property could vary considerably from one decade to another, and taxation tended to fluctuate in inverse proportion to the fortunes of surrounding nobles, clerics, exempted groups, and urban residents.

By the middle of the sixteenth century the *taille* levies occasioned by the French expeditions in Italy had increased dramatically. Normal levies of around 41, 51, or 61 *livres* for each *feu* were multiplied by five, ten, and twenty. These increases occurred in two stages: first in the 1530s, when Francis I imposed forced loans that soon became regularized as extraordinary levies to support twenty thousand and eventually fifty thousand foot-soldiers, then when a second extraordinary levy was imposed in the mid-1540s. By the beginning of the religious wars the fifteenth-century levy of 20,000 *livres* a year had increased to a minimum imposition of 47,658 *livres*. The creation of the extraordinary levies provides a further indication of the type of unilateral intervention in provincial affairs practised by the French Crown.[17] The amounts of the new extraordinary taxes were far more substantial than the regular ordinary levies.

The new wave of *taille* increases provoked a movement to readjust the fiscal levies in such a way that the privileged and exempted groups maintained and even extended their exemptions. The levy for each *feu* increased from 8 *livres* in 1535 to 20 in 1536, to 58 in 1537, and to 80 in 1538,[18] and assessments became more and more unjust. The town of Montélimar, which had been placed on regular *taille* rolls in 1525 and 1527, argued that such impositions had been forbidden by the treaty of annexation through which the town had become an integral part of Dauphiné. Montélimar's contention was upheld eventually in letters issued by Francis I in 1539 and by an agreement reached at the Estates of 1542. The 1542 document stipulated that the town was to pay any military costs, such as for garrisons and passage and quartering of troops, but was to be exempt from all other levies.[19] Crest, Gap, and Embrun were among other towns that benefited from similar exemptions.[20] In a second category the nobles and clerics, although exempt from regular *taille* levies, had contributed traditionally to extraordinary taxes. In 1529, at the time of the *grande crue* for the ransom of the king-dauphin, the levy was distributed only among *roturiers* and a few of the exempted groups. In succeeding years the few members of the privileged orders who paid the 1529 imposition went before the parlement to be discharged from the obligation to contribute to such levies in the future.[21]

The same sort of manoeuvre to escape taxes was undertaken by the walled towns in 1542. At the Estates of that year they asked for changes in the structure of the specific taxes designed to maintain the 1,500 troops stationed in the province. Up to that point each town had been responsible for quartering and nourishing the troops stationed within its walls. The town representatives at the Estates argued that this was unfair, since the troops served all the province. In 1542 they succeeded in passing a measure by which the maintenance of a garrison in a walled town would be assured by tax levies upon the inhabitants of the surrounding countryside as well as upon the town residents.[22] Thus, at a point when extraordinary levies became heavier and heavier, their full weight became more and more concentrated upon the rural *taille*-paying groups.

Between 1540 and 1543 the weight of the *taille* levies was reduced considerably, and the full effect of the reapportionments was not felt until the second wave of extraordinary taxes, which were added to the *taille* between 1543 and 1546. From levies of 6 or 9 *livres* per *feu* between 1540 and 1542, the rate increased to 64 *livres* in 1543, 53 *livres* in 1544, and 45 *livres* in 1545.[23] The pressure placed upon the population by such *taille* increases was aggravated by the fiscal readjustments, which increased the relative burden placed upon the rural areas. In addition, the poor harvests and exceptionally high grain prices in 1543, 1544, and 1545 created general economic difficulty.[24] It was in this context that there developed a concerted effort among the villages to reduce the privileges and exemptions that had exaggerated the weight of rural *tailles*.

Blocked by a 1538 decision of the provincial Estates from unilaterally taxing certain exempted groups,[25] several villages in the mid-1540s turned to the judicial branch of the government. They lodged an official request before the parlement of Grenoble to register all *roturier* property in *cadastres*. Such action was most clearly directed against the rural exemptions accorded to townspeople, since the nobles and clerics would have remained exempt even with the introduction of *cadastres*. This concentration upon the rural acquisitions of town residents reflects the fact that cities such as Grenoble, Valence, Vienne, Romans, Crest, and Montélimar were the generators of economic activity for their surrounding regions.[26] The considerable interest of their residents in acquiring rural holdings seems to have provoked the contestation movement in the villages.[27]

This context was particularly clear at the 1547 Estates. Claix, Jarrie, and Montbonnot, three villages in the Grenoble region, engaged *avocat* De Dorne to contest the exaggerated weight of *tailles* in the rural areas. De Dorne even went beyond the question of *tailles*, arguing that impositions for maintaining troops and garrisons had impoverished the village residents and led them to sell their holdings to town residents. His arguments were aided by the intervention of the president of the parlement, Bellièvre, who asked the Estates to deal with the rural problem. Bellièvre noted that in the past few years the courts had received numerous complaints from villages concerning the distribution of tax levies and the fact that town residents were purchasing more and more rural holdings on which they refused to pay taxes.[28]

The information available on property acquisitions in the village of Montbonnot, one of the leading centres of the contestation, demonstrates that there was considerable interest in rural land among exempted officials from the surrounding area. In the 1540 *dénombrements*, or lists of property owners, and in the 1541 acts of *homage* for Montbonnot, sizable exempted holdings were owned by two councillors to the king who were *avocats* in the parlement, by one of the presidents of the parlement, Joffre Carle, and by the *auditeur* in the Chambre des comptes. Smaller holdings had been acquired by an *avocat* and notary and by four clerics. All were from Grenoble.[29]

Following the complaints of Claix, Jarrie, and Montbonnot, a committee of the Estates was named by the representatives of the towns and villages to study the question. The only solution it could offer was to undertake a re-evaluation (*revision*) of the *feux* in order to redefine the tax base. Acting as spokesman for the committee, the *vicaire* of Valence contended that without a total revision of the tax base it would be impossible to measure the amount of the old *feux* estimate that should be deducted from each village and added to each town to compensate for the rural purchases of town residents. He proposed that the revision be made at the least expense possible and that it respect all of the traditional privileges of each order, including the principle that townspeople could be taxed only at their place of residence.[30] Despite hesitations on the part of the representatives of the towns, the conclusions of the committee were accepted by a plurality of votes.

Dussert, one of the leading historians of the Dauphiné Estates, considers that despite the committee recommendation to revise the tax base, the underlying decision to maintain all aspects of the existing tax structure constituted an unacceptable solution for the rural areas. He notes that in 1547 the quarrel between towns and villages had not yet become vehement, and the fact that each of them chose representatives of the first two estates to form the negotiating committee shows their willingness to accept some form of a compromise. However, the resulting decision undermined the confidence of the villages in the privileged orders. By deciding to maintain exemptions on rural property owned by townspeople, to continue taxing the villages for the upkeep of town garrisons, and to retain the traditional exemptions for the nobles, clerics, and tax-exempt groups, the committee sided decisively with the towns.[31]

A year later no action had been taken on the recommendations of the 1547 committee. The Italian struggle continued, and Henry II had again asked for a sizable *taille* levy. The 1548 Estates were held during the period when the king was to pass through Grenoble on his return from Italy. The village demands for changes in the system of *taille* levies were again on the agenda. Prior to the meeting each group chose representatives to defend its case.[32] Since the expenses of third-estate representatives were not paid by the Estates, village delegates received approval for a series of local meetings in each *bailliage* to collect funds to pay their expenses and at the same time to consult the other villages on the strategy and arguments to be presented.[33]

The meeting with Henry II produced results. Two months after meeting the Estates the king issued an *arrêt* in which he tried to correct certain injustices of which the villages had complained. In the decision, rendered before the Conseil privé, Henry ordered that the *feux* should be revised but that the revision should incorporate the principle that townspeople were to pay taxes on all rural property that they had acquired in the last thirty years. The *arrêt* further ordered that neither clerics nor nobles should use their exemptions to buy or hold *roturier* property on behalf of others, the king thus responding to village complaints that the bourgeoisie frequently purchased property under the cover of noble exemptions. Finally, the edict specified that any future changes in the existing tax structure that might involve heavier taxes should be submitted to the governor of the province before being presented to the Estates so that he could determine whether the change affected all or merely one of the estates and therefore who should bear the weight of the tax. This clause was intended to respond to the third-estate complaint that traditional town expenses were being placed in the *universel*, or general provincial levy, and being charged to the villages.[34]

Reactions to the decision were divided. The towns were furious. In the first of several attempts to annul the *arrêt*, they appealed its provisions before the parlement of the province. The villages were more satisfied, and they accelerated their meetings and consultations to try to work out a system by which the *arrêt* could be implemented and through which the *feux* could be revised most easily and accurately.[35] The 1548 decision marks two important initiatives: first, that the Crown had gone above the head of the provincial institutions and had interceded directly in favour of the villages; and second, that despite the differences in their social and political weight, the towns and villages were to be treated on the same fiscal footing. The new alliances that eventually resulted from this decision upset the traditional power structure, in which the Estates had been seen as the supreme arbiter of provincial affairs and the representatives of the three orders in the Estates had generally reached some form of compromise on every issue.

After the 1548 decision the villages of the province viewed the king as their protector, and this view was reinforced in 1550, when, in letters patent concerning the edict of 1548, Henry recommended that the villages be given permission to name a *commis*, or representative from each *bailliage*, to assist at the accounting sessions that followed each meeting of the Estates. In the past at these sessions representatives of the towns and privileged orders had divided up the *taille* levy that had just been voted among the different towns and villages of the province; they then continued to sit in order to collect payments. The villages had long contended that since they were not represented at these sessions of the *commis*, the towns and privileged orders assigned them the heaviest load of the tax levies. At their 1550 meeting the Estates grudgingly accepted the royal recommendation and accorded permission for each *bailliage* to elect a representative to assist at the accounting sessions, but they stipulated that this permission was accorded only for 1550 and should not establish a precedent.[36] In fact, the position was not renewed at the following session.[37] Thus, it became clearer and clearer to the rural

communities that the king was their natural ally and that the provincial
elite was not. Their realization of this state of affairs was demonstrated
in the 1550s, when they appealed regularly beyond the Estates to the
king and sent and maintained numerous delegations at the royal court
to argue their cases.

The other result of the 1548 decision was that the town residents,
who up to that point had benefited from a special tax category for their
rural possessions, were placed in the same fiscal category as the other
roturier groups. Within the provincial Estates the towns were the most
important members of the third estate: they dominated third-estate representation at the meetings of the Estates; they named the *commis* who
sat for the third estate on the standing committee of the Estates, and
they formed the Assemblée des villes, which could speak for their order
between the full meetings of the Estates. Up to 1548 the towns had
hesitated to undertake or even to participate in any outright attack upon
the *taille* structure or upon the exempted groups, since they too possessed
a privileged fiscal status. But after 1548 the major towns of Grenoble,
Vienne, Valence, and Romans began to re-evaluate their own position.
They saw commonality of interest with other members of the third estate
in the problem of the declining tax base, a decline that became more
and more critical as tax levies became heavier.[38] For the first time one
of the major components of the provincial Estates began to adopt an
attitude of clear opposition to the other two orders. This new role of
the towns led to a destabilization of the social consensus that had permitted the harmonious functioning of provincial institutions. The towns
began to assume a leadership role in the agitation for the introduction
of *cadastres* throughout the province. In practical terms their actions were
oriented towards obtaining a reduction in the number of those eligible
to hold exemptions. Their particular targets were the *avocats consistoriaux*
of the parlement and the other officials who benefited from exemptions
as a result of their functions.

The third-estate challenges to the two privileged orders are not evident in the minutes of the Estates for 1550 and 1551. The contestation,
however, seems to have started during those years. In 1550 the third-
estate leaders sent delegations to Provence and Languedoc to look into
the legal implications of the *taille réelle* as applied in those provinces.
Assemblies were held in the towns and *bailliages* to approve, finance, and
co-ordinate these new initiatives. Finally, in December of that year a
mission composed of an *avocat*, town councillor, and village merchant
was sent to the royal court to seek the king's intervention.[39]

In 1551 the king, reacting to this pressure, threatened to intervene if the province did not try to resolve the problem of the excessive tax levies imposed upon the third estate. In the face of this direct threat it was decided that the provincial Estates of 1552 would take up the matter.[40] On 4 March the *procureur général*, François Roux, introduced the question, noting that the issues that divided the Estates over the *taille* problem threatened to bring the intervention of outside forces into provincial affairs. Such intervention, he argued, might have unfortunate consequences upon the ability of Dauphiné to maintain its independent laws and customs. In the ensuing discussion it was decided to form a committee of arbitration composed of four distinguished individuals named by the first estate, four by the second estate, and eight by the third estate.[41] Apparently showing their continuing desire to co-operate with the privileged groups to reach a negotiated settlement, the third estate nominated a mixture of lawyers and members of the second estate. After four days of deliberations the committee was unable to reach an agreement. They decided to continue discussions with the view to try to present a solution to the Estates the following year. They asked that in the meantime no innovations, such as *cadastres*, be introduced by any of the groups involved in the dispute, that no new delegations be sent to the king or the governor, and that no illegitimate assemblies be convened.[42]

While these discussions were taking place to try to settle the dispute, the third estate remained divided internally by the town-village problem. Romans and its surrounding villages could not agree on the revisions and transfers to be carried out in their *feux* evaluations in the light of the 1548 decision. After a lengthy discussion in the Estates the *procureur du pays*, along with a representative elected by the towns and one elected by the villages, was mandated to meet with both parties concerned in order to negotiate an acceptable re-evaluation of the *feux* in the region.[43]

At the 1553 Estates the double dispute between the towns and villages and between the third estate and the privileged orders continued to dominate discussions. On the town-village issue it was decided that the existing agreements between the two parties should remain in effect until the next Estates. On the question of the third-estate protest concerning the purchases of village property by nobles and clergy and the increasing number of tax exemptions granted to officials, the three estates worked out a compromise proposal. The agreement accepted the lands purchased by the nobles as tax exempt, and it proposed that the exemptions accorded to the *docteurs d'université* and to the *avocats consistoriaux* be limited strictly to four *docteurs* and twelve *avocats*. In addition it stipulated that these exemptions were *personnelle* – that is, they were to apply only to the property that the *docteurs* or *avocats* acquired during their lifetimes and under no condition should the exemptions be extended to their families or heirs.[44] The *avocats* perceived the threat to their social status and ambitions. Most of them counted on transforming the exemptions granted during their lifetimes either to permanent exemptions or to a form of ennoblement that would benefit their families and heirs. They attacked the agreement immediately. The parlement heard their appeal and suspended application of the settlement. The duke of Guise, governor of Dauphiné, agreed to delay application of the compromise until the Estates of 1554.[45]

In response to this setback the towns sent Ennemond Charvet and Gabriel Loyron, councilmen at Grenoble and Valence, to appeal to the king. At the royal court they seem to have concentrated their efforts upon convincing the duke of Guise of the merit of their case.[46] Locally, town and village representatives held numerous assemblies to consider new moves by the third estate and to support the actions of their delegates at court. It appears, however, that the *avocats* acted directly through the *procureur* of the province. The *procureur* advised the king of the legal problems connected with the proposal to alter the tax status of the *docteurs* and *avocats*, and on 4 August the king accepted the *procureur's* advice. He upheld exemptions for the *docteurs* and *avocats*, but he specified that the clerics should pay the *taille extraordinaire* for their *roturier* holdings.[47]

In the midst of this controversy the Dauphiné Estates were convened at Grenoble for the beginning of February 1554. In the absence of the minutes of this meeting it is difficult to evaluate exactly what transpired. We possess only a copy of the agreement on the *taille* question, which was adopted by a majority vote and became the basis for the eventual settlement. In that document the third estate accepted officially the principle of personal *taille* exemptions for nobles and for officials – members of the parlement, *avocats consistoriaux*, *procureurs généraux*, members of the Chambre des comptes, correctors, controllers, clerics, secretaries, the treasurer, and the *receveur général*. This exemption applied to present and future acquisitions both in towns and in the countryside.

The delegates to the third estate also lost ground on the question of clerical exemptions. In 1553 they had obtained clauses that rendered the property of all non-noble clerics *taillable* and that prevented future acquisition of *roturier* property by tax-exempt clerics. In 1554 exemptions were confirmed for the holdings of church foundations and livings, but chapels, colleges, and religious and charitable orders were to sell their rural lands within the next two years or they would be transferred automatically to the village parishes. Individual priests who benefited from canonical exemptions were to pay no taxes for their personal holdings, but those who did not possess such immunity were permitted to hold only a house and garden exempt of taxes. The only concession by the privileged orders was that all nobles and clerics were to be taxed for reparations on community walls, bridges, fountains, public roads, and so on. Finally, the third estate reserved the right to continue its legal contestation of *avocats consistoriaux* and *docteurs d'université*, but it renounced the concessions that it had obtained in the 1553 proposal.[48]

It is difficult to explain the third estate's sudden reversal of its position between the short-lived agreement of 1553 and the so-called 1554 *transaction*. Its representatives' acceptance of the principle of the *taille personnelle* system in 1554 undermined their whole argument on the *taille* question. The pamphlets published by third-estate leaders during the late 1590s and early 1600s proposed two explanations for this about-face: either the nobles had stacked attendance at the meeting or force had been used to compel the representatives of the third estate to sign the document.[49] As for the question of attendance, it is clear from the list of representatives who voted the *transaction* that the nobles in attendance or voting by proxy had assured their order of almost a controlling vote; there were twenty-eight nobles, fifteen clerics, most of whom were nobles, and seventeen representatives of the third estate.[50] Attendance at these meetings had always varied considerably from one year to another depending on the interests of the orders in the questions to be discussed. In 1549, when the villages were particularly interested in pursuing their 1548 victory, twenty-six village representatives were listed in attendance at the Estates.[51] In 1551 'many individuals' claiming to represent villages arrived at the Estates without the required credentials, and the assembly voted by a 'plurality' to admit them.[52] It appears therefore that the stacking of the 1554 meeting alleged and contested by the third estate in the pamphlets produced in the 1590s revolved around the presentation of proxy votes by the nobles. In fact the vote simply reflected the use of procedure by the nobles, since they had the right to send a majority of delegates to the Estates. They presumably decided to use this majority to put an end to the *taille* discussion.[53] There does, however, appear to be evidence that force or coercion was used to obtain passage of the *transaction*. Dussert notes that in addition to the repeated accusations of noble intervention contained in the pamphlets, the minutes of the Grenoble town council meetings for February 1554 mention official protests against the intimidation used in the Estates.[54]

Third-estate reactions to the 1554 *transaction* were contradictory. Dussert notes that in this mood of pessimism town-village divisions resurfaced and towns began to quarrel among themselves over third-estate objectives. For Grenoble, where the *avocats consistoriaux* resided, the question of obtaining the repeal of their exemptions was primary, whereas Valence with its university and Valence and Vienne with their numerous clergy argued that the exemptions accorded to the *docteurs d'université* and to the clerics should receive far more attention.[55] By contrast, Chorier, a seventeenth-century historian and president of the Chambre des comptes, who reflected the attitudes of the upper classes, wrote that after the 1554 *transaction* the determination of the third estate to win its case was even greater than before.[56]

In fact, both reactions seem to have co-existed. Dussert finds evidence of the increasing internal divisions in the registers of town council meetings, but to all outward appearances the third estate and especially the towns continued to present a vigorous common front. During the month of February 1555 Grenoble, Vienne, Valence, and Romans began planning strategy and produced in reaction to the 1554 *transaction* a counter-proposition that was presented to the bishop of Embrun, the representative of the third estate at the *taille* negotiations.[57] The document conceded the totality of the exemptions that had been recognized for the nobility and the members of the parlement and the Chambre des comptes in the 1554 *transaction*. The new document differed, however, in its treatment of two problems: quotas for *avocats consistoriaux* and the *docteurs d'université*, and the question of arbitration in disputes between different estates.

For the *avocats consistoriaux* and *docteurs d'université* the towns demanded that the type of quotas agreed to in the 1553 compromise should be respected and the number of avocats benefiting from exemptions should be limited to twelve, elected and named by the parlement. As for the *docteurs*, the towns conceded ten exemptions; six at the Université de Valence and four at the Université de Grenoble. This figure represented six more than had been conceded in 1553. The question of arbitration was also important, given the number of disputes that had arisen between towns and villages and between seigneurs and communities after the order to revise the *feux*. The document proposed that the cost of such arbitration should be paid out of the general funds of the province (*l'universel*) and not exclusively by the third estate.[58]

In order to obtain these new demands the third estate dispatched Jean Laurent and M de Combes to the royal court, where they met with the governor of the province, the duke of Guise, in June.[59] They reported that Guise had told them that this was the first time he had heard their arguments against the exemptions held by the *avocats* and *docteurs*.[60] Despite the *transaction* Guise was anxious to pacify the third estate, and to this end he appointed his lieutenant-governor, the duke of Clermont, to head a new commission to arbitrate the affair.[61] The commission met on the second of December 1555 and was again unable to propose a solution that would satisfy the increasingly divided parties. Finally, after all the meetings and commissions had failed to produce an acceptable compromise, the duke of Guise asked that all the documents relating to the case be sent to the royal court. Once again it became clear that the ultimate decision was to come from the king. Henry II promised to study the different court judgments, the minutes of the Estates, and the proposals of the different conciliation committees and to pronounce on the matter by the end of May.

In the Edict of Fontainebleau, published in June 1556, Henry restated the numerous efforts that had been made to resolve the problem. He then listed the articles of the settlement upon which he had decided. In addition to the articles contained in the 1554 *transaction*, which entrenched the principle of exemptions for nobles and clerics, the 1556 edict retained the idea of quotas for official exemptions, although these quotas were far more generous than the third estate had proposed: twenty-one *avocats consistoriaux* and twelve *docteurs d'université* were to benefit from exemptions. In the concessions that were made, the clergy were the group most affected. They were declared exempt in principle from ordinary *tailles*, but they were to contribute for their rural holdings to all extraordinary levies. Non-noble clergymen were to be taxed on the basis of all their holdings for any expense of common interest to the community. Finally, the edict restated the obligation of all nobles and clerics to contribute, along with the third estate, to all *tailles* for the maintenance of walls, roads, bridges, fountains, community ovens, and so on.[62]

The process of fiscal centralization was also extended in the 1556 edict. The king profited from the occasion to widen the scope of ordinary *tailles*. In the future, military taxes for the *augmentation de la solde* and funds granted to local garrisons and for the *commutation des utencilles*, originally a tax to furnish linen and utensils to the soldiers, were to be added to the regular provincial *tailles*.[63] Further, in addition to declaring that the third estate alone was subject to *tailles*, the edict automatically increased the weight of those *tailles* by reducing the number of individuals subject to the new and heavier impositions. The decision had a devastating effect upon the third-estate leaders. They had already experienced some difficulty in mobilizing their forces after the setback they had received in 1554, and the 1556 edict broke the back of the contestation. With the exception of a brief resurgence in 1560[64] the *taille* struggle remained subdued until its second major offensive in the 1570s.

Over and above the fiscal motivations to escape or reduce the ever-increasing tax levies, the *taille* question reflected the breakdown of the social hierarchy that dominated the institutions of the province. The 1548 decision consecrated the transfer of the town elite from the protected and partially exempted social categories to the same fiscal level as the other *roturier* groups. Given the privileged place held by the towns within the institutions of the province, the new role of town leaders as opponents of the traditional fiscal structure upset the social harmony that had previously existed within the institutions of Dauphiné. It paved the way for the social polarization that became so evident in the 1570s, in the 1590s, and in the early part of the seventeenth century.

In the past, peace and harmony among the diverse social groups represented in the Estates had been maintained by compromises proposed by the clergy and nobility. This operational pattern broke down in the case of the *taille* dispute, for clergy and nobility were in precisely those groups that had the most to lose. The clergy and nobility stood firm; they refused to budge in the face of rural and town pressures, and their rigidity forced the Crown to intervene more and more regularly in the affairs of the province. In short, in the face of important tax increases each order stood defiantly for its own interests, paving the way for royal initiatives and undermining the provincial liberties that the three estates claimed to defend. This struggle over taxation ended momentarily with the 1556 edict, but the fragmented social order that resulted from the first stage of the *taille* confrontation became a permanent fixture of the provincial Estates and one of the major elements of social division during the civil and religious wars.

Royal interventions into provincial jurisdictions in early sixteenth-century Dauphiné ran the gamut of opportunities available to centralize political and fiscal power despite the conditions stipulated in the treaty by which the province had been acquired by the French Crown. The first series of interventions was directed at restructuring the internal institutions of Dauphiné; later interventions sought to submit these reformed institutions to the checks and controls of Paris-based structures. At every turn, however, these initiatives were met by the resistance of provincial, seigniorial, and municipal bodies, such that the Crown was involved in a continuing series of negotiations, compromises, and legal manoeuvres aimed at blocking new policies. The *taille* dispute introduced a powerful element of discord into the group that up to that time had presented a unified front in the face of Crown interventions. In the late 1540s and throughout the 1550s municipal, seigniorial, and clerical institutions became the scene of confrontations between groups whose particular interests were at stake and groups that constantly appealed over the heads of local and provincial bodies. The king was asked and virtually forced to intervene in 1548 and 1556 because of the incapacity of provincial institutions to produce a compromise acceptable to all the parties involved. The dangers of the appeals over and above the Estates and parlement of the province were evident even to contemporaries and were underlined by the *procureur général* at the 1552 Estates. The king became established clearly as the arbiter of all problems and was seen by some elements of the third estate as their protector. Thus, rather than having to force its reorganizations and interventions upon hostile provincial institutions, the Crown was henceforth offered a pretext to intervene and to reform provincial laws and institutions.

In contrast to the movement of absolutism as it has been studied by historians who focus upon its rise within the Conseil du roi, the chancellery, or the Parlement of Paris, in the case of Dauphiné, it is clear, the occasions for the king to intervene were opened up within provincial structures. In the continuation of the *taille* struggle during the second half of the sixteenth and the beginning of the seventeenth centuries, provincial institutions remained ineffective, and the Crown became more and more involved in provincial jurisdictions as it tried to resolve the different facets of the dispute.

2

The Crisis of 1579:
A Historiography of Taxes,
Social Protest, and Rebellion

The Wars of Religion in Dauphiné (1560–98) were aggravated by the occupation of the Rhone Valley by the forces of the Catholic League in 1589 and by the invasion of upper Dauphiné by the duke of Savoy in 1591.[1] In the midst of these conflicts, in 1579–80, the *taille* controversy flared up again, suddenly and most spectacularly. Stimulated by the excesses of the war years and in particular by the exorbitant fiscal demands of the military machine, the new series of contestations led to two distinct types of protest. The first was characterized by legal initiatives and cahiers of grievances submitted through official channels. These were debated within the institutional structures of the province and kingdom. The second began as a defensive alliance among rural villages and culminated in a popular revolt. It fused peasant leagues with the artisans and *menu peuple* of the towns in a violent confrontation with the official governing structure.

This period of the *taille* controversy has attracted the attention of numerous historians: Lacroix, Romans, Dussert, Cavard, and more recently Vital Chomel, Le Roy Ladurie, and L. Scott Van Doren.[2] Most of them have analysed the implications of the popular revolt and referred only secondarily to the *taille* conflict. Nevertheless, three convergent aspects of their theses are of considerable importance to the fiscal protest: first, the role of the fiscal squeeze in provoking the contestation; second, the part played by the local elites in renewing the legal protest movement; and finally, the origins and the social composition of the popular revolt that shook the province in 1579–80.

It is L. Scott Van Doren who has produced the most original research upon the first of these points, the fiscal origins of the contestation. Van Doren's examination of the official *taille* levies leads him to argue that

as armed confrontation became increasingly intense, the secondary effects of the warfare became more evident. Though numerous communities escaped attacks, pillage, and destruction, none escaped the ever-
increasing weight of *tailles* and impositions destined to support the opposing armies. Confirming this fact, the official *taille* levies as calculated
by Van Doren took a major jump between 1573 and 1576. From an
average of 46 *livres* per *feu* from 1563 to 1572, provincial *taille* levies
rose to 77.7 *livres* per *feu* between 1576 and 1582. They declined to 59
livres per *feu* from 1583 to 1588, then sky-rocketed to 435.7 *livres* per
feu from 1589 to 1595.[3] Comparing Van Doren's *taille* levies with the
price of wheat at the Grenoble market, however, Le Roy Ladurie has
demonstrated that the take-off in *tailles* was not as dramatic as it appears
for the period prior to 1589. Pointing out the effect of inflation and
devaluations upon the currency, he notes that the levies of the 1570s
and 1580s were, in fact, lower than those of the 1540s when measured
in terms of the purchasing power of wheat (see Graph 1).[4] It is, of course,
evident that for the period after 1589 *taille* levies dramatically outpaced
those of the 1540s.

Both of these analyses are based upon official *taille* levies, and it is
not at all clear that they do not underestimate the real fiscal squeeze.
Evaluating the real level of taxation during the religious and civil wars
remains very difficult. It is clear that official rates are deceptive, and
despite many studies of the *taille* levies paid out by various groups during
or even after the wars, the subject remains controversial.[5] There are
discrepancies on two levels: first, between the amounts that were received
by the royal *épargne*, or treasury, and those claimed to have been levied
by provincial officials; and second, between the levies approved by the
provincial Estates and the amounts that the villages claimed to have paid
out. There appears to have been a syphoning of funds from the time
the levies were collected to the time the royal *épargne* registered their
receipt. The Crown seems to have received only a fraction of the monies
that the village syndics and provincial treasury officials claimed to have
paid out.[6]

The budget of 1581 presents a useful example of the problem. After
analysing and revising the budget résumés of Forbonnais and Sully,
Albert Chamberland concluded that Dauphiné had contributed 7,500
écus to the *recette d'épargne* in 1581.[7] Van Doren studied the *taille* levies
authorized by the provincial Estates and collected in some of the major
towns and villages. He concluded that Dauphiné had levied 154,018 *écus*
in 1581 and that this levy was based upon an evaluation rate of 77 *livres*

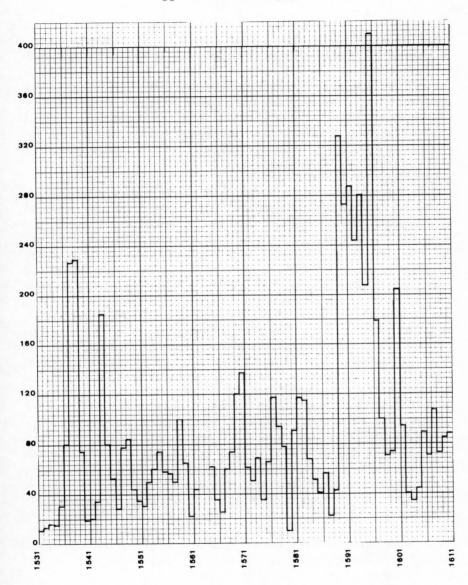

Graph 1 Official *taille* levies in Dauphiné from 1531 to1611, expressed in *quartals* of wheat

10 *sous* for each *feu* of property value.[8] On the local level, a series of 152 village cahiers, drawn up for the most part in the 1590s, listed the taxes collected in each community and demonstrated a third and even higher evaluation of *taille* levies. The variations from village to village were considerable. Condorcet claimed to have paid out 174 *livres* per *feu* of property value; Vaunaveys submitted claims for 153 *livres* per *feu* and Châteauneuf-de-Mazenc paid 364 *livres* per *feu*.[9] If these three levels of taxation are accurate, then it is obvious that the real amounts paid out by the taxpayers were considerably higher than the official *tailles* that were supposed to have been levied by provincial officials, or that were eventually received by the royal *épargne*.

The differences in these three levels of *taille* receipts are owing partly to the patronage system, under which the salaries of tax collectors and provincial treasury officials were deducted from the amounts that they collected. The discrepancies also arise from embezzlement by both groups. The third estate levelled charges against both these practices in the cahiers that they presented to the provincial Estates in 1573 and in 1579 and to the Estates-General at Blois in 1576.[10] The disappearing funds can also be explained by the regular use of *taille* revenues at local and provincial levels in order to meet valid and approved local responsibilities. The majority of the amounts collected in *taille* levies were used to meet the previously approved salaries of provincial forces headed by the lieutenant-governor or his subalterns, the mercenary troops brought into Dauphiné by the provincial government, and in some cases to provide maintenance for Huguenot garrisons. Communities, too, had the right to be reimbursed for expenses, such as the maintenance of *étapes*, or relay posts at which royal armies could stop for food, lodging, and supplies, and for the upkeep of garrisons, although as early as 1565 both of these items tended to be transferred back to the district (*mandement*) in the form of *aides*.[11] The difficulty of isolating the *tailles* that were used to cover these enlarged local and provincial responsibilities makes it impossible to evaluate the real contributions that the provinces and *élections* made to the Crown during the religious wars, or even during the first part of the seventeenth century. It is clear, however, that the royal budgets are a poor reflection of the taxes levied. The sums listed in the Crown receipts for Dauphiné represent only a small fraction of the amounts actually collected in the province.

On the provincial level, the differences between the levies calculated by Van Doren from the official royal *lançons* and the taxes that the officials of the local communities claimed to have been obliged to collect

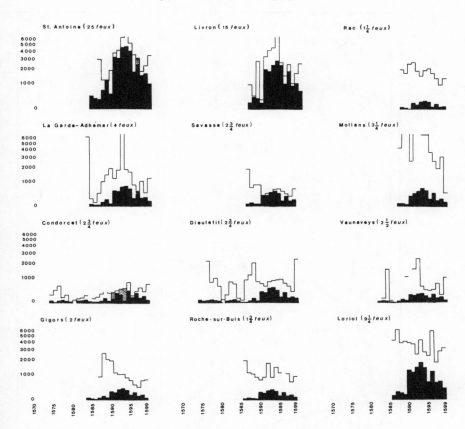

Graph 2 Official and unofficial *taille* levies in twelve villages between 1573 and 1599. The solid areas represent the official levies that can be traced from the *taille lançons,* and the lines above them represent the impositions collected in the villages according to the third-estate cahiers. The sliced areas represent the difference in cases where official levies were higher than the amounts actually collected. All of the levies are in *écus,* and the graphs are represented as a semi-logarithmic progression. The twelve villages represented on the graph are located geographically on Map 2.

from their inhabitants are just as great as the gap between Crown and provincial receipts. Graph 2 illustrates this difference. For twelve villages located in different regions of the province, the graph shows the level

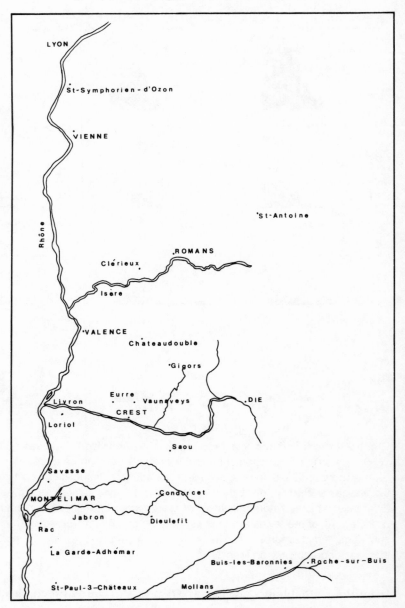

Map 2 The Rhône Valley region of Dauphiné

of *tailles* that should have been apportioned to each village according to the levies approved in the Estates and listed in the *lançons*. The graph also demonstrates the level of taxes that each of the communities claimed actually to have collected as official and unofficial *taille* levies and as military impositions.

The graphs of the two different sources of *taille* information illustrate dramatically the discrepancy between the official levies, duly approved by the Estates and by the king, and both the non-official levies, which were coerced exactions from communities, and the illegal levies that the king imposed without following the prescribed procedure. Of course one must be very prudent in accepting the accuracy of the village cahiers. Prepared by the members of the third estate to demonstrate their fiscal difficulties, the cahiers were frequently cited during the *taille* affair. Charles Tilley, Regine Robin, and Roger Chartier have all demonstrated the extent to which the third-estate elite manipulated the preparation of similar cahiers in 1614 and 1789.[12] Are the cahiers of 1598 any more trustworthy?

It is true that the framework and the principal grievances of the 1598 cahiers were imposed upon the communities by the third-estate elite just as in 1614 or 1789.[13] But if the village protests cannot be used as an indication of individual community problems, the data that they provide concerning the problems identified by the elite constitute an invaluable source of information. They are one of the first indications of actual taxation levels available for the period of the Wars of Religion. As to their accuracy, it can be tested for the case of St Antoine, a small village in lower Dauphiné between Vienne and St Marcellin. The secretary of the village, Eustache Piémond, drafted official cahiers for St Antoine in 1596 and 1598, but more important than the cahiers was his personal journal. Extending from 1572 to 1608, the journal contains entries and comments upon the most important events to affect the village, including most of the important tax levies.[14] Piémond's laconic comments upon individual impositions clarify the differences that are so apparent in Graph 2 and confirm the general level of third-estate claims.

According to the *lançons* for 1594 located by Van Doren, the official, approved levies should have amounted to 71 *écus* per *feu* for the village of St Antoine. Piémond, however, records that St Antoine paid out much more. The village collected levies of 130 *écus* per *feu*. Further, troops had demanded 42,019 *écus* in the form of impositions upon future village *tailles*. Most of these *tailles* were irregular and non-official, to the point that Piémond frequently confused the two types of levies. According to his journal, the village actually received *lançons* approved by the Estates for levies of 7 *écus* 30 *sous* per *feu*, 9 *écus* per *feu*, and 59 *écus* per *feu*. In fact, according to the *lançons* located by Van Doren, the Estates had approved levies of 10 *écus* per *feu*, 59 *écus* per *feu*, and 2 *écus* per *feu*; it is probable that Piémond neglected the levy of 2 *écus* per *feu* and confused the legal levy of 10 *écus* with non-official levies of 9 *écus* and 7 *écus* 30 *sous*. Over and above the *tailles* that he characterized as official, Piémond noted that provincial officials had demanded payments of two impositions of 10 *écus* in May and June and that four military companies had arrived before the village demanding that the consuls accord them advances upon future *tailles* or they would set up camp in the village or confiscate the supplies of its inhabitants.[15]

It is clear from Graph 2 that it is impossible to depend only upon uniform official levies to detect periods when the fiscal squeeze was turned on, or when the monetary demands of the war machine escalated, or when peasants were most likely to resist tax increases. In effect, in the period from 1585 to 1595 taxation levels varied from village to village. In most places from 1585 to 1589, when official demands had not yet attained their highest point, non-official levies and military impositions were considerable; however, when the official *tailles* increased dramatically from 1590 to 1594, non-official levies were reduced proportionately. It is probable that once the villages had paid the exorbitant official levies, there was simply no further money in village coffers to pay non-official levies. The village cahiers of the 1570s also show that the increases in real taxation occurred earlier than the *lançons* indicate and were already considerable in the period prior to the popular revolt.

In his treatment of the French fiscal system during the Wars of Religion, Martin Wolfe claims that the discrepancy between the actual sums paid out and the real receipts at either the provincial or national levels serves as an indicator of the sums that were injected directly into the war machine.[16] He is only partly right. His theory is complicated by the fact that there was considerable confusion over what a legal *taille* was: Who could levy it? Who had to approve it? To what expenses could it be applied? How was it to be collected?

Piémond's journal demonstrates this confusion. In the entries for 1588, when official levies amounted to only 21 *écus* per *feu*, St Antoine had paid out 437 *écus* per *feu*. Piémond noted that during the month of May the village had been forced to levy two *tailles*, one for 33 *écus* per *feu* and the other for 3 *écus*. Lieutenant-Governor Maugiron had imposed these levies arbitrarily and illegally despite the fact that the Estates had refused to vote them. Towards the end of August Maugiron had again ordered payment of a *taille* of 10 *écus* 20 *sous* per *feu*. On learning of this new *taille*, Captain Mesplex of the royalist forces demanded an advance of 400 *écus*. But the village coffers were empty. Not to be denied, Captain Mesplex took the community councilmen as hostages until the payment was made. It is also clear from the 1588 entries that numerous expenses that were not official *tailles* were none the less listed under the *taille* category. In this way impositions, or advances on *tailles* paid out to the Huguenots or to local military companies, as well as village levies for the maintenance of bridges, fortifications, and community buildings, were entered as regular *taille* levies.[17]

From this comparison of Eustache Piémond's journal with the village cahiers and official *lançons*, it is clear that while the *lançons* reflect the verifiable minimum *taille* demands of the wartime period, the cahiers reflect the more probable maximum levels of taxation. The cahiers and the journal establish that the official *taille* payments were a minor problem compared to the levels of non-official forced payments seen in the military impositions. A second important issue that emerges from a comparison of the three sources is the confusion over when a non-official levy could be considered a *taille* payment. One of the most important aspects of that confusion concerned military impositions and the increasing difference between their theory and practice.

In theory, all sums that the military imposed directly on the villages were deductible from future *taille* levies. The *foulles*, or military taxes, were viewed by the armies as advances upon official *taille* payments. The company provided the village with a receipt of payment, and the village councils paid their *tailles* with a combination of money and receipts for the payments that they had made directly to troops during the preceding year. They made these payments to the *commis du pays*, the permanent committee of the provincial Estates.[18] The impositions of Huguenot armies fell into the same category. Several of the truces negotiated during the war years stipulated that the official *taille* levy should be divided between royalist and Huguenot troops. The draft of a 1578 agreement noted that 6,200 *livres* a month should be reserved for expenses related to the maintenance of Huguenot garrisons.[19] The sums of money set aside for the Huguenots were not paid directly to the Protestant Council of War. Just as any other military imposition, they were to be collected directly by Huguenot armies from towns and villages. It was for this reason that St Antoine counted non-official advances they had made to Huguenot armies as official *tailles*.

The difficulties with this system became evident as the sums of money that a village paid out in advances on its *taille* levies began to represent more important sums of money than the official levy from which the advances were to be deducted (see Graph 2, where the unofficial levies are almost always higher than the official levies). In theory the general funds of the province (*l'universel*) were intended to balance out the inequalities of the chaotic collection methods. When the financial statements of the Estates, or *parcelles*, were approved initially, authorities always set aside certain sums for the *universel*. A village from which troops had collected more than their due should have been compensated by the *tailles* reserved in this general fund. The surplus payments from the villages that had been untouched by the military should have compensated for the deficits accumulated by the more unfortunate communities. Two obstacles prevented this system from functioning. The first was the creation of three *receveurs particuliers*, each responsible for collecting *tailles* in different regions of the province. From their creation in 1574 to their suppression in 1577 these new offices broke down the global treatment of village payments and interrupted the functioning of the system of compensations.[20] The other more permanent obstacle to the compensatory system was the fact that as the wars dragged on, fewer and fewer villages arrived with surpluses after the advances had been deducted from their *taille* levies. By the middle 1570s the deficits accumulated by the villages exceeded the amounts reserved in the *universel*, and the advances were refused more and more frequently.

All decisions concerning the acceptance or rejection of non-official advance payments were to be made by the *commis du pays*, a group whose composition the rural communities had always contested. No village representative was included among the six nobles, two clerics, and ten town representatives who constituted the theoretical make-up of the committee. Village contestation increased in the 1570s as the *commis* refused frequently to accept the villages' military receipts as deductions from *tailles*. This problem resurrected the *taille* disputes of the 1550s. Village representatives complained that more and more town expenses, such as for the maintenance of garrisons, *étapes*, and *passages*, were being made deductible from *tailles* or transferred to all the communities of the district, or *mandement*. They brought this complaint before the Estates in 1569, but the assembly ruled that such decisions rightly belonged to the *commis*.[21] Finally, the deductions claimed by towns and villages reached a point where the Estates declared more and more frequently that no military payments (*foulles*) would be deductible from the taxes they voted. Among the meetings of the Estates for which minutes or résumés can be located, those of 1575, 1576, 1586, and 1587 suspended deductions.[22] In other years the *commis* simply refused to honour the village receipts. It is clear that while in theory the military impositions did represent deductible advances on the *taille*, in fact they were interpreted more and more as sums to be added to the *taille* levies.

Another aspect of wartime taxation that was reflected in the confusion over the *tailles* was the question of what constituted a legal *taille*, as opposed to an illegal levy. From the comments of Eustache Piémond and the work of Van Doren it becomes evident that government officials sought to expedite the imposition of *tailles*, bypassing traditional procedures of approval.[23] Under those procedures the king sent out letters patent calling for a meeting of the Estates to consider his request for the right to levy additional taxes. Then the Estates drew up a financial statement (*parcelle*), listing the sums that they agreed to pay. Thereafter, an official of the Estates went to the royal court and presented the *parcelle*. It was studied by the privy council, which generally authorized the tax levy. The Dauphiné official then returned to the province, where the *parcelle* and the royal letters were verified by the parlement and the Chambre des comptes. The Chambre des comptes then distributed the *taille* among the communities according to their *feux*, in the presence of the *procureur*, treasurer, and *commis* of the Estates. *Lançons* were printed to announce the amount of the taxes due from each community and the date upon which payment was due. These *lançons* were handed over to the *huissier*, or messenger of the Estates, for delivery to the villages.[24]

Van Doren notes two changes in the *taille* procedure that illustrate the illegal tendency to short-circuit provincial and local taxation prerogatives and to concentrate fiscal power in the hands of the king and his agents. Evidence of this movement towards what Van Doren calls 'fiscal absolutism' can be seen in the 1572 imposition in Dauphiné of a *taille* levy that for the first time did not have the prior consent of a provincial assembly.[25] In July 1571 Charles IX had ordered that all provinces pay a special three-year subsidy. Dauphiné was assessed at 120,000 *livres*, payable in three equal instalments. When the Estates did not act upon the request, the law court (parlement) acted unilaterally to attach a two-year assessment to the 1572 *parcelle*. Other *tailles* were imposed in the same way in 1577, 1580, 1590, and 1591, either because the Estates did not have the time to meet or because they had not approved the requested levies.[26] This method of imposing *tailles* without the prior consent of the Estates became more and more common and was reflected in the village protests against 'illegal' levies.

Immediately following the initiatives of the parlement to impose *tailles* unilaterally, the Crown attempted to make this method a permanent, legal system for approving *taille* levies. Even more destructive of provincial prerogatives, this system would permit the Crown to bypass the Estates systematically in presenting *taille* demands. *Tailles* would be levied by the law courts, acting upon the orders of the lieutenant-governor or some other royal official. The first such successful, albeit contested, levy was imposed in March 1573, and it was followed in June of the same year by a far more substantial demand. Both of these requests were attached to a *parcelle* that had been processed properly by the Estates. They had the effect, however, of doubling the *taille* that had been approved. In the face of opposition from the Estates the method was modified, and in 1574 and 1575 *taille* demands were addressed to the *commis du pays*, the standing committee of the Estates. This committee's involvement preserved a semblance of consent from the Estates but actually increased the Crown's access to direct taxation.[27] In the future the king only needed the consent of the *commis*, which was generally composed of a majority of members from the non–tax-paying first and second estates.

To add to the confusion, in January 1576 the Estates committed a serious blunder. They granted a subsidy for support of the infantry to which they added, for reasons that are not clear, a resolution allowing the lieutenant-governor to levy additional *tailles* 'should there be any need of them.' In February 1576 and in January and May 1577 the lieutenant-governor invoked this concession, asking the parlement to impose additional *tailles*. In November of 1577 he deemed the additional subsidy offered by the *commis du pays* to be insufficient. He therefore ordered the courts to approve a levy three times greater than that approved by the *commis du pays*. Of the four levies collected to support the military operations of the duke of Mayenne in Dauphiné, the last two were imposed illegally by Mayenne and the lieutenant-governor of the province without the consent of any assembly.[28] Given this problem of who could levy taxes and how they were to be approved, it is not suprising that the village lists of *tailles* do not conform with the *lançons*. A comparison between the village cahiers and Piémond's journal indicates that St Antoine levied and paid all the impositions demanded. The distinction between legal and illegal, official and non-official levies seems to have been strictly academic.

The tendency towards fiscal absolutism and the centralization of *taille* initiatives in the hands of the Crown coincided with the decentralized collection of taxes. The Catholic and Protestant armies and the groups of armed maurauders who demanded food, shelter, and salaries from the already hard-pressed population were not interested in the official distinctions between legal and illegal levies. To be secure from attack, a village or a seigniory had to pay the levies requested by every armed group that passed through. Thus Huguenot leaders figure regularly on the *taille* rolls of Catholic villages, and vice-versa.

The role played by these security payments is illustrated in the memoirs of Captain Thomas Gay, a Huguenot. Gay wrote that when the seigneur of Paris died in 1574, the Huguenots of the Diois seized all his lands. The Huguenot leader Montbrun, however, ordered that the confiscated holdings be returned to the seigneur's widow. He justified the repudiation of his followers by arguing that the seigneur of Paris, although a Catholic, had rendered equal service to all passing armies.[29] This example demonstrates that those who met the demands of the soldiers were spared from attack, while the villages and seigniories that were too poor to pay the required levies were susceptible to destruction and confiscation. The example of the seigneur of Paris is corroborated by a 1582 report on the damage done to various communities in the Valentinois-Diois by the previous years of warfare. The report noted specifically that La Roche, Montoison, Comps, Vesc, and Montjoux had all escaped damage because their seigneurs had ensured that the villagers met the financial demands of every passing army.[30]

The local nature of such impositions explains the considerable variations between the amounts paid out by each village (see Graph 2). The communities placed along strategic routes and the poorer villages, which lacked adequate defence installations, tended to be the hardest hit by military demands. The variations between the *taille* levies that the different villages claimed to have paid resulted from the varying intensity of regional conflicts and from the confusion over the classification of military payments.

From this examination of different aspects of taxation between 1570 and 1600, it is obvious that Van Doren is correct when he argues on the evidence of the *lançons* that *tailles* rose considerably prior to the outbreaks of social confrontation. In fact the increases seem to have been even more important than he has shown. The actual tax payments of village and town residents were much closer to the levels reflected in the more politicized village cahiers than to those of the royal *épargne* or the provincial *lançons*. The official approved levies were minimal compared to the unofficial payments: the forced loans and military impositions demanded by Huguenot and royalist-Catholic troops; taxes for the construction of walls and fortresses as well as for the maintenance of garrisons; the outright confiscation of money and foodstuffs. The sums that reached the royal *épargne* or the Grenoble Chambre des comptes represented only the tip of the iceberg.

Van Doren also notes the development of fiscal absolutism during the period of the wars, a movement characterized by the centralization of arbitrary taxation powers in the hands of the king and his representatives.[31] It becomes clear, however, that not only the Crown but also the towns, garrisons, and war-lords stepped in to demand increased revenues from the communities. The traditional fiscal structure was under attack both from above and from below. This explains partly the series of inquiries into *taille* levies and collection procedures that was instigated by Sully following the Wars of Religion. These commissions were directed at studying abuses in the traditional levy procedure. Influenced by Crown desires to strengthen the central government, however, they generally interpreted these abuses as coming from below, from the financial demands of the towns, villages, and provincial Estates. They ignored Crown abuses as they confirmed and consolidated the illegal initiatives that had been taken by royal officials to impose *tailles* directly upon the population.[32]

On the question of the links between tax increases and social protest, Le Roy Ladurie has downplayed a causal relation, arguing that the official, approved *taille* levies of the 1570s were less important than those of the 1540s and were not sufficient to explain the widespread popular protest movement. For him the protests can only be explained by the fact that the injustice of the fiscal system magnified the effects of the levies.[33] Le Roy Ladurie is correct in noting the fiscal injustices, but he too underestimates the real weight of taxes. Throughout the period of the wars the unofficial levies paid by towns and villages and expressed in the third-estate cahiers represented two to thirty times the amounts of the official *tailles*. On the specific problem of the unrest in the 1570s, the graphs for Condorcet and Dieulefit show that the combination of official and unofficial taxes did, in fact, result in even higher levels of taxation than in the disastrous years of the 1590s. It is clear that the fiscal squeeze played an important part in the contestation, both non-violent and violent.

After the question of the fiscal system as a cause of social unrest, the second major debate concerning the *taille* issue in the 1570s revolves around the origins of the moderate protest movement and the involvement of local notables in the contestation. This debate confronts the thesis of Le Roy Ladurie with that of Van Doren, Cavard, and Dussert. In discussing the legalist, moderate movement to contest the weight and distribution of *taille* increases within the institutions of the province, Le Roy Ladurie personalizes the conflict. He attributes an overwhelming role to Jean de Bourg, characterizing the archepiscopal judge of Vienne as the 'liberal intellectual' leader of the third-estate forces, the figure who almost single-handedly led the fight against the *taille* up to 1578, when widespread popular interest stimulated a wave of local assemblies and district cahiers.[34] Le Roy Ladurie places great emphasis upon the fact that de Bourg was responsible for drawing up the cahier presented by the third estate of Dauphiné at the Estates-General at Blois in 1576, a document that stands out among the cahiers prepared for that meeting as a masterpiece of humanist and classical reasoning. He was also one of the principal leaders of the third estate during the *taille* debates in the Estates of Dauphiné at the time of the peasant uprisings and of the queen mother's visit in 1579.

It is true that de Bourg was very influential in the third-estate struggle, but he was not alone. Van Doren and Cavard have demonstrated that the third-estate contestation was marked by organized rural resistance movements well before 1578 and even before de Bourg became involved actively. In fact the cahiers presented by de Bourg in 1576 were based upon grievances previously voiced at numerous village and regional meetings as well as upon a 1574 cahier drafted by the third estate. The clearest proof of continuity on this question can be seen in the series of regional meetings on *taille* increases, in the local discussions of extending the tax base, and in the cahiers that the third estate had drawn up prior to the Estates of Blois in 1576. As early as 1571 a series of regional assemblies was held in the Baronnies, situated south of Die in the mountains that surrounded the Eygues River Valley. In a letter sent to the consuls, or village officials, of Nyons it was noted that the next scheduled assembly was to seek 'the advice of the largest possible number of communities' to contribute to the preparation of *mémoires*. The letter deplored the fact that Nyons often neglected to elect representatives to these meetings, and it threatened sanctions if no delegate from the town was present.[35] Assemblies were also held to consider more specific problems. In 1572 the consuls of Grenoble asked permission to assemble the cities of the province to discuss the propositions to be submitted to the provincial Estates.[36] Châteauneuf-de-Mazenc convoked an assembly of villages at Montélimar in 1575 to discuss the financing of the *étape* at Montélimar.[37] A number of villages prepared cahiers addressed to the provincial Estates, protesting tax increases and listing the names of nobles who had purchased *roturier* holdings in their communities. This type of 'documented' cahier became a model for the third-estate protests later in the century.[38]

Beyond the discussion stage, concrete propositions were studied in the municipal council at Châteauneuf-de-Mazenc in 1571, propositions aimed at negotiating an agreement with Montélimar whereby the town consuls could 'include gentlemen in the *taille* lists.'[39] In 1573 Grenoble studied a proposal to tax ecclesiastical benefices and the property of those nobles 'who, speculators of the tragedy, have not performed their duty by presenting themselves under arms to Mgr de Gordes.'[40] At a 1574 meeting of the cities of the province, Vienne, Valence, and Romans demanded that the members of the parlement and all others enjoying exemptions should contribute to war costs.[41]

These local efforts to resist *taille* increases and to reform the taxation structure were blocked regularly at the level of the provincial Estates. Even third-estate efforts to suggest alternate funding methods fell on deaf ears. In 1569, meeting apart from the two other estates, third-estate representatives discussed the financing of garrisons and proposed that in the future the cost of maintaining garrisons should be paid in part from the salt tax. The full meeting of the Estates, however, only agreed to have the *commis du pays* study this proposal.[42] The same decision was made concerning the complaints of Vienne, Die, Quirieu, and Gap that they were obliged to maintain large garrisons out of city funds. The decision was left to the *commis du pays* and to the lieutenant-governor to see whether the size or number of the garrisons could not be reduced.[43] The third estate seems to have become increasingly frustrated by such decisions. Later in the same meeting they protested the judgments of the *commis* regarding the deductibility of the military impositions. These impositions had not been allowed since 1567, particularly in the case of the *foulles* imposed by Protestant forces. The representative of the Valentinois declared that he would go before the courts to obtain the restitution of these payments.[44]

The *commis du pays* and officials of the Estates seem to have obstructed systematically the initiatives of the third estate. As the official institution comissioned to draw up and interpret the budget approved by the three orders, the *commis du pays* arbitrarily increased the amounts of the *parcelles* voted by the delegates, decided for each village which impositions could or could not be deducted from their levy, and approved or rejected expenses submitted by garrisons and by officials of the legal, military, or administrative structure. In theory the consuls of the ten major cities of the province had the right to participate, alongside the *procureur général* of the Estates, the two clerics elected by the first estate, and the six nobles elected by their peers, in the meetings of the *commis du pays*.[45] However, a number of the town consuls complained regularly that they were unable to attend. The meetings were held at Grenoble, where the noble and clerical delegates resided, and it was difficult for representatives from Briançon, Gap, Embrun, Crest, Die, and Montélimar to travel that far. In addition, the meetings were convened on very short notice, and travel expenses for the third-estate delegates could not be refunded.[46]

The split in the third-estate delegation between rural and urban interests was a second and perhaps more fundamental reason why the spokesmen who sat as *commis du pays* from the ten cities did not do more to further the village demands for alternative methods of *taille* imposition. Sequels to the city-village disputes of the 1540s and 1550s were still evident. In addition, the structure of the major consulates, the governing bodies of the towns, made their delegates suspect in the eyes of the rural members of the third estate. Although the delegates from Grenoble, Romans, and Vienne to all third-estate meetings were *taille*-paying members of the third estate, the consulates were generally presided over by nobles of the sword or of the robe, and at least in Grenoble the voice of the first consul, a noble, was of considerable importance. Before sending a delegate to any third-estate meeting, the Grenoble consulate discussed the issue to be debated and gave a precise mandate to its delegate.[47] For this reason the major cities sided rarely with the rural demands, and there tended to be a breech in the third-estate delegation that sat as *commis du pays*. The largest cities, Grenoble, Romans, Vienne, and Valence, were not all that dissatisfied with their representation, and they worked with the delegates from the privileged orders to protect their own interests. The rural third estate, the lesser cities, and the walled towns, however, had considerable difficulty working within the framework of the provincial Estates. Their dissatisfaction was particularly evident in 1573, when the three estates submitted a common cahier of grievances to the king. The long-standing complaints of the rural third estate concerning *tailles* and exemptions were taken up in only one of twenty-seven articles. In addition, the article was exemplary for its banality, remarking only that the third estate deplored the fact that nobles and town residents were exempted from *tailles* when they owned the best lands in the villages and that the recent creation of *anoblis* and exempted royal officials was worsening the fiscal situation of the third estate.[48]

With the exception of the delegates from the large cities, the third estate was dissatisfied with the common cahier, and a year later third-estate leaders refused to have their grievances buried in a similar document. At the provincial Estates held at Grenoble in March 1574, they met separately from the other estates and asked the king to reverse the decisions of the *commis du pays* concerning *foulles* and new taxes.[49] Later, in October 1574 they appealed to the king for permission to assemble apart to discuss their grievances. At that meeting they drafted a cahier of thirty-two articles that was submitted to the king and his council.[50] This cahier is particularly interesting in the light of the previous difficulties of the third estate, for its two major themes were the structure of the Estates and the problem of the distribution of *taille* levies.

The structure of the Estates was one of the principal targets of the cahier. The document questioned the objectivity of the *commis du pays* in establishing the distributions of the *tailles* voted in the Estates. It argued that the *commis du pays* was in obvious conflict of interest in determining what part of the levy should be carried by the towns, how much should be placed as *taille extraordinaire* to which the nobles and clergy contributed, how much as *taille ordinaire* should be levied only on the third estate, and what expenses should be taken out of the general levy.[51] Articles ten and seventeen of the cahier deplored the fact that often the *commis du pays* divided up the budget in the absence of all the third-estate representatives, and asked the king to invalidate the decisions of such meetings. Reflecting the frustration of communities other than the large cities with the Estates' structure, articles eighteen and nineteen presented a demand that became one of the constant preoccupations of the third estate in the 1570s: the third estate demanded to meet and organize its assemblies separate from those of the other estates. The articles proposed that a special *procureur* be elected by the third estate to convoke and preside over its meetings and to become a member of the standing committee of the *commis du pays*.

The other major preoccupation was fiscal: the traditional problem of the distribution of *taille* levies. The initial articles of the cahier exposed at great length the third-estate argument that wartime taxes were at least as oppressive to the peasants as was the destruction wrought by Huguenot and royal armies. They contended that the first and second estates actually profited from the wars by selling goods to the armies at the same time that their tax exemptions and their control over the Estates' structure permitted them to escape *taille* levies even for military expenses. Articles ten and sixteen noted that the unjust tax distribution made by the *commis* was aggravated by dishonest tax collectors, by moneylenders who lent peasants the funds to pay their taxes at high rates of interest, and by judges who upheld exemptions for *présumé* nobles. Despite all these complaints the cahier remained ambiguous concerning solutions to the problem, suggesting only that the king keep a closer watch on the exemptions accorded to officials, that he reduce the number of officials, and that *tailles* continue to be levied on *roturier* lands that had been bought by tax-exempt individuals within the previous fifty years.

During the rest of the decade the cahiers in which de Bourg participated reflected the two basic arguments of the 1574 demands. As a corrective to what Le Roy Ladurie implies, it is important to note the close collaboration of town, village, and *bailliage* representatives in establishing the priorities for the subsequent cahiers. Local assemblies were consulted regularly to establish the third-estate arguments. These procedures were particularly evident in the case of the cahiers prepared for the 1576 Estates-General at Blois. Between August, when letters of convocation were sent out, and 6 December, when the Estates were opened officially, representatives of the cities and *bailliages* met with their communities to elect representatives and to formulate a series of regional grievances. These were sent to Grenoble on 24 October and used in the preparation of a new third-estate cahier to be presented to the Estates.

The Archives départementales de l'Isère possesses a copy of the Vienne cahier composed by Antoine Giffard. This cahier documents the steps taken in the organization of the consultations. Its four folios list the complaints that had been submitted by village representatives of the *bailliage* of Viennois. The cahier notes that the complaints were to be transmitted to Grenoble and that, at an upcoming meeting, the delegates of every region of the province would decide which grievances would be included in the cahier that was to be drafted for Blois.[52] A similar assembly of the villages of the *bailliage* of St Marcellin was convoked for 10 October to prepare a list of their grievances.[53] In the Graisivaudan, continuing town-country differences were reflected in the fact that two competing assemblies were held, one at Vif and the other at Grenoble. After negotiations between the two elected delegations, the Grenoble city council recognized the Vif delegates as the legally elected representatives of the *bailliage*, and in return the Vif delegates agreed to support the pretensions of the bishop of Grenoble to preside over the provincial Estates, a right contested by the bishops of Vienne and Embrun.[54]

From these local and regional cahiers the third estate, under the direction of Jean de Bourg, prepared the final cahier that was to be presented at Blois. Refusing to have its document buried in a common list of grievances from the three estates of Dauphiné, the third estate selected five delegates to go to Blois and defend its demands. Among the five was Jean de Bourg.[55] While de Bourg was not alone in preparing the third-estate cahier, it is clear that his ideas and arguments led to a reorganization of the 1576 and later of the 1579 cahiers. Under his guidance the lists of grievances from the local assemblies were turned into logical and well-documented arguments for change. The de Bourg cahier contained one hundred articles. It has been analysed masterfully by Le Roy Ladurie, even though he isolates it from the wider protest movement that preceded and inspired the document. In effect the cahier presented at Blois developed in more detail and in more scholarly language the two basic third-estate grievances of the early 1570s: the structure of the Estates and the unjust distribution of tax levies.[56]

The cahier proposed a revision of the provincial Estates' structure whereby the third estate would become a separate entity, responsible for its own affairs. The 1574 request for a separate *procureur* was repeated, and the cahier elaborated upon the position. The *procureur* was to be assisted in the two *bailliages* and the *sénéchaussée* of Valentinois by local representatives (*commis*), responsible for transmitting information to and from the communities. As in 1574 the cahier asked that the *commis du pays* be forbidden to meet without the presence of the proposed *procureur* of the third estate and of its representatives. The Blois cahier suggested a new tax-collection procedure that would deprive the existing tax collectors and assessors of their high commissions to assess villages and to deliver the *lançons*. Instead the communities of each *bailliage* or *sénéchaussée* would elect a *récepteur*, or tax receiver, who would be responsible for such tasks. Finally, it was argued that since it was the third estate that paid the *tailles*, its representatives should carry the *parcelle* to the royal court for approval, thereby giving the third estate an ideal opportunity to expose its grievances directly to the king.

Most of the proposals and suggestions that were made at Blois for restructuring the Estates were a direct carry-over from the 1574 cahier presented at Grenoble, but the Blois document was more specific. It elaborated a more coherent structure for the third estate, producing extended arguments from classical authors in favour of the proposed organization and trying to foresee and reply to any objections from the Crown. The third estate's request that its own representatives carry the tax *parcelle* to the royal court and negotiate their grievances directly with the king shows that just as in the 1550s and in the 1574 cahier, the third estate viewed the Crown as a more favourable interlocutor than it did the privileged orders of the province.

The second major element of the cahier concerned the long-standing *taille* controversy. In contrast to the proposals for reorganizing the Estates, the cahier essentially approached the question of the *taille* as it always had, through a list of abuses and grievances. It noted the increasing number of tax-exempt nobles, *anoblis*, *présumé* nobles, and officials who were buying up the holdings of ruined peasants, thereby removing them from the taxable lands listed in the village cahiers. A new aspect was the denunciation of seigneurial justice. The cahier claimed that in rendering justice in their own names, the seigneurs were reclaiming their traditional rights to communal lands, mills, ovens, and presses, rights that the peasants had appropriated or acquired since the fifteenth century. Article seventy-seven even contended that the seigneurs were interfering with the efforts of the third estate to organize community assemblies.

In addition, the Blois cahier was marked by contradictions on the town-country question. As a representative of the town of Vienne, where one of his relatives was first consul, de Bourg did not support the fiscal demands of the villages upon town residents who bought rural holdings. Article 89 of the Blois document defended the old town contention that all taxes should be imposed and paid at one's place of residence, even for holdings that were located in outlying villages. It held that the nobles, clergy, and officials were exploiting the peasants by their exemptions, but it maintained that similar exemptions accorded to the townspeople did not amount to exploitation. This gap in the logic of the Blois cahier was to be rectified only in 1583, when urban and rural representatives concluded an agreement concerning rural purchases.

The town-country cleavage indicated in the 1576 cahier remained one of the most divisive factors within the ranks of the third estate throughout the 1570s. It resurfaced in 1578 during debates on a new *taille* levy. All communities except the ten cities appear to have taken up their old argument that townspeople were not paying taxes on their rural holdings and that the *commis du pays* was distributing traditional town expenses over the whole third estate while refusing to allow the villages to deduct *foulles* and impositions.[57] To remedy this situation, two propositions were passed. The first specified that the cities and villages would name arbitrators to negotiate acceptable terms for the application of the 1548 edict, which had specified that townspeople were to be taxed in each village where they held property. The second proposition asked for the creation of one additional *commis*, to be elected annually by the villages and to assist at all regular meetings of the *commis du pays*. To assure adequate representation, each *bailliage* or *sénéchaussée* would have its turn to elect the proposed representative.[58] Both propositions were accepted by the Estates.

The creation of a *commis* for the villages constituted a very important step because, from the very beginning of the *taille* controversy in the 1540s, the villages and walled towns had complained of the favoured treatment accorded to towns in the distribution of *taille* levies by the *commis du pays*.[59] That the whole problem was discussed and accepted with so little apparent opposition in 1578 seems to indicate two things. First, it indicates that the rivalry within the third estate between towns and villages was still present and that the privileged orders that controlled the Estates perhaps tried to aggravate these differences by supporting the request of the rural delegates. Second, the rapid acceptance of the proposal may have been an attempt to appease the rural population, which was affected particularly by the wars and by the numerous acquisitions of tax-exempt nobles, officials, and usurpers. This gesture was especially significant in 1578, for the villages were beginning to discuss armed resistance to the excesses of the soldiers, seigneurs, and tax collectors.

A year later, in 1579, the second de Bourg cahier was drafted in the midst of what could be called a crisis situation. Local and regional resistance had become widespread, and many third-estate communities had even taken up arms to combat the excesses of the unorganized and undisciplined military. The king had refused to accept the terms of a 1578 provisional treaty with the Huguenot leader Lesdiguières to end the fighting, and both Huguenot and royalist forces had spent the remainder of the year trying to gain ground militarily in order to strengthen their bargaining positions.[60] It is this period of 'armed peace' that Le Roy Ladurie sees as the immediate cause of the 1579 peasant risings. Military banditry hit a new high. Under the direction of commanders La Prade, Bouvier, and La Roche a network of pillaging soldiers was formed, attached to neither Huguenot nor royalist camp. From their strongholds in Châteaudouble, Pont-en-Royans, and Roussas these brigands terrorized peasant and merchant communities in lower Dauphiné and along the Rhone Valley.[61]

Having ignored the previous grass-roots contestation, Le Roy Ladurie holds that the heavy taxes levied in 1578, combined with the raids and pillaging visited upon the rural population, led to the first widespread round of village meetings. While it is clear that 1578 did not mark the first series of such meetings, the assemblies held that year did take far more dramatic actions than in the past. Eustache Piémond, one of the syndics who represented his village at the new round of meetings, reported that the communities around Montélimar had begun to form a secret alliance, a 'union' or 'league,' whose aim was to refuse to pay future tax levies and to pledge support for the renewed third-estate efforts to force the privileged orders to pay a part of the *taille*.[62] This union or league took two immediate actions. First, many communities resorted to arms by organizing vigilante groups to oppose any future incursion of regular or irregular soldiers into their areas. This movement led eventually to the peasant revolt of 1579, which will be treated in the following section. The second initiative of the league was to open discussion and reformulate the grievances that had been presented at the provincial Estates in 1575 and the Estates of Blois in 1576.

The provincial Estates that had been convoked to meet at Grenoble on 19 April 1579 provided the occasion for local assemblies to debate and revise the third-estate cahiers. Once again Jean de Bourg was part of the group that drafted the final document.[63] As in previous cases the group appears to have worked from individual documents submitted from different towns and regions.[64] The cahier that resulted from this renewed consultation was presented at the Estates during a session punctuated by the violence of the popular risings.[65]

Divided into forty-four articles, the new cahier repeated previous demands for reorganizing the provincial Estates, reducing the number of officials, restoring Crown domains, and ending fiscal abuses concerning the distribution, levy, and collection of the *taille*.[66] Far more significant, however, were the initial articles of the cahier. For the first time they went beyond a mere list of the individual exemptions they contested; instead, the first seven articles established a clear argument against the *taille personnelle* system. They traced the historical basis of the *taille* in

Dauphiné from the *transport* of 1349, which specified that the inhabitants of the province would continue to be exempt from *tailles*. Having outlined the historic right of the inhabitants to such exemption and the extreme poverty of the population, the cahier went on to ask in article eight that the king cease to impose the *taille*. However, in documents that describe the oral presentation of the cahier at the Estates, it is clear that the third estate recognized that it was impossible to suspend the *taille*. The third-estate delegates envisaged a compromise that would have allowed the *taille ordinaire* to continue but would have stopped the *extraordinaire* impositions and would have introduced the principle of the *taille réelle* in the distribution of levies. Article ten and the surviving notes on the Estates' meeting further demonstrate that although the cahier did not propose specifically the *taille réelle*, the third-estate leaders formulated their demands around the principle of this system. They asked that *cadastres* be prepared for the rest of Dauphiné just as they existed for the *bailliage* of the Montagnes.[67]

Articles nine to thirteen set forth the criteria to be applied to the landholdings of old nobles, new nobles, and officials in view of the establishment of these *cadastres*. Under the proposed system the *roturier* holdings acquired by old nobles during the last twenty years were to be included in the *cadastres*, and *tailles* were to be collected on these lands in the future. New nobles were defined as those who had acquired their titles within the last hundred years. According to notes on the discussions in the Estates, new nobles were to be taxed in the future for all their non-noble acquisitions since 1518, and they were to pay back taxes on such acquisitions since 1560. As for the exempted officials of the parlement, Chambre des comptes, treasury, and the like, article twelve demanded that their numbers be reduced to their traditional level, as the king had promised at Blois. Further, article thirteen held that they should be taxed for the *roturier* holdings that they had acquired in the last twenty years. No mention was made of the controversial question of townspeople being assessed at their places of residence for rural holdings.

When compared to the third-estate demands of the 1540s, the cahiers of 1574, 1576, and 1579 demonstrate the progress made by the third estate in clarifying and defining its desires. From complaints and appeals to the king and the courts concerning the functioning of the Estates, the third estate had moved so far as to propose a new system in which it would benefit from a separate and autonomous status. From lists of grievances and complaints concerning the *taille* exemptions of nobles, *anoblis*, officials, and townspeople, it had gone on to opt clearly for a reorganization of the *taille* system and the adoption of *cadastres*, the principal characteristic of the *taille réelle* system.

Certainly, Jean de Bourg played a considerable role in this intellectual and political evolution. The more logical formulation of third-estate demands after 1576 and the more thorough documentation of those demands through legal arguments and classical references were clearly contributions by de Bourg. Nevertheless, Le Roy Ladurie overemphasizes the responsibility of the archepiscopal judge from Vienne for the contestation process. Van Doren, Cavard, and Dussert are quite correct in underlining the continuing work of the local notables. From 1571 to 1579 bailiffs, *sénéchaux*, *châtelains*, village syndics, and town consuls organized meetings, drew up cahiers, and protested regularly in the provincial Estates and at the royal court against the abuses of the existing *taille* system. Their basic demands were evident well before the Blois cahier. The local meetings over which they presided seem to have been just as important as the actions of de Bourg in maintaining the momentum in the third-estate contestation.

These local and regional assemblies initiated the *taille* dispute, and the role they played constitutes one of the principal differences between Dauphiné and most of the other French provinces whose local institutions have been studied. The existence of such regular, defined channels of communication between villages, districts, and *bailliages* in Dauphiné contrasts singularly with the simplicity and isolated nature of rural institutions in such regions as the Lyonnais or in Burgundy.[68] Local and village structures in Dauphiné seem even more extended than in Provence, where the towns dominated the powerful assemblies of the *communauté d'habitants*.[69] This well-developed rural organization constituted the backbone of the *taille* contestation in Dauphiné throughout the sixteenth century. It furnished the opponents of the *taille personnelle* system with institutions and recognized delegates who participated in the structures that governed the province and who were capable of slowing down or paralysing those structures. The existence of these local institutions may well be the key to explaining why the communities of Dauphiné were able to sustain such a long-term contestation of the fiscal system while the equally hard-pressed villages of other provinces mounted minimal opposition to the new taxes.

The third major topic of historiographical debate over the social unrest of the 1570s concerns the popular revolts of 1579–80. The major problem arises in defining the economic and social dividing line between those who rebelled and those who supported the government attempts to quell the disturbances. In particular, historians and contemporaries differ over the role played by the moderate town and village leaders who spearheaded the legal contestation efforts throughout the decade.

Eustache Piémond is the only contemporary observer who does not implicate the moderate third-estate leaders in the violent confrontations that marked the popular revolts throughout the province. In all the other sixteenth-century accounts the preparation of the third-estate cahiers is linked with the origins of the more radical contestation, and the moderates who prepared the cahiers are included among the instigators of the revolt. The most outstanding of these accounts is an unsigned memoir on the disturbance in Romans that has been attributed by Joseph Romans to the *éminence grise* of the city, Judge Guérin. Later ennobled for the role he played in crushing the revolt, Judge Guérin produced a politically inspired report that whitewashed his friends and condemned his enemies. In the memoir he associated the moderate contestation with the popular revolt, and he noted that in the presence of the queen mother, Paumier, one of the leaders of the Romans revolt, had identified himself with the third-estate cahiers, declaring 'that he had been elected leader by the third estate in order to try to obtain [acceptance of] the articles that had been presented to the assembly that had met in Grenoble.'[70] Of the social origins of the participants in the popular revolt, Guérin left little doubt. Paumier was 'bad mannered and rude'; his aides were 'the most evil people who could be found,' and they imposed their 'perverted ideas of order' upon the people. On the other side were the 'gens de bien,' the 'notables,' the 'consuls,' and the nobles who tried to contain the excesses of the Paumier clique.[71]

The other important witness to these events was the queen mother, Catherine de Médicis. Sent to the province during the summer of 1579 to negotiate an end to the *taille* dispute and to try to reach an agreement with the Huguenot armies, Catherine sent daily reports back to the king.[72] Even before arriving in Dauphiné she had accepted the nobles' version of the contestation, identifying the third-estate cahiers with the demands of the villages and towns that were in revolt. Writing from Agen, she told the king that

very upsetting movements have begun to take place in Dauphiné; according to what I have been told, all the towns have banded together; all the soldiers, your own as well as those of the Huguenots, have been chased out of their garrisons ... they say that they don't want any other king than you, but they want to live in peace and they don't want your treasurers manipulating their taxes; on the contrary, they want to be responsible for collecting and sending their taxes to your coffers in the Louvre in Paris; they don't want to pay any more taxes than they paid during the reign of Louis XII ... they say they have no other leader than the towns and villages. As you can see, if these things are true, they are of great importance and very dangerous.[73]

Her analysis of the dangers of the movement changed little once she began negotiating with the third estate. She singled out as the social groups responsible for the revolt the nobles, clergy, and bourgeois leaders who had failed to take vigorous action against the rebels. She accused the delegates of the third estate of collaboration with the armed rising. At every opportunity during her visit Catherine chided those whom she considered to be weak leaders, notably the bishop of Valence and the notables of Romans. She tried to stimulate them to take a stronger stand against the agitators.[74] At the same time she scolded the rebel leaders of Montélimar, Valence, and Romans, accusing them of substituting themselves for the legal authorities. During a special session of the provincial Estates called to discuss the *taille* question, Catherine accused de Bourg 'and all the other troublemakers' among the third-estate delegation of promoting the very dangerous leagues and of opposing her peacemaking efforts.[75] In other words, she dealt with the third estate as a totality, an order, and the whole order was responsible for the actions of the radicals.

The recent analyses of Le Roy Ladurie, Vital Chomel, and L. Scott Van Doren have cleared up a number of points that the more politically oriented sixteenth-century reports had misrepresented. As to the origins of the popular rising, it appears true, as Catherine de Médicis believed, that the violent aspect of the contestation grew out of the same regional concerns and to some extent out of the same organization that produced the third-estate cahiers and the *taille* protests. Catherine's contention is borne out by evidence from a meeting at Marsans on 25 March 1578. A group of village officials came together in the same manner in which they had met to draw up their cahiers; only this time they concluded their assembly by requesting permission of the lieutenant-governor to defend themselves against groups of soldiers, companies, and garrisons that had tried to tax them in violation of the peace treaty of 1577.[76]

During the summer and fall of 1578 the communities remained in close contact, providing each other with advance notice of any passing troops.[77] Their desire to avoid conflicts with provincial officials and to act through official, legal institutions was evident when they presented a summary of their initiatives to the municipal council of Montélimar on 1 November 1578. A representative of the village union claimed that the villages had approached Lieutenant-Governor Maugiron and had offered to work under the authority of the parlement to see to it that robbers and thieves would be brought to justice. But Maugiron had replied that the union should consult the towns concerning their actions. The village representatives reported that the resulting contacts had produced support for the leagues from Valence, Crest, and Romans, the latter still under the direction of Judge Guérin. At the conclusion of the assembly Montélimar too joined the movement.[78]

Le Roy Ladurie notes that in this initial stage the Montélimar league stayed scrupulously within the bounds of the moderate protest movement, though elsewhere organizers were less prudent. In the barony of Clérieu, to the west of Romans, a similar league had turned to open attacks by June 1579. First to fall into the peasants' hands was a company of light cavalry commanded by Jean de Bourrelon, governor of Embrun. Upon entering the village of Marsas the company was attacked and forced to seek refuge in the château of Jarcieu before it could retire to Lyon. Next was the company of the grand prior of France, commanded by the governor of Provence, an illegitimate son of Henry II. The surprised troops retreated and were dispersed by the peasant bands from Marsas.[79]

The fusion of municipal protest movements with the rural contestation further radicalized the leagues. By February 1579 the towns of Valence and Romans had turned out their garrisons, and by the middle of March Grenoble too demanded the expulsion of its soldiers.[80] About the same time the united rural and urban leaguers in Montélimar under the command of the vice-sénéchal of Montélimar, Jacques Colas, had undertaken a siege of the brigand fortress at Roussas.[81] This initiative was almost immediately imitated by the leader of the league in Romans, Jean Seve, surnamed Paumier. The Romans forces marched against the brigands in Châteaudouble, and the château was captured on 15 March, after Lieutenant-Governor Maugiron came to Paumier's aid.[82]

The leagues, therefore, appear to have originated in the same type of local meetings that produced the third-estate cahiers. As Scott Van Doren claims, the long series of third-estate protests before the provincial Estates served an educational role for the peasant communities that took up arms in 1579.[83] Guérin and Catherine de Médicis do not appear to have been accurate, however, when they identified the leaders of the legal-contestation movement with the eventual actions of the popular leagues. Even if their initial goals had been similar, fewer and fewer town and village notables continued their association with the league movement as the actions of the leaguers became more radical.

Initially, the demands set before the Estates in the cahiers of the third-estate notables were merely translated into action by the leaguers. They sought to stop the exaggerated impositions of the military, to obtain the proclamation of the peace treaty of 1577, and to remove unwarranted garrisons. They wanted to ensure regular audits of provincial and municipal accounts to prevent embezzlement. They tried to obtain the restoration of alienated Crown lands so that the personal revenues of the king would be sufficient to abolish *tailles*.[84] But as the leagues continued, the official third-estate leaders found their support increasingly embarrassing. Several aspects of the league movement met with disapproval. In particular the attacks upon the municipal structures of the province and the violent manner in which the leaguers pursued their goals began to alienate third-estate leaders from the movement.

In Montélimar the urban leaguers had begun by contesting the weight and the distribution of *tailles* as well as the accuracy of municipal fiscal records. In short, they accused the municipal council of embezzlement.[85] The same refrain was repeated at Romans, where the leaguers went even farther and contested the political structures of the town. Romans, just as most other communities in the province, was governed by a corporate structure that camouflaged the exercise of power by the third-estate elite. In theory the town's political institutions represented the four social divisions of its citizens: the notables ('nobles living nobly, nobles of the robe, lawyers, medical doctors, or bourgeois living from their investments without engaging in commerce'); the merchants and the men of professions; tradesmen and artisans; and ploughmen (*laboureurs*). Supreme political power was vested in four councillors, one representing each social group. This executive was assisted by two secondary councils, one composed of forty members, ten from each social category, and the other composed of twenty-four, or six from each category.[86] Each of these positions was renewed annually.

In practice two obstacles blocked the proper functioning of this political apparatus in Romans. The first was that since 1542 the representatives of the different social categories were no longer elected by their constituents; they were co-opted. The forty-member assembly had become the body responsible for naming new councillors or new representatives on the town councils. The second obstacle was the emergence of a strongman, Antoine Guérin, the royal judge and the author of the report on the Romans revolt. Through his social and political connections Guérin came to dominate the political structure. Since the position of judge and its attendant police power were permanent, Guérin was able to supervise and control the rotating positions on the town councils.[87]

Just as in Montélimar, charges of excessive taxation and embezzlement were levied against the Guérin-controlled town council. The Paumier faction contended that it was necessary to reform the town's political structure in order to remedy the alleged fiscal abuses. The type of reform Paumier supported was not at all in conformity with the interests of the moderates among the third-estate leaders. Upon returning from his 'victory' over the brigands at Châteaudouble, Paumier and a large number of his supporters confronted the municipal council. At a meeting held to elect four consuls for the upcoming year, the Paumier clique demanded that the municipal council be enlarged before any new elections were held. Judge Guérin protested the presence of the crowd, arguing that their demands violated the town statutes, which prescribed that all elections were to be carried out by the council of forty. Guérin's protests were overruled, and twenty 'extraordinary' councillors were permitted to participate in the election.[88] Guérin noted in his subsequent report on the revolt that most of the twenty were leaguers who were 'as unworthy of this position as a shoemaker is of being president of a sovereign law court.'[89]

This introduction into town government of greater representation of the more important artisan groups, whom Van Doren has termed the 'new men,' and the questioning of the principle of co-option were certainly not in conformity with the goals of the third-estate leaders, all of whom were either consuls or the representatives of the consulates of their towns. Municipal governments were very important within the institutional structures of both the third estate and the province. Since all of the towns possessed the same type of political structure as Romans, they reacted negatively to the reforms of the leaguers. The municipal council of Vienne feared that a similar coup might be organized there and, in response to Maugiron's appeal for troops to aid him in the siege of Châteaudouble, replied: 'we have been warned that it is very dangerous during these popular *emotions* to empty the town of men, and in doing so the members of the *menu peuple* would be in danger of flaming up and being stirred into action.'[90] The Vienne council was presided over by Laurent de Bourg, a relative of the third-estate leader Jean de Bourg. Though Vienne had always been in the forefront of the movement to contest the *taille* privileges of the second estate, the town took its distance from the league. On 19 May the council refused a series of proposals from Jacques Colas, the league commander in Montélimar. It replied that the articles 'tended more towards sedition and war than anything else.'[91]

The acts of violence that became a mark of the revolt separated the third-estate moderates from the leaguers. Just as the Estates of 1579 were meeting to consider the third-estate cahiers, the leaguers at Clérieu murdered a judge, a *châtelain*, and a clerk. They looted and burned the châteaux of nobles Dorbain, Dubois, and Gaste. At nearby Hauterives they attacked a tax farmer.[92] During her visit the queen mother castigated the leaguers for these actions and noted that she would hold Paumier personally responsible for any future excesses in the Romans region. The report written by Judge Guérin implies that Catherine's meetings with the 'gens de bien' constituted a turning point in the Romans revolt. Her encouragement of their plans to move against the rebels permitted the traditional elite to re-establish control over the town. In so doing they set the stage for the murder of Paumier and for the eventual massacre of the remaining leaguers at Moirans on 28 March 1580.[93]

The excesses of the leaguers facilitated the condemnation of their actions by the moderate third-estate leaders both at the April meeting of the Estates and in the presence of Catherine de Médicis.[94] Despite these denunciations, however, the third estate and its cahiers remained highly suspect. That the cahiers emanated from the same current of protest that produced the leagues, that they contained most of the demands made by the leaguers, and that the leagues had always expressed full support of the documents compromised the efforts of third-estate leaders to establish a distinction between themselves and the leaguers. That certain delegates, and in particular Jean de Bourg, had threatened to refuse the queen mother's mediation efforts made them 'troublemakers' and accomplices of the leagues in her eyes.[95]

In the absence of complete and accurate lists of those who revolted, it is very difficult to assess the exact social composition of the league forces. Both Le Roy Ladurie and Van Doren conclude that participation was very fluid and that support for the leagues was reduced considerably after the violent attacks carried out in the spring of 1579. The only reliable documents available for evaluating participation are the official lists of those who were condemned by the special commission of the parlement sent to Romans after the revolt had been crushed in 1580.

These documents, of course, indicate only those who were present in the league forces in Romans up to the end and do not reflect the broader social spectrum that was represented at the beginning of the movement.

In analysing the list of twenty-six individuals condemned by the commission, Van Doren identifies one notable, eighteen artisans, and seven ploughmen. He notes that the relative wealth and upward social mobility of a number of these 'new men' makes it difficult to classify them as members of the lower classes, that is, the *menu peuple* and other marginal members of the community, who Guérin claimed were behind the revolt. For this reason Van Doren hesitates to conclude that the 1579 rising represented a clear-cut class conflict.[96]

Le Roy Ladurie, in his *Carnival of Romans*, goes beyond the lists of condemned leaders, the demands of the rebels, and the reports of Guérin and Catherine de Médicis. He analyses the folklore of the carnival, which served as a setting for both the revolt and the repression. From this approach he concluded that in terms of totems, signs, and symbolism there were, in effect, two folklores that confronted each other in the 1579 rising, one elite, the other popular. He notes that while the revenues of Paumier and the other leaders of the leagues were superior to those of an average artisan, the leaguers were still members of the popular movement by virtue of their professions and backgrounds. The symbols of the Paumier group were those of the lower classes. The group organized its initial rebellion within the festivities of St Blaise Day, the feast of the patron of both the textile and the agricultural workers. Paumier was elected chief of the celebration. He presided over games and competitions in which his followers pursued capons, hares, donkeys, sheep, and bears, animals clearly associated with the lower classes. It was from the basis of this 'kingdom' that Paumier led the attack upon the town elite. In contrast, the Guérin group organized its festivities under the elite symbols of eagles, partridges, and roosters. The Guérin counterattack on 15 February 1580 began as a costume ball to celebrate Mardi gras. Le Roy Ladurie argues that the carnival games reflect a fundamental confrontation between rich and poor. The symbolic organization of the two sides reveals the upper crust of the bourgeoisie, the lawyers, the men of professions, and the merchants aligning themselves with the privileged orders against the artisans, *menu peuple*, and agricultural workers.[97]

By 1579 the elite of the third estate had successfully dissociated itself from the more radical turn of the league movement. It had maintained its credibility in the eyes of the provincial leaders, for immediately fol-

lowing the suppression of the rising its leaders were permitted to reunite
the local assemblies of the third estate. In the new series of meetings the
contestation issue became secondary to a major effort to reconstitute the
internal unity of the order. The meetings concentrated upon resolving
internal third-estate differences and in particular upon reconciling the
division between the town and village elites. The principal dispute between the two groups centred upon the 1548 edict, in which Henry II
had rejected the custom of exempting the rural holdings of townspeople
from taxation. For several years after 1548 the cities had opposed the
decision and refused to ensure its application. As a result, numerous
aspects of the edict remained subject to dispute: Could the tax upon
rural holdings be levied by the cities in which the owners resided? Were
the owners of such holdings obliged to contribute to both ordinary and
extraordinary *tailles* for their possessions? How were they to be taxed
for the grain, livestock, and supplies that the villages were obliged to
furnish to passing troops?

In the absence of clear regulations the problems of applying the 1548
decision had resurfaced frequently, often during the periods when the
third estate was trying hardest to present a united front in the *taille*
dispute. In 1554 and 1579, both critical years in the third-estate campaign, the differences between town and village had flamed up in the
Estates. The request of the villages in 1550 and 1578 for a separate
commis to represent the rural communities of the third estate had stemmed
from these differences. By the late 1570s the village-town problem appeared more and more frequently before the courts. In 1579 the consuls
of St Auban contested the right of the inhabitants of St Euphémie to
possess holdings in the village without paying *tailles*.[98] The city of Vienne
contested the right of the villages of Septème and Pinet to place Vienne
residents on their rolls for the *taille extraordinaire*.[99] In 1581 the consuls
of Piégros petitioned the duke of Mayenne. They argued that all the
neighbouring towns and cities obliged them to contribute to the upkeep
of royal troops but that these same towns refused to let Piégros levy
taxes upon their residents for the property that they had purchased in
the village.[100]

Prior to the Estates of 1581 the villages had raised these problems in
a long petition to Mayenne. They noted that the weight of rural taxes
had been aggravated by a decision of the 1565 Estates that village wartime
expenses would no longer be added to the general provincial expenses
(*l'universel*) in order to be apportioned equally to all taxpayers. The
villages noted that they had appealed numerous cases concerning city

residents to the provincial courts but that the decisions had varied due to the vagueness of the 1548 document. They added that at the 1578 Estates it had been argued that both parties would name arbitrators to negotiate their differences, but that the towns had refused to co-operate. The villages, therefore, asked Mayenne to intervene and to oblige the towns to name negotiators.[101] Mayenne, who represented the king at the Estates of 1581, discussed the issue and gave the towns fifteen days – that is, up to the formal opening of the Estates – to name their negotiators.[102] The towns hesitated, questioning the ability of nobles to serve as arbiters of the dispute, since they too owned rural holdings. Finally, on the opening day of the Estates, they selected the members of the parlement of Grenoble to argue their case.[103] Although we do not possess any documents tracing the progress of these negotiations, that they continued is evident from a preamble to the 1582 tax roll for Grenoble. The text rejected village claims that town residents were not being taxed for their village possessions. It noted that they were listed in the *forain* section of the city *cadastre* for *tailles extraordinaires* but that since 1581 Grenoble had left taxation for ordinary levies to the villages.[104]

The numerous points at issue were finally settled during the assembly at Romans on 24 October 1583. It is not altogether clear how the agreement was reached. The final document was signed by six representatives of the king, the Estates, and the parlement together with sixteen delegates from the towns and twelve from the villages.[105] These were not at all the same negotiators named in 1581 by the villages and towns. That the 1583 résumé of the provincial Estates refers to the arrival of royal commissioners confirms a note in the 1583 agreement, that the matter had been submitted before the *généraux des aides* in Paris. It appears likely that the 1581 negotiations had broken down and that when the issue was submitted before the Cour des aides, the king dispatched commissioners and pressed Maugiron to expedite a settlement.

The agreement of Romans contained twenty articles that specified the means by which the principle of the 1548 decision should be applied. The initial eight articles established that town residents of *roturier* status who had acquired property in rural villages since 1518 were to pay to the village all taxes that were imposed upon their property. They were to pay their share of the ordinary and extraordinary *tailles* and of the sums imposed for the upkeep of garrisons, passage of troops, *étapes* (depots for provisions required by troops in transit), and *utencilles* (a tax originally levied to provide troops with lodgings, linen, and utensils). The only exceptions to this rule were for town residents who had ac-

quired their holdings before 1518 or who had acquired rural property
from a noble who had owned the holding since 1518.[106] The remaining
articles of the agreement concerned specific village complaints about the
grain, livestock, and supplies that the villagers were obliged to furnish
to the passing armies. The towns did not agree to contribute to any of
these expenses, but they did agree to support the rural claims that these
impositions should be deducted from the *universel*.

This agreement, accepted by the Estates of March 1584, was of great
significance in re-establishing the unity of the third-estate forces under
the leadership of the village and town notables. Both towns and villages
accepted the full consequences of the 1548 edict and began the work of
planning a new attack upon their common problem of the unjust distribution of *taille* levies among the different social orders in the province.
This desire to re-establish internal unity after the events of 1579–80
explains the major concession of the towns to the villages. Despite the
fact that the towns had obtained favourable legal judgments concerning
their rights to levy extraordinary *tailles* on the rural possessions of their
residents, they conceded these rights to the villages. The villages, however, gained little ground on the question of taxing town residents for
the goods furnished to troops.

The unity exemplified in this document brought an end to the divisions in the leadership of the third-estate forces, divisions that had reached
a climax in the 1579 revolt. The document represents more of a political
alliance destined to unite moderate third-estate forces against the privileged orders than a veritable economic and social contract. Divisions
remained clearly drawn among the moderates and radicals within the
third estate, and these divisions were just as profound as the town-
country cleavage that had appeared so often in the meetings of the
provincial Estates. It was perhaps the defeat of the more radical elements
in the spring of 1580 that permitted the more moderate political representatives of the town and village elite to reach the 1583 compromise.

The concessions of the major towns in 1583 were no less significant.
The small towns and villages had been the sources of all the major
complaints lodged by the third estate since the 1540s. They were at the
origin of the contestation of the *taille* system as well as of the structures
of the Estates and the *commis du pays*, which approved and distributed
the levies. The third-estate leadership had always been divided over the
exact presentation of the village complaints. Its cahiers had always hesitated to accept village claims to the right to assess and collect taxes upon
the rural lands owned by townspeople. The leadership had also skirted

the question of appointing a village representative to the *commis du pays*. The 1583 concessions appear to have been directed towards restoring third-estate unity and consolidating urban leadership over the third-estate forces.

In treating social structures at the end of the sixteenth and during the seventeenth centuries, several historians have emphasized recently the relative independence of the third-estate elite from both the lower classes and from the first and second estates.[107] Certainly, the social alliances that can be perceived in the 1579–80 revolts confirm this. Throughout the 1570s considerable pressure was placed upon the elite of the third estate: town consuls, village syndics, judges, officials, lawyers, and merchants. In the face of the exaggerated legal and illegal *taille* levies, town and village officials were the ones responsible for voting and collecting payments from their constituents. If they refused, troops often took them as hostages, as was the case at St Antoine in 1588. When they accepted, they were often accused of complicity with the troops or of embezzlement, as was the case in Montélimar and Romans in 1579. The cahiers and the meetings through which third-estate leaders protested the excesses of the wartime profiteers were denounced by the privileged orders as seeking to divide the social groups in the province. The same cahiers, however, were seen by their constituents as minimum demands. It was in the face of the slow negotiation of these legally expressed grievances that the contestation process was radicalized. The lower classes of the third estate and the overtaxed villages took direct action not only against brigands, recalcitrant nobles, and officials but also against the notables of their own order, as was the case at Romans.

The social composition of the leagues fluctuated between 1579 and 1580, but the work of Le Roy Ladurie and Van Doren on Romans shows that before the summer of 1579 most of the notables of the third estate had withdrawn from the movement. The notables were viewed with suspicion both by the leaguers, who accused them of collaboration with provincial officials, and by the queen mother and certain Crown officials, who associated their actions with the leagues. It was for this reason that Guérin's report tried to whitewash the actions of the town notables by placing such emphasis upon their efforts to defeat the rebels in Romans. It was also for this reason that the 1583 agreement between the towns and villages was so important to the third-estate elite. After the rejection of its leadership in the events of 1579–80, this agreement constituted a proof of its credibility in the face of both constituents and critics. Through this agreement, the village and particularly the city notables regained their control over the lower elements of the third estate. The subsequent stages of the *taille* contestation demonstrate the effectiveness of their leadership.

3

From Rural to Urban Contestation

The 1583 agreement between the cities and villages marked a turning-point in the *taille* struggle. After its conclusion the village syndics slowly withdrew from the leadership of the contestation, and the renewed third-estate offensive was increasingly directed towards the priorities of the ten cities. Leadership now fell to their designated representatives. They were the ones who conceived and drafted the grievances and cahiers. No longer were these itemized in wide-ranging village, *bailliage*, town, and district consultations. The tight circle of consuls who became the new spokesmen for the third estate reflected the restricted social base upon which urban political structures were erected. It was within these narrow corridors of bourgeois power that the *taille* offensive of the 1590s unfolded.

Up to the 1570s the villages had been the principal instigators of the *taille* challenges. In 1538 the villages had tried to impose taxes unilaterally upon the rural holdings of nobles, clerics, and townspeople. In the 1540s the villages began to appeal the question regularly before the provincial Estates and the courts. The moderate and radical contestation movements in the 1570s were set off by the villages too. But after 1579–80, though present within the contestation movement, the villages were no longer responsible for the major initiatives. They withdrew into the background, leaving the leadership of the *taille* contestation to the cities. Why? Several factors seem to have contributed to their withdrawal. The first was a certain psychological exhaustion in the face of the long and difficult struggle that the village leaders had waged only to obtain a *commis des villages* in 1578 and the application of the 1548 edict concerning the taxation of townspeople for their rural holdings, which was accorded in 1583. The second important factor in the political retreat of the villages was the dramatic failure of the popular rising and the judicial prosecution of numerous leaders of the villages and *bailliages* who had been accused of recruiting or organizing the peasants. Closely linked to these causes was the intensification of the military conflict in the 1580s, particularly after 1585. The villages appear to have resigned themselves to the increasing taxes, debts, and troops that were imposed upon them.

There are numerous indications that the burdens imposed upon the rural communities after 1585 were the heaviest of the war years. As Graph 2 in chapter 2 shows, the level of illegal *taille* levies was at its highest between 1585 and 1589. After 1589, legal levies increased by 700 per cent. Village debts began to accumulate in direct relation to these levies. In order to meet the demands of the Crown, the provincial government, and the local military, communities either levied heavy taxes or resorted to accepting substantial loans from nobles and members of the town elite. Generally they combined both practices. At the end of the wars the village of Gigors had accumulated a debt of close to 5,000 *écus*; Châteauneuf-de-Mazenc owed 15,000 *écus*, St-Paul-Trois-Châteaux 14,000, and Livron 12,000.[1] The cahiers prepared by the villages in 1596 and 1598 indicate that the great majority of the communities began to accumulate these deficits in the course of the 1580s (Graph 3). The semi-annual interest on the debts varied from 8 1/3 to 16 per cent, and frequently village syndics were obliged to seek additional loans simply to meet regular interest payments.[2]

Between 1584 and 1593 the fiscal situation of the rural communities was aggravated by the mediocre or poor level of harvests. The journal kept by Eustache Piémond contains monthly meteorological data concerning his village. He recorded a bleak succession of cold rainy summers for the last fifteen years of the century (Graph 4). This poor-weather cycle, also observed in Languedoc and in most of western Europe, seems to have been a factor in the stagnating agricultural production and the general economic contraction that affected France in the second half of the sixteenth century.[3]

A partial consequence of the rural debts, the adverse weather, and the resulting poor harvests was the slow and constant emigration from villages towards the walled towns and cities.[4] Every region of France registered high death tolls as a result of the crop failures and epidemics that haunted the second half of the sixteenth century. In the villages of Dauphiné the effects of the mortality were aggravated by the departures. Initially apparent in 1547 during the early stages of the *taille* debate, the

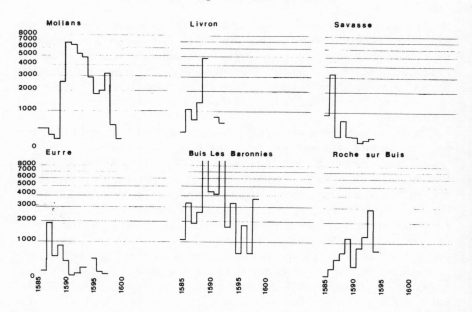

Graph 3 Annual loans negotiated by six towns and villages. The debts are expressed in *écus* and represented in a semi-logarithmic progression.
Source: Third-estate cahiers, AM Vienne, CC 42, 43

emigration problem worsened during the Wars of Religion. Though reliable statistics on the question are rare, town deliberations refer frequently to the difficulty of controlling the influx of peasants. The rapidity with which the population levels of cities and towns bounced back after severe demographic setbacks indicates their dependence upon this new source of population. The city of Romans with a population of 8,334 in 1557 declined to 7,853 in 1566 and to 6,742 in 1578 because of the wars and the epidemics of 1564 and 1580. By 1583, however, the population had jumped back to a level of 7,998, before registering a new and dramatic decline due to the plague of 1586.[5]

Urban population-replacement patterns may be traced in the baptismal registers of the Church of St Sauveur in Crest for the year 1587. During that year the royalist commander La Valette waged an intense campaign in the countryside around Crest, burning and sacking villages. Immigration into Crest increased dramatically. The baptismal registers list births to parents from the villages of Mirabel-en-Diois, Vachières,

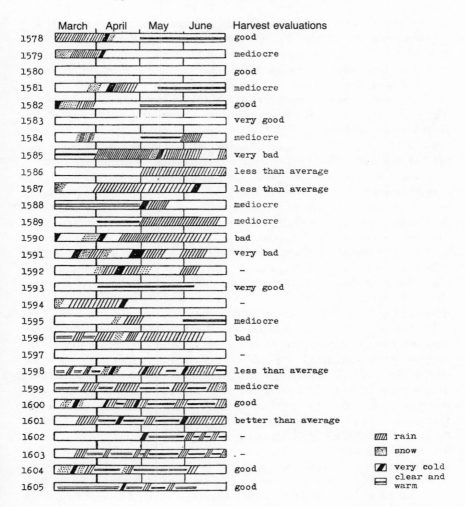

Graph 4 Annual weather and harvest conditions in Dauphiné, 1578–1605;
based upon the observations of Eustache Piémond, notary at St Antoine

Eurre, Allix, Saillans, and Saou, all of which had been overrun by La
Valette's troops. Twenty-eight per cent of the births recorded that year
were to these 'foreign' parents; in ordinary times this figure would have
represented only one per cent.[6]

The direct interaction between these economic indicators and the psychological attitudes of the peasants can be evaluated from Eustache Piémond's journal. Frequently, Piémond added his own remarks at the end of an entry concerning taxes, the quartering of troops, the outbreak of epidemics, and the like. A staunch Catholic, though a superstitious man, he was an astute observer of natural phenomena and of people. Throughout his journal Piémond always regrets the 'sufferings of the poor people' and the 'excesses' of the soldiers and Huguenots. He generally sees a ray of hope in any number of isolated incidents, such as a tax reduction accorded by the lieutenant-governor, or a new peace treaty, or a good harvest. Nevertheless, his journal entries for 1586 to 1590 contain absolutely no optimistic note. Piémond, himself a village official, expresses continual dismay at the quandary of the apparently powerless provincial leaders. Concerning the preparation of cahiers for the Estates of 1586, he notes, 'it's foolish to complain to those who have no pity on us.'[7] A 1588 illegal *taille* levy by Captain La Roche brings the comment that '[La Roche] obliged payment by force and with such violence and determination that the people did not know where to turn.'[8] Finally, in the face of another non-official levy in 1590 he comments, 'the only defence for the people was the consolation that they took in God.'[9]

Piémond's laconic comments upon the powerlessness of provincial and worldly institutions translate the agony and decline of the village community as a financial and political entity. He enumerates the succession of events that contributed to the ruin of his village: taxes, quartering of troops, epidemics, and poor harvests. The decline experienced in St Antoine seems to have been common to most rural communities in Dauphiné and in the rest of France. It is this same period that Pierre de St-Jacob and Jean Jacquart have singled out as a turning-point marking the decline of village political influence throughout the kingdom and its replacement by urban structures.[10]

The towns, by virtue of their superior means of defending themselves, were not as seriously affected by the exorbitant illegal *taille* levies of the 1580s as were their rural counterparts. They were never subjected to the coercion payments, military impositions, and direct *taille* collection so frequently demanded of the villages by regular and irregular military units. The towns were forced to make loans to their military governors, loans that were never reimbursed, but the amounts of these payments were inferior to the sums imposed upon the rural areas.[11] The fiscal structure of the province even allowed the towns to distribute their expenses for maintaining garrisons, repairing fortifications, and quartering troops over the rural communities of their district. Town residents benefited from this privileged fiscal regime up to 1589. Thereafter the official *taille* rate sky-rocketed. From an average 59 *livres* per *feu* from 1583 to 1588, the *taille* attained an average of 435.7 *livres* per *feu* from 1589 to 1595. The new increases brought the official *taille* rate of the 1590s up to the level of the combined official and unofficial levies of the 1580s. Indeed, due to the new official fiscal squeeze, the illegal *taille* levies were reduced noticeably.[12] For the villages the change made little difference. The towns, however, had never paid as much in non-official levies, and for the first time they were subjected to the same exorbitant level of taxation suffered by the villages. Within this new context it was the turn of the towns to undertake a concerted attack upon the fiscal structure of the province.

The new wave of *taille* protest dated from 8 September 1590, when the town consuls asked the lieutenant-governor for permission to assemble deputies from the cities and villages. Their meeting, held at St Marcellin, produced a cahier of thirty articles, which was submitted to a meeting of the Assembly of the Ten Cities held at Voiron on 21 November.[13] In fact the Voiron meeting took the form of a miniature Estates, since representatives of the towns and villages attended along with delegates from the nobility. The *taille* dispute was resurrected timidly.

The new cahier was not in any way a reproduction of the outspoken and clearly developed demands of the 1570s. In its insistence upon co-operation within the hierarchy of orders in the province, it belonged to a much older tradition. The third estate was once again submitting its grievances to its superiors, asking for justice. The village delegates at the meeting even presented a text that pleaded for unity among the three orders of the province. Using the metaphor of a river-boat piloted by nobles of the sword and the robe, the text noted that by their 'intelligence' and 'good judgment' the pilots could 'avoid the perils of the great rapids with which we are continually assailed.' The text went on to ask each social group, and especially the nobles, 'to inventory their names and goods and to give up and discharge themselves of any excesses so that the whole vessel could stay afloat,' an obvious reference to the exemptions of the privileged orders.[14] Yet the thirty grievances submitted by the third estate referred only obliquely to the question of the special *taille* status of the nobles and clergy. The cahier did, however, list concrete demands. It called for the suspension of levies, the control and verification of the amounts imposed by military companies and by tax collectors, the reduction of the size of regiments, and the limiting of the number of garrisons. In the case of debts, the cahier demanded that it be forbidden to seize the work animals of peasants, to take hostages, or to impose forced loans upon the solvent members of the rural communities to compensate for those who could not pay.[15]

At the Voiron meeting the nobles drafted their reply to the third-estate cahier with great tact. This was a critical period. Lesdiguières, commander of the Huguenot forces and later lieutenant-governor of the province, and several important Protestant leaders were present for the first time among the sixteen noble delegates. This obvious integration of the Huguenots into provincial institutions came just as the challenge from the Catholic League threatened the province. Totally distinct from the peasant leagues of the 1570s, the Catholic League in Dauphiné, was linked to a national movement led by the duke of Guise to depose the new Huguenot king, Henry IV. The leaguers had seized Grenoble and had taken Lieutenant-Governor Ornano hostage. Within this context the nobles replied that, given the new threats to the peace and tranquillity of the province, they could not suspend *tailles*, reduce military companies, or limit the number of garrisons. But they did promise to contribute more equitably to wartime expenses through the *ban* and *arrière-ban* (the feudal army organization by which holders of fiefs were called upon to perform the obligatory military service that was attached to the possession of their fiefs), and they did agree that the rural holdings acquired by the exempted groups should be retained on the *taille* rolls. They also agreed with the third estate that certain tax collectors and military companies had exaggerated the levies that they imposed upon the villages. They asked that commissioners be named to audit the accounts of such *receveurs* and that heavy fines be imposed upon soldiers who left their garrisons without written permission and tried to levy taxes or seize animals or foodstuffs without written orders from the lieutenant-governor or his delegates. On the proposals to find substitutes for the *tailles* to support garrisons and wartime expenses, the nobles were less affirmative. On the use of the salt tax, *gabelles* on merchandise, and the receipts from the *péages*, or toll stations, they replied that the lieutenant-governor should study the issue, this despite the fact that the salt-tax proposal had been studied several times since its original submission in 1569.[16] In other words, at Vioron the nobles conceded the principle that the third estate was overtaxed, but they were not ready to take any concrete steps to alleviate the fiscal disparities.

In 1591 the conflict between the two groups became more apparent. The third estate protested more explicitly the problem of the increasing number of rural acquisitions by tax-exempt groups. At the Assembly of the Ten Cities prior to the Estates meeting, third-estate leaders organized their strategy. They drew up a cahier focused upon the exemption problem. It noted that abandoned fields and excessive community debts had resulted from the purchases of *roturier* holdings by the privileged orders.[17]

At the meeting of the provincial Estates that began on 18 May, the cahier was presented and debated at great length. André Lacroix believed, on the basis of a vague reference by Nicolas Chorier, a seventeenth-century historian of Dauphiné, that the 1591 Estates had witnessed the introduction of lawyers to argue the cases of the third estate and the privileged orders.[18] Nothing in the official summary of the meeting bears out this claim. Only the official delegates of each order appear to have taken part in the discussions. The third estate agreed grudgingly to a *taille* levy of 10,000 *écus* but repeated its previous protests against the excesses of the soldiers and garrisons, asking that the number of men-at-arms be reduced. On the *taille* issue, the third estate once more criticized the privileged orders for not assuming their share of the financial burdens of the wars. Third-estate delegates again raised the issue of the confiscations for debt of the peasant's work animals and agricultural instruments. Among the newer articles in their cahier was a demand that the province apply the clauses of the Ordinance of Blois relating to the acquisition of *roturier* holdings by *taille*-exempt officials.[19] The edict had specified that *roturier* land purchases by exempt officials within the last twenty years should be reintegrated into *taille* rolls and that all such future acquisitions should remain subject to the *taille*. The issue of increasing noble purchases of village lands was also discussed at great length, and a report on the question was submitted by the sieur de la Motte.[20]

The real financial difficulties of the province seem to have been the decisive element in the debate. Felix Basset, the president of the Estates, intervened along with the president of the Chambre des comptes to deplore the long-term reduction in *taille* revenues that had occurred over the previous twenty years because of the transfers of *taillable* into non-*taillable* holdings.[21] The assembly produced a series of proposals on the subject. Notably, an article asked the king to name a number of independent judges to apply the Blois ordinance concerning *taille* exemptions for officials. A second vague article was voted in which the nobles allowed that the problem of the acquisitions of *roturier* holdings should be presented to the king.[22] Nicolas Chorier, who generally reflected the opinions of the privileged orders, believed that the 1591 agreement would have resolved the *taille* question 'if it had been carried out.'[23]

By the Estates of 1592 it had become clear that no action had been taken on the 1591 resolutions and that the *taille* levies had continued to increase. The new meeting abandoned the spirit of compromise that had characterized the 1591 session and marked the beginning of a new period of confrontation. The third estate asked to meet separately from the privileged orders, and it assumed a more aggressive attitude both towards the exempted groups and towards the *taille* levies. Over two hundred villages assisted at the Estates convened at Grenoble on 25 January. Their delegates described at length 'the great misery and poverty ... to which they had been reduced, principally because of the holdings acquired and occupied in their villages by the nobles and by those exempt from *tailles*.'[24] The consuls of Romans and those of the other cities protested against the increasing number of individuals who claimed exemptions from *tailles*, adding that two people often claimed to be exempt for the same office. The third-estate *procureur* brought up the issue of rural debts and the abuses that continued to be committed in villages by creditors, soldiers, and tax collectors. Finally, the third estate declared that it would not vote any new *taille* levies until the other two orders had announced how much they would furnish.

From 1592 to 1595 the meetings of the Estates were paralysed by such confrontations. Arguing that the privileged orders should assume a more substantial part of the imposition, the third estate refused to vote subsidies requested by the lieutenant-governor at three consecutive meetings in 1594 and 1595.[25] Of course such refusals did not block the *taille* levies, since the government had many years of experience in imposing *tailles* that had never been voted.[26] The successive refusals were important, however, in that once again they showed the inability of provincial institutions to resolve provincial problems and the necessity of increased intervention by the Crown. During this period the third estate maintained a continual dialogue with the court through a series of ambassadors sent to explain its case and to seek royal support. Valence sent Achilles Faure four times between 1592 and 1595, and Romans sent Jean Bernard in 1595.[27] As early as September 1594 the Grenoble consuls introduced plans at a meeting of the Assembly of the Ten Cities to place the whole *taille* affair directly before the king.

Despite last-minute attempts on the part of the privileged orders to keep the conflict within the confines of provincial institutions, third-estate plans to appeal to the king were realized in August 1595, when Henry IV agreed to hear the case during his visit to Lyon.[28] Both the third estate and the nobles held preliminary meetings to plan their strategies. At a meeting of the Assembly of the Ten Cities the third estate selected Ennemond Marchier, an *avocat* from Grenoble, to present its arguments. Its leaders invited a large number of impoverished communities to attend the audience to demonstrate the plight of their villages to the king. On 14 September 1595 over sixty village representatives made the trip to Lyon and assisted at the audience.[29]

Marchier's address to the king resurrected most of the grievances that had been presented in the cahiers of the 1570s. The only major issue left aside was the reorganization of the Estates. The exemptions of the nobles constituted the principal preoccupation of the speech. Marchier argued that they had never been exempted from extraordinary taxes and that during the war years they had abused their tax-exempt status to acquire considerable *roturier* holdings. He underlined the fact that the size of the exempted group had been increased regularly by *annoblissements* and by the creation of new exempted *parlementaires* and officials, all of whom placed an additional strain upon the tax-paying third estate. All this led Marchier to conclude that to restore the social and fiscal equilibrium of the province, Dauphiné should adopt *cadastres* and the *taille réelle* system, the same conclusion that Jean de Bourg had reached in 1579. Among the newer accusations contained in Marchier's speech were his attacks upon the parlement. He denounced the reticence of the exempted *parlementaires* to allow the *taille* problem to be presented to the king. As an interested party he asked, 'how can they judge equitably the protests of others when in the face of the Privy Council they argue that they should be both judges and defendants for their own case?'[30]

The nobles, too, selected eminent lawyers to plead their case. *Avocats* Jean Aquin from Grenoble and Julien Dufos from Toulouse presented the legal articles upon which the privileges of the second estate depended. They argued that privileged orders were the backbone of all organized societies. Dufos noted that similar attacks upon social hierarchies had undermined the Roman republic and the Greek empire. Going even further, he linked the Marchier speech with the 1579 popular rebellion, which had tried to overthrow both the structures of noble power and the institutions of the Crown. He recalled that it was the nobles who had suppressed the rebellion, and he argued that if the privileges of the nobility were now reduced, the defence of the province would be jeopardized.[31] The king sent both sides away with the traditional reply, 'I deplore your difficulties; I will render you justice; be loyal subjects and I will be a good prince for you.'[32]

On 9 October the king's council rendered its decision. It recognized the validity of the third-estate grievances and declared that it would hear the case. The arguments and supporting documents were to be presented to the council in the course of the next three months. On more immediate issues, the king's council ordered that no new impositions were to be levied in the province without the king's orders, that levies for the present year should be reduced by ten months for the garrison districts and by eight months for the others, that communities should not be obliged to pay on the principal of any debt for the next six years, and that none of the overdue *tailles* should be collected.[33] In fact most of the king's measures merely repeated previous unkept promises, and Eustache Piémond noted that the decisions of the parlement again prevented the application of the royal edict. The third estate had no illusions concerning the impartiality of provincial institutions, and its leaders set out to prepare their case for the Conseil privé.

In the initiatives taken by the third estate between 1590 and 1595, the same basic grievances were presented as in the 1570s; the difference lay in the organization and strategy of the third estate itself. In the 1570s it had been the rural villages that organized meetings to prepare cahiers of grievances, but in 1590 it was the Assembly of the Ten Cities that provoked the new round of confrontations with the privileged orders. At the Estates of 1591 it was this assembly that reintroduced the question of acquisitions by the exempted groups, and in 1594–5 it decided on the tax boycotts and the appeals to the king. The Assembly of the Ten Cities was the pivotal element of the new offensive.

The organization and role of this assembly as a provincial institution was not new. Generally composed of one or two representatives of each of the recognized cities of the province, it served traditionally as a meeting-place where delegates could co-ordinate their positions prior to the sessions of the provincial Estates and where they could select one delegate from each of the towns to sit as a member of the *commis du pays*. Between sessions of the Estates the assembly was authorized to speak for the third estate on any important issue. Its meetings were loosely structured. They were preceded by a request to the lieutenant-governor for permission to assemble, and they were held in the presence of a royal official. Before the 1590s these meetings do not appear to have produced either minutes or summaries of their deliberations. The best indication of the assembly's decisions can be found in the cahiers that delegates from the ten cities drafted or in the arguments that they presented in the provincial Estates.[34] The increasingly official role played by the assembly became evident in 1592, when the lieutenant-governor himself summoned the ten cities and assisted at their assembly.[35] During the remainder of the 1590s and in the early 1600s their sessions were held frequently in the presence of Lesdiguières, the former Huguenot leader appointed lieutenant-governor by Henry IV.

The membership of the Assembly of the Ten Cities varied. Up to the middle of the sixteenth century it was made up of designated representatives of the eight recognized cities of the province. When Gap and Montélimar were recognized officially as cities, it gained its official designation as the Assembly of the Ten Cities (for locations, see chapter 1, Map 1).[36] Each of the cities generally sent its first or second consul or both of them. Given the town procedures for selecting first and second consuls, this normally meant that the meetings were attended by nobles of the robe, officials, judges, lawyers, *procureurs*, and merchants. When the questions to be debated were particularly important, as in 1590, 1594, and 1595, the Assembly of the Ten Cities was enlarged to include delegates from other towns and villages. The enlarged meeting was sometimes designated an *assemblée du pays*. The interests of the walled towns (*villes closes*) were particularly important in the enlarged meetings. There were twenty to thirty walled towns in the province, towns such as Cremieu, Beaurepaire, St Marcellin, Loriol, Pont de Beauvoisin, La Tour du Pin. Each of them contained garrisons and benefited from most of the fiscal and defensive privileges of the ten cities.[37] Although their representatives were not invited to the regular meetings of the assembly, they assisted at all of the enlarged meetings and played a considerable part in debating the priorities of the third estate in the renewed *taille* controversy.[38] Nevertheless, the rural communities participated less and less actively in the organizational meetings. Despite the reported presence of two hundred village delegates at the 1592 Estates, their representation was limited generally to the *commis des villages*.

It is not easy to single out the individuals who revived the third-estate fiscal protests during the period from 1590 to the beginning of the legal contestations in 1595. Only in 1594 do the résumés of the Estates meetings list the delegates in attendance. Similar lists for the assemblies of the ten cities are available only for the extraordinary meetings of 1597 and 1602. Beyond that, the Estates left minutes or summaries of their deliberations, but in these it is only possible to verify the presence of a delegate if he spoke out on a major issue. The only other source for reconstituting the lists of those who attended these meetings are the municipal records, which frequently note the names of the delegates sent to the provincial meetings.

While the lists that can be reconstituted do not reveal the presence of any specific leader of the contestation in the early 1590s, a few individuals do reappear frequently at the meetings of the Estates and at the assemblies where the *taille* affair was discussed. They must have ensured a certain continuity to the debate. The social and economic backgrounds of these activists is indicative of the urban constituency and power-base of the new challenge.

Among the representatives whose names are mentioned in the summary of the 1591 Estates were Aymar Pellisson from Vienne and Achilles Faure from Valence. Both continued to work for the third-estate cause throughout the decade. Pellisson came from an eminent family of Vienne. He was a doctor of law and an *avocat*. In 1591 he was neither young nor rich, and his past involvements demonstrated a humanitarian interest in the underprivileged. As early as 1578 he had been *avocat* of the poor in Vienne, and as such he often came into conflict with Bishop Pierre de Villars over such matters as giving out tickets for grain distribution and providing the poor with legal advice on their grievances. Pellisson and the bishop clashed over the hours for the *bureau des pauvres*, an institution devoted to the poor. The bishop argued that by opening Sunday mornings, the *bureau* conflicted with the Mass, and he proposed that it be opened only on Sunday afternoons. Pellisson replied that it was important that the morning hours be retained, for the consulate met Sunday mornings and the grievances of the poor could only then be submitted directly to the consuls. Despite these objections the hours of the *bureau* were modified. Pellisson returned to the attack in 1594, arguing that the new hours made no difference to Mass attendance since 'men don't go [to mass]; women go!' His persistence again went unrewarded, and the local judge ruled that the bishop could continue to schedule the *bureau des pauvres* on Sunday afternoon.[39]

Pellisson's political career seems to have been just as controversial. In 1584 he turned down the position of consul after a disputed election that had pitted him against his cousin Louis Pellisson. His reasons for refusing the post were that he was a widower and that his financial situation was difficult. He noted that his cousin was an 'homme de bien' who had the means to carry out the responsibilities vested in a consul.[40] Things seem to have improved for Pellisson between 1584 and 1591. In

1591 he accepted the position of consul, and as such he participated at the Estates of that year.[41] Between 1591 and 1602 he appeared often at meetings of the Estates or of the assembly. Pellisson attended the 1599 Estates as a *député du pays*. In 1601 he was among the delegates sent to the court to plead the *taille* case, and in 1602 he participated in the Assembly of the Ten Cities as a representative of Vienne.[42]

Achilles Faure was more involved in the *taille* contestation. Besides representing Valence as consul in 1591 and 1592, he was present at the 1594 and 1595 Estates and at virtually all the meetings of the ten cities between 1595 and 1602. This regular and prolonged assistance at third-estate meetings accounted for his selection in 1595 as one of the delegates to present the third-estate case before the king. His role in the negotiations was to assure a liaison among the cities, towns, Estates, and the royal court. To do so he travelled from town to town co-ordinating third-estate actions, informing the consuls of the latest proposals, and requesting funds to continue the delegation.[43] Even after the royal decision in 1602, Faure continued to pursue third-estate demands that community debts be reduced. In 1604 this led him to be accused by the nobles of using his position to embezzle town and village funds, a charge upon which the privy council refused to act.[44]

The economic and social background of Achilles Faure suggests a decided contrast with the humanitarian inclinations of Pellisson. Faure was not a lawyer, and he was always listed as a 'bourgeois' in official documents. He appears to have been a *rentier*, indulging in credit operations and managing his investments as well as those of others. This can be established from a series of notarial minutes concerning contracts between Faure and inhabitants of Valence.[45] The clearest indication of his money-lending activities emerges from records of the deliberations of the Valence consulate in 1593 and 1594. The city council expressed its regret to Faure concerning the financial losses he had suffered due to the ordinances on the *pinatelles*. The city eventually reimbursed him 1,004 *écus* for his losses.[46] The *pinatelles* were base money, generally made of copper or tin. They had no intrinsic value, and their worth depended upon the exchange rate fixed by the government. Between 1591 and 1593 the Crown carried out two drastic devaluations of the *pinatelles*, the first reducing their value by three-quarters and the second by a half. The reason for these devaluations is significant: the *pinatelles* seem to have been the money in which community debts were contracted and paid. The letters patent argued that the devaluations were intended to reduce these debts.[47] A controversy followed the royal interventions as creditors protested the devaluations, and eventually, in 1609, the Crown ordered that the rates be revised upwards.[48] From this controversy and from the reimbursement that Valence made to Faure, it appears that Achilles Faure had invested in the debts accumulated by the communities of the province during the 1580s and 1590s. It is certain that he had loaned to Valence the 1,004 *écus* that were reimbursed in 1594, and he had probably loaned much more.

If one can judge from Faure's assessment on the Valence *taille* rolls, his affairs seem to have prospered. On the roll for 1588 his wealth was a little above the average for those in his fiscal category. The average assessment paid by those on the bourgeois *parcelle* was 2 *écus* 10 *sous*, while Faure paid 3 *écus* 26 *sous*.[49] On the 1606 roll Faure's finances were again better than average. He paid 17 *livres* 4 *sous*, compared to the average assessment of 7 *livres* 7 *sous*.[50] In 1615, the last available *taille* roll during Faure's lifetime, he paid almost three times the average assessment, 27 *livres* 3 *sous*, compared to 10 *livres* 16 *sous*.[51]

Socially, Faure seems to have been well integrated into the oligarchy that governed Valence, and he appears to have been closest to those in the middle or lower fiscal brackets of the bourgeois *parcelle*. The parish registers of St Jean reveal that he married the daughter of Jean Sepolet, a 'bourgeois' whose *taille* assessment was only 40 *sous*.[52] The same register indicates that either Faure or his wife was frequently a godparent for 'bourgeois' who paid average or below-average assessments on the *taille* rolls. His power-base within this social group explains his election as consul and the fact that after his two years as second and first consul, he figured regularly among the city councillors. Faure's popularity and leadership role within the city of Valence seem to explain why he was the only third-estate representative without legal training to be sent on missions to the royal court.

Among the other individuals who became involved in the *taille* contestation between the 1591 Estates and the official appeal of the case before the king's council in 1595, the most influential were Moyne Charbotel, Henri Martinon, and Antoine Rambaud. Clearly a member of the social elite, Moyne Charbotel was a doctor of law and the *avocat* of the *bailliage* of Vienne. Politically, he seems to have been very versatile in the exercise of power. Elected as a consul in 1593, he was elevated to the position of first consul in 1594, when the duke of Nemours took Vienne in the name of the Catholic League. A year later, when the Crown retook the city, Charbotel was retained as first consul by the duke of Montmorency.[53] His role as first consul made him the automatic delegate to the provincial Estates, but when he first assisted is not clear. The summary of the Estates of 1593 is missing, and Vienne appears not to have sent a delegate to the Estates in 1594, because of its links with the league. It was at the Estates of 1595 that Charbotel was first mentioned as representative from Vienne. At that meeting he assumed a major role, replying for the third estate to the delaying tactics of the nobility. The second estate wanted to reach a compromise on the *taille* question without going before the king's council, but once again the nobles were ready to make only minor concessions.[54] Charbotel noted that when the duke of Montmorency, the constable of France, had asked the two sides to try to reach an agreement, his remark had been aimed particularly at the nobility, and it was up to them to make concessions that could serve as a basis of negotiations.[55]

At the conclusion of the 1595 Estates Charbotel was sent with Achilles Faure and another third-estate representative, Gaspard Billionet of Grenoble, to pursue the *taille* case before the royal court, a role that Charbotel exercised up to June of 1597, when he became ill and asked to be replaced.[56] Despite his withdrawal from the official delegation Charbotel remained interested in the *taille* question, and he represented Vienne at the important Assembly of the Ten Cities in October 1597 and again in July 1602.[57]

Grenoble did not participate in the *taille* negotiations with as much fervour as Vienne or Valence, perhaps because the privileged orders of Grenoble held the important position of first consul. One of the most active representatives of the city on the *taille* question was Henri Martinon. Elected second consul in 1594, he represented Grenoble at the Assembly of the Ten Cities and at the Estates of that year as well as at the estates of St Marcellin in 1598. In 1597, when the third estate organized its appeal to the king at the Assembly of the Ten Cities at St Marcellin, Martinon was named one of the syndics of the third estate. Along with Faure, Martin from Romans, and Sambein from Vienne, he was responsible for co-ordinating correspondence, information, and fund raising for his district.[58]

Martinon was a *procureur*, a member of one of the legal professions that so dominated the political and fiscal structure of Grenoble. Despite the importance of their numbers, the functions of the *procureurs* were relatively minor within the legal machinery. They resembled the English solicitors. They were retained by plaintiffs to seek information and documentation for their cases and to advise them on legal procedure. Trained as apprentices, without any university formation, they could not plead cases before the courts. In general, legal historians have considered them, as their contemporaries did, to have been professionally and socially inferior to the *avocats*, but this inferiority may be overstated in the case of Dauphiné.[59] Alain Balsan has found that they were well respected within the social orders of Valence, and in Grenoble their average tax assessments were only a fraction lower than those of the *avocats*.[60]

When compared to the majority of the Grenoble *procureurs*, Martinon was not rich. He paid assessments of 2 *écus* 20 *sous* in 1591, when the average *taille* assessment for *procureurs* was 4.7 *écus*.[61] In 1610 he paid 5 *écus*, again only about half that of the average *procureur*.[62] He resided in the Portetreyne district, one of the streets of the town where *procureurs* accounted for over half the tax-paying population.

The age and social position of Henri Martinon can be approximated from various indicators. Grenoble parish registers do not extend back far enough to furnish his birthdate, but we do know that Martinon's wife gave birth to a daughter in 1598[63] and that Henri Martinon died between August 1613 and December 1614, when his tax assessment was transferred to his heirs.[64] In all probability Martinon was only in his thirties during the *taille* contestation in the 1590s. Socially, Martinon and his family were tied closely to the village and town political leaders. In 1597 he was asked to advise a group of forty village notables, assembled at St Marcellin, on the progress of the *taille* dispute.[65] Martinon's connections in the towns of the province led him to be retained by Valence in 1599 to prepare its case for the parlement concerning the grievances of the town's Huguenot population.[66]

From a very different social and political category was Antoine Rambaud. Pellisson, Faure, Charbotel, and Martinon were all local notables who represented clearly defined social elements of their respective towns. Rambaud's career and social connections transcended Die, of which he was a consul and a delegate at the provincial Estates of 1594. Educated at the University of Valence, Rambaud had begun by studying the classics before he turned to law. In 1595 he became established as *avocat* to the parlement of Grenoble. Throughout the period, however, he continued to sit for Die at the provincial Estates.[67] At the assembly of St Marcellin in 1597 he was selected to represent the third estate in the presentation of the *taille* case before the king's council, a task that he pursued with great zeal up to 1614. Contrary to the belief of André Lacroix and A. Rochas that Rambaud retired from the case after the 1602 judgment, a 1606 letter from the nobles of Dauphiné to Chancellor Bellièvre noted the renewed initiatives of Rambaud to contest their privileges, and a cahier of grievances signed by Rambaud was submitted to the Estates of 1611.[68] In effect his withdrawal from the *taille* controversy seems to have been much later than 1602. It appears to have coincided with his nomination as episcopal judge for the diocese of Die in 1614.[69]

Socially, Rambaud's family was well established both in Die and in the province. His father, Gaspard, had arrived in the town towards 1549 from nearby Châtillon-en-Diois. Doctor of law and *avocat*, Gaspard Rambaud was elected member of the consulate of Die in 1562, and in 1567 he became one of the consuls.[70] The brother-in-law of Antoine Rambaud was the Grenoble lawyer Ennemond Marchier, who pleaded the third-estate cause before the king in 1595.[71] Rambaud's father-in-law, the doctor Louis Villeneuve, was close to the provincial governing elite. Villeneuve held the title of Physician to the King, and he was ennobled for his medical services in 1603.[72]

Among his biographers Rambaud has the reputation of a polemist who engaged himself rapidly in controversy.[73] This assessment is readily borne out by his writings in the *taille* controversy. In 1599 his *Plaidoyé pour le tiers estat du Dauphiné* argued that the judicial officials of the province were 'hypocrites,' existing 'like warts on a sick body; they live like semi-gods, like Lucullus; build like Crassus and speak like Cato; they have no other objective than that which is useful to them, nor other goal than to enrich themselves, most often at the expense of the public; they earn excessive wages; they are not equitable in their judgments; without them the world would be much happier than it is.'[74] The privileged orders exploited rapidly this excessive language and accused Rambaud of being a troublemaker (*boutefeu*) who attacked the integrity of the king's justice and tried to open the way for rebellion and the establishment of a 'popular state' in the province.[75] In a series of published letters and in his *Second plaidoyé* Rambaud was forced to backtrack on this and several other of his accusations.[76]

This motley group of five delegates from the different towns of the province seems to have ensured a certain element of continuity to the third-estate cause from meeting to meeting between 1591 and 1595. None of them represented rural communities, and it is clear that none of them came from the marginal or minority groups that are so often depicted as the source of discontent and unrest in early modern France. On the contrary, these five delegates from the different towns of the province came from representative social elements of the urban elite. Four of the five were associated with the practice of law, and their range of influence extended from Pellisson, the humanitarian lawyer who worked

TABLE 1

Socio-economic breakdown of the Grenoble *taille* roll, 1591. Assessments are listed in *écus* (é) and *sous* (s).

	Number	% of city total	Assessment	% of city total
LEGAL PROFESSIONS				
Procureurs	88	9.10	419 é, 22 s	16.68
Notaires	21	2.17	36 é, 22 s	1.44
Avocats-praticiens	15	1.55	76 é, 20 s	3.03
Clercs	11	1.13	35 é, 50 s	1.42
Huissiers	3	0.31	21 é, 44 s	0.86
Total	138	14.26	589 é, 38 s	23.43
OFFICIALS				
Army, sergeants, etc	26	2.69	30 é, 27 s	1.21
Govt Treasury, Crown, Estates	11	1.13	25 é, 14 s	1.00
Total	37	3.82	55 é, 41 s	2.21
MERCHANTS	52	5.38	276 é, 7 s	10.98
Total	52	5.38	276 é, 7 s	10.98
NOTABLES				
Widows and heirs				
(no professions listed)	113	11.69	394 é, 38 s	15.69
'sieurs' and 'maîtres'				
(no professions listed)	54	5.59	301 é, 5 s	11.97
Total	167	17.28	695 é, 43 s	27.66
MEDICAL PROFESSIONS				
Médecins, chirurgiens, barbiers	7	0.72	31 é, 40 s	1.25
Apothicaires	11	1.13	70 é, 10 s	2.79
Total	18	1.85	101 é, 50 s	4.04
TRADES AND ARTISANS				
Leather workers				
Cordonniers	82	8.48	101 é, 21 s	4.03
Couroyeurs	4	0.41	5 é, 50 s	0.23
Total	86	8.89	107 é, 11 s	4.26
Textile workers				
Tailleurs	20	2.07	47 é, 28 s	1.88
Tisserands	11	1.13	3 é, 20 s	0.13
Couturiers	27	2.79	17 é, 49 s	0.71
Merciers, Epingliers	8	0.82	27 é, 46 s	1.10

	Number	% of city total	Assessment	% of city total
Chapeliers	9	0.93	12 é, 50 s	0.51
Cordiers	6	0.62	12 é, 20 s	0.49
Teinturiers	2	0.20	19 s	0.01
Chaussetiers	4	0.41	2 é, 57 s	0.10
Total	87	8.97	124 é, 49 s	4.93
Artisans				
Potiers	5	0.51	9 é, 40 s	0.37
Peintres	3	0.31	5 é, 5 s	0.20
Total	8	0.82	14 é, 45 s	0.57
Metal workers				
Serruriers	6	0.62	4 é, 19 s	0.17
Armuriers	3	0.31	23 s	0.01
Quincailliers, cloutiers	5	0.52	17 é, 35 s	0.70
Peyrolliers	4	0.41	21 é, 44 s	0.11
Total	18	1.86	25 é, 1 s	0.99
Construction				
Maçons	7	0.72	1 é, 41 s	0.06
Charpentiers, menuisiers	24	2.48	34 é, 48 s	1.38
Total	31	3.20	36 é, 29 s	1.44
Provisions				
Affameurs	6	0.62	2 é, 52 s	0.11
Meuniers	8	0.82	13 é, 56 s	0.55
Boulangers	49	5.07	83 é, 23 s	3.31
Bouchers, Rôtisseurs	16	1.65	24 é, 16 s	0.96
Celliers	9	0.93	5 é, 57 s	0.23
Total	88	9.09	130 é, 24 s	5.16
Services				
Naucher-bateliers	5	0.51	1 é, 18 s	0.05
Changeurs de monnaie, Orfèvres	9	0.93	10 é, 59 s	0.43
Muletiers	6	0.62	5 é, 9 s	0.20
Hôtes, cabaretiers	42	4.34	47 é, 54 s	1.90
Revendeurs	20	2.07	15 é, 33 s	0.62
Total	82	8.47	80 é, 53 s	3.20
Total identified	812	83.89	2,238 é, 52 s	88.87
Total unidentified	160	16.56	275 é, 11 s	10.94
Total on taille roll	966	100.45	2,514 é, 03 s	99.81*

* Percentages have been rounded off within each category; therefore, the totals do not equal exactly 100 per cent.

for the urban poor, to Rambaud, the *avocat* in the parlement who was closely tied into the socially mobile new provincial elite. Each of them came from a social group that played an important part in the political structure of his town, and they all possessed networks of friends and relatives who kept them in close contact with third-estate complaints.

The question arises, however, as to why these elite groups were so interested in the *taille* question. Historians in the past have interpreted their action as strictly humanitarian. For Charles Laurens, in the nineteenth century, it was a question of darkness against light, and the advocates of the popular cause were on the side of righteousness.[77] André Lacroix noted that the delegates of the third estate argued the cause of 'the people' at great personal expense to themselves. According to Lacroix, Antoine Rambaud ended up sacrificing his health, while one of his colleagues in the *taille* contestation, Claude Delagrange, died in pursuit of the cause. As a result of his father's activities Delagrange's son was refused succession to his office.[78] Even for Le Roy Ladurie in his short supplement on the 1590 *taille* question, the advocates of the third-estate cause were 'forerunners of equality,' forward-looking lawyers who prefigured the ideological struggles of the French Revolution.[79]

How accurate is this portrayal? One tool useful to developing a more adequate understanding of the reasons for the wholesale implication of the urban elite in the *taille* discussions of the 1590s is the surviving *taille* rolls. These rolls demonstrate that in contrast to what is frequently implied or argued, the impoverished day laborers and the artisan class of the town were not those most affected by the tax increases.[80] A breakdown of the *taille* rolls for Grenoble, Valence, and Romans shows that it was precisely the legal, merchant, and 'bourgeois' groups that were the most heavily taxed by the urban fiscal structures (see Table 1). In Grenoble the legal professions, which had seen their numbers grow by the creation of the parlement in 1453, dominated the tax-paying elements of the city.[81] They constituted 14 per cent of the individuals listed on the 1591 *taille* roll, and they paid 23 per cent of the taxes.[82] Among the other major categories of the third-estate elite, the 5 per cent of the taxpayers listed as merchants were assessed 10 per cent of the *tailles*, and the 'bourgeoisie,' living from their investments and identified only as 'sieur' or 'maître,' constituted 5 per cent of the taxpayers and paid almost 12 per cent of the taxes. At the other extreme of the *taille* lists, the artisans and workers of the leather professions, who constituted 8.9 per cent of the total number of taxpayers, paid only a little over 4 per cent of the taxes, and the textile workers, 9 per cent of the taxpayers,

TABLE 2
Social categories in the Valence *taille* roll, 1588, and in the Romans *taille* roll, 1578–9

	Number	% of city total	Assessment	% of city total
VALENCE 1588				
Merchant-bourgeois *parcelle*	240	23.50	519 é, 8 s	49.95
Trades-artisans *parcelle*	456	44.66	319 é, 36 s	30.73
Ploughmen, *main-d'oeuvre agricole parcelle*	325	31.83	200 é, 27 s	19.28
Total	1,021	99.99	1,037 é, 11 s	99.96
ROMANS 1578–9				
Lawyers, notables: officials, bourgeois *rentiers*	51	3.92	284 é, 48 s	12.94
Merchants and men of professions	132	10.15	379 é, 19 s	19.72
Tradesmen and artisans	640	49.23	765 é, 8 s	39.77
Ploughmen (*laboureurs*)	477	36.69	494 é, 31 s	25.70
Total	1,300	99.99	1,923 é, 46 s	98.13

were responsible for only 4.9 per cent of the assessments.[83]

In other towns where *taille* rolls are available, it is impossible to provide such a breakdown of occupational categories. Nowhere else are there clear indications of the professions or trades of individuals. Nevertheless, the *taille* rolls for Valence and Romans do give some insight into the social breakdown of fiscal categories. The rolls are divided into the official categories that participated in the selection of consuls: bourgeois-merchants, tradesmen, ploughmen (see Table 2). From these rolls it is again obvious that the members of the bourgeois elite bore the heaviest tax burden. In Valence the 240 individuals listed on the bourgeois-merchant *parcelle* in the 1588 *taille* roll constituted 23.5 per cent of the tax-paying population of the town, yet they paid close to 50 per cent of the *tailles*.[84] In Romans, where the 1578 roll was the last to list inhabitants by their social categories, the taxpayers in the first two *parcelles* (notables, professionals, and merchants) constituted 14 per cent of the total list and were assessed for almost 33 per cent of the *tailles*.[85]

Given the amount of the tax burden that the elite shouldered, it is clear that the involvement of large numbers of *procureurs, avocats*, merchants, and bourgeois *rentiers* among the advocates of the third-estate *taille* propositions indicates far more than their highly developed social consciousness. The 'forerunners of equality' were far more than generous intellectuals defending the poor and exploited peasants.[86] The *procès des tailles* interested them much more than as an abstract intellectual confrontation. They saw their tax payments rising and their future investments compromised due to the fiscal structures of the province.[87]

In each of the major towns the groups that paid the heaviest fiscal impositions also controlled the political structures. Like the system of Romans, so attacked during the popular revolts of 1579, electoral procedures in the other cities of the province were based theoretically upon the dominant medieval socio-economic categories. City governments, however, were in a period of evolution. They had moved away from strict adherence to the electoral lists defined by adherence to medieval corporations, but they had not yet been influenced by the regular Crown interventions, nominations, and ordinances of the absolutist period. During the sixteenth century in Dauphiné, as in the other regions of France, control of the urban consulates was disputed between the dominant economic and social groups in each town, generally the merchants and the legal or official groups.[88] Eventually, control of the towns tended to become vested permanently in small cliques of notables, since new consuls were not elected by the group that they represented but were co-opted by the preceding government.

The most outstanding example of the functioning of such urban oligarchies is furnished by Vienne, where in 1551 the merchants excluded all other third-estate groups from participation in the selection of consuls. Seven of the eight consuls were chosen by merchants after 1551, and they elected five of the six consuls during the Wars of Religion.[89] In Grenoble the legal profession established practical control over the city by more discreet but just as effective means. According to the fifteenth-century regulation under which the consulate operated, the first consul should have been a *docteur-en-droit*, the second a bourgeois or noble, the third a merchant, and the fourth an artisan.[90] But by the end of the sixteenth century the first consul was alternately a noble of the sword or an *avocat consistorial* (an ennobled *avocat* to the parlement), the second a *procureur* or an *avocat*, the third a merchant, and the fourth a *procureur*, notary, clerk of the courts, or apothecary. The changing appropriation of the seat of the fourth consul illustrates the social evolution of the city and of the consulate. Reserved originally for artisans, the fourth seat was held generally by merchants towards the beginning of the sixteenth century. By the 1570s the legal professions began to monopolize the position.[91] As a result of this evolution the non-ennobled legal groups held regularly the seats of the second and fourth consul, and in the case of the *taille* contestation they were supported consistently by the merchant groups that held the third seat. Nevertheless, there always remained the influential first consul, representing the nobles, who opposed the active involvement of the city in the *procès des tailles*.

In Valence the nobles were not represented on the city council up to the time of its reorganization by the monarchy in 1610.[92] In the 1590s the city was divided into three social categories, each of which had its own *taille* roll and its own consuls. The second consul represented the bourgeoisie (*rentiers, avocats,* medical men) and the merchants, while the third consul was selected from the masters and artisan groups. The fourth consul came from the ranks of the *laboureurs* or agricultural workers. In order that continuity would be ensured, the outgoing second consul (*consul ancien*) became automatically first consul in the new consulate.[93] This assured the merchants control of the seats of the first and second consuls, which was generally enough for a majority, since the fourth consul assisted rarely at meetings.

Behind the apparent democracy of the annual election of new consuls, the indirect electoral mechanisms provided the means by which town governments were controlled by certain families or social groups. In both Grenoble and Valence the outgoing consuls and councillors met together to designate four or five choices for their successors, and the enlarged council elected one of the designated nominees. In Grenoble two of the outgoing consuls were retained as councillors in the new government, while in Valence, as previously noted, the outgoing second consul automatically became the new first consul, and all of the *consuls anciens* were retained, generally among the eleven municipal councillors.

The smaller towns reflected the reduced popular participation and the tendency towards oligarchical rule observed in the cities. In St Marcellin, for instance, the election procedure only appeared more democratic. Elections were held to choose between two preselected nominees of the outgoing consuls. Since the town was not divided into social categories, the new consuls were elected by a general assembly at which any inhabitant listed on the *taille* roll could participate. Despite this apparently more open procedure, the nomination system restricted the candidates, and participation in the final electoral assembly was very limited. Between 1588 and 1603 attendance averaged only 52 persons. In that same period the *taille* roll of 1592 listed 329 individuals eligible to vote, and that of 1599 contained the names of 325 eligible voters.[94]

It is not at all surprising that the principal targets of these town oligarchies were the massive tax increases that were forced upon them and that were exaggerated by the exemptions held by their privileged colleagues, the nobles, clergy, and officials who escaped the new impositions. In effect, the financial and social division was very fine between the exempted groups and the non-exempt elite, as evidenced by the number of ennoblements that were distributed towards the end of the sixteenth century.[95] The members of the urban elite who paid the new impositions accused their exempted colleagues, and particularly the new nobles, of being partly responsible for the increases in their levies. They noted that they had to make up the difference in the *taille* levy for each new noble who was scratched from the rolls.[96]

In terms of urban space and sociability, both the exempt and non-exempt elites were clustered together in certain districts and on certain streets of each town. One of the best sources available for demonstrating the patterns of urban occupation during this period is the *taille* rolls, especially in the case of Grenoble. The *taille* roll lists taxpayers, their occupations, and their streets of residence. From this document it becomes evident that the streets in the centre of the town, such as rue Chenoise, Revenderre, Mal Conseil, Peyrollerie, Neuve, Palharey, and Portetreyne, were strongholds of the noble, merchant, and legal elite. The average assessment on these streets varied from 231 *écus* on rue Chenoise to 278 *écus* on Revenderie and Portetreyne (see Map 3). By contrast, in the outlying sections such as the St Laurent district, or on the other side of the Isère, or in the Très Cloître or St Jacques districts, which were dominated by *laboureurs*, presumably agricultural workers, the average amounts paid varied from 22 to 100 *écus*.[97]

The residences of merchants, artisans, men of professions, and nobles were interspersed, although here also certain groups tended to dominate particular streets. The richer merchants, nobles, and artisans seem to have been concentrated on rue Chenoise and Revenderie, where the *taille* lists show numerous tailors, haberdashers, leather workers, and innkeepers. On Mal Conseil and Peyrollerie, shopkeepers and dealers in hardware and leather goods were mixed with legal groups, clerks, *procureurs*, and *avocats*. Finally, rue Neuve, Palharey, and Portetreyne were strongholds of the legal professions. Lawyers, *procureurs*, or officials constituted 18 of the 37 taxpayers on rue Neuve and Palharey and 38 of the 73 individuals assessed on Portetreyne.[98]

While the breakdown in the occupational structures of Grenoble differs from that of the other towns of the province because of the presence

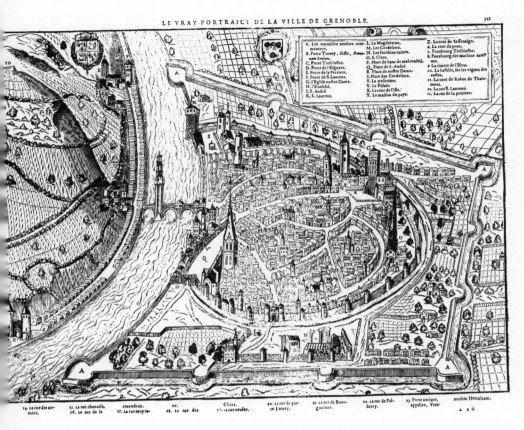

Map 3 Grenoble in the late sixteenth century: streets and districts
Source: BM Grenoble, Pd 4.10

of so many lawyers, solicitors, and clerks who gravitated about the parlement and the Chambre des comptes, the general socio-economic resi-
dential patterns seem to have been very similar in other cities of the
province. It is obvious that in Romans, where the 1595 *taille* roll was
organized by district, the merchants, artisans, professional groups, and
ennobled officials had clustered in the centre of the town. Just as in the
1578 roll analysed by Le Roy Ladurie, these notables occupied the tri-
angle extending from Place des Cordelliers to Place St Bernard and

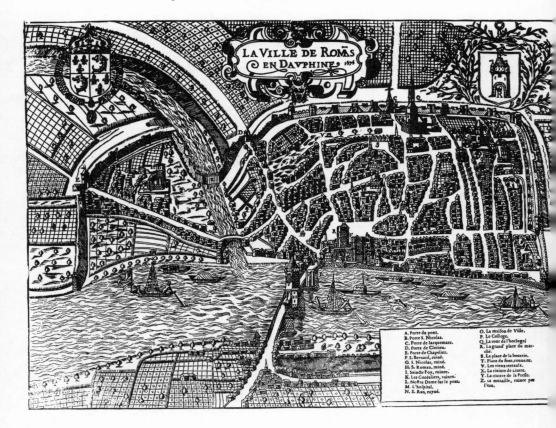

A. Porte du pont.
B. Porte S. Nicolas.
C. Porte de Iacquemare.
D. Porte de Clerieu.
E. Porte de Chapelier.
F. S. Bernard, ruiné.
G. S. Nicolas, ruiné.
H. S. Roman, ruiné.
I. Saincte Foy, ruinée.
K. Les Cordeliers, ruinez.
L. Noſtre Dame ſur le pont.
M. L'hoſpital.
N. S. Rus, ruyné.

O. La maiſon de Ville.
P. Le College.
Q. La tour de l'horlogei
R. Le grand' place du mar-
ché.
S. La place de la boucrie.
T. Place du foſſé, couuerte.
V. Les vieux rextaulx.
X. La riuiere de Lizere.
Y. La riuiere de la Preſle.
Z. La muraille, ruinée par
l'eau.

Map 4 Romans in 1575: streets and districts
Source: *Cosmographie universelle de Munster enrichie et augmentée par François de Belleforest* (1757), Bibliothèque de l'Arsenal, Paris

Place Jacquemart (see Map 4). Between them and the city ramparts, the St Nicolas, Chapelier, and Clérieu districts were inhabited by artisans, textile workers, peasants, and agricultural workers.[99]

In the Valence *taille* roll for 1588, the *parcelles*, or lists drawn up for the bourgeois and artisan groups, actually included the names of several men who had been recently ennobled and whose tax listings had been

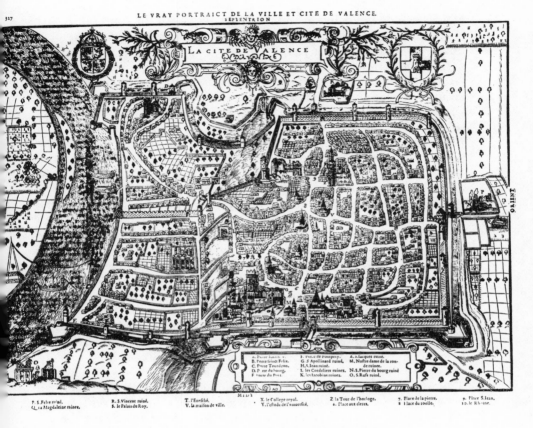

Map 5 Valence in the late sixteenth century: streets and districts
Source: BM Grenoble, Pd 2.21

scratched. From the *parcelles* it can be shown that the taxpayers with the
highest assessments and best social standing lived along the Grande Rue
in the area extending from Place des Clercs to Place St Jean and into
Place de la Pierre, Côte des Chapeliers, and the St Félix district (see Map
5). The separate roll of the *laboureurs*, which listed principally agricultural
workers, demonstrates their concentration around the ramparts: the
first, second, third, and fourth quartalets, the rue des Oches, Cros de

Malric, rue de la Vacherie, and the lower section of the town bordering on the river. Only one *laboureur* lived on the rue des Chapeliers, and only four lived on rue St Jean.[100]

The *taille* offensive of the 1590s would appear to have been provoked largely by these urban social cleavages that were essential fiscal. The rivalry between those members of the elite who were *taillable* and those who were exempt was exacerbated as taxes increased. Both groups resided in the same districts, often exercised the same professions, and possessed approximately the same revenues, but one group paid the *taille* and the other did not. René Pillorget has noted in his studies of Provence that disputes between such social elites were one of the basic elements in the outbreak of both violent and non-violent contestation in the late sixteenth-century urban context.[101] In the case of Dauphiné the rivalry between the two elite groups is clear. They regularly confronted each other at the meetings of the provincial Estates, and the third-estate elite forced the town consulates to examine scrupulously each new exemption that was proposed in order to try to reduce the number of tax-exempt inhabitants on the existing *taille* rolls. During the month of January 1592 four such cases were debated and contested by the Grenoble city council.[102] In 1593, according to Chorier, Grenoble tried to reincorporate into its *taille* rolls all officials and their descendants who had benefited from ennoblements since 1523.[103] In Valence a similar offensive began in 1592, when the city began complex legal proceedings to block the exemption of Claude Frère, a *lecteur* at the University of Valence. The town argued that the Edict of Fontainebleau, issued in 1556, had allowed only six exemptions to the university and that Frère represented the seventh.[104] Valence won its case and proceeded to contest the exemptions of other *lecteurs*. On 30 October they even invited a series of outside examiners to test the competence of Claude Frère to retain his position at the university. Among those invited was Jean Vincent from Crest, one of the future defenders of the third-estate cause.[105]

If the dominant political groups in the towns were not successful in imposing taxes on their exempted neighbours, the question arises why they did not try to shift the fiscal weight of the *tailles* towards the more marginal groups. The answer is that they were under constant scrutiny by the lower orders. The outbreaks of urban protest in Montélimar and Romans in 1579 had stemmed from suspicion that the notables were embezzling funds. The continuing tax increases in the 1590s provided one of the principal excuses for the popular orders to question and even contest oligarchies that controlled the towns.

In the mid-1590s there were obvious signs of this discontent. A letter from the consuls of Montélimar noted that in 1594 the urban governments were caught between the excessive tax demands of the provincial officials and the possibility of violence in their towns if they levied the full impositions.[106] This tension was evident at another level. In the 1596 election of the new consuls in the town of St Marcellin, Hugues Russet and Clément Vachebat barely defeated Pierre Pain and Jean Lantelier in a very close election. The new consuls announced that they could not accept their seats without trying to assure themselves of additional support to resolve the 'internal disputes' that divided the town.[107] These disputes seem to have revolved around the attitude to adopt in the face of the new waves of taxation. The newly elected consuls had apparently been accused of being too soft on the question of the new *taille* levies. Among their opponents was Bertrand Delagrange, a relative of Claude Delagrange, one of the principal lawyers charged with defending the third-estate *taille* challenge. The St Marcellin election was resolved finally when Russet and Vachebat promised to negotiate to stop payment of the tax for wood and candles (*bois et chandelles*) levied by the town guards and to try to reduce the *taille* allocation of the town.[108] After that, they were invested officially, but a special committee of thirty notables was named by the chancellor of the town to 'aid and advise' the new consuls.[109] It is clear from this example that the taxation issue threatened town leaders. To retain power they had to be very cautious in imposing higher levies upon their towns. As a result they had to be adamant in opposing new provincial levies.

The *taille* challenge, renewed by the urban elite, appears to have eased if not eliminated the frictions within the third estate between towns and rural villages and between lawyers, merchants, artisans, and the *menu peuple* of the cities. Unlike other areas of the kingdom, notably the southwest and Provence, where divisions within the third estate over the taxation question led to scattered individual initiatives and violence, Dauphiné remained free of disturbances during the fiscal squeeze of the 1590s.[110] By taking aggressive legal action against the new levies, the new town oligarchies consolidated their leadership over villages and *bailliages* as well as over their own populations.

During the fifteenth and sixteenth centuries the changes within the town consulates of Dauphiné relfected the political, social, and fiscal evolution that took place in the rest of the kingdom. Everywhere the political influence of the towns was reinforced by their economic and demographic momentum, and the role of the villages became more and more marginal. Within the town political structures the role of the artisans and *laboureurs* was reduced, and the merchants continued to dominate the consulates. At the same time, the new legal class composed of officials, lawyers, and *procureurs* had acquired a position of financial and social importance, and its members were applying increasing pressure to obtain an equivalent political role. This pressure was evident not only in Grenoble, which the legal class came to control, but in Valence and Vienne as well. The result of these transformations was the concentration of urban power in the hands of town obligarchies formed of rich, talented, and competent lawyers and merchants.

Once again, in Dauphiné it was the *taille* contestation that distinguished the socio-economic evolution of the province from that of the other areas of the kingdom. After 1590, when urban taxes increased dramatically, the economic interests of the new town oligarchies were at stake. In order to challenge the tax increases these groups invoked the precedent of the long-term contestation of the fiscal structures, and they used representative institutions, such as the Assembly of the Ten Cities, to obtain direct access to the governing bodies of the province. The more important role played by the urban groups in the renewed contestation is evident in the fact that the Assembly of the Ten Cities became the pivotal element of the protest movement of the 1590s, replacing the more democratic system of regular consultations of village, *bailliage*, and town meetings.

The weight of the new oligarchies is apparent in the character of the social groups that spearheaded the renewed *taille* challenge. The delegates most in evidence at the assemblies of the ten cities or at the meetings of the provincial Estates were lawyers, *procureurs*, or merchants tied closely into the groups that dominated the town consulates. Their contestation was not just aimed at defending the interests of the 'poor people' or the overtaxed villages, as some historians have argued. Analyses of the urban tax roles show that the leaders of the challenge were precisely those most affected by the tax increases. Therefore, it is not surprising to see that it was the elites who reinstituted the *taille* protests. In effect, the *taille* challenge of the 1590s pitted the new socio-economic elite of Dauphiné, the upwardly mobile lawyers, *procureurs*, merchants, and men of liberal professions, against the traditional elite, the nobles, clergy, and exempted officials.

4

The Lawyers:
Rhetoric and Reality

During the sixteenth and the early part of the seventeenth centuries, the social structures of the kingdom felt the effects of the upward social mobility of those groups that had profited from the wars. Lawyers, merchants, and military men sought a higher status for themselves. The lawyers provide one of the clearest examples of the breakdown of the traditional divisions among classes, orders, or estates. The new phase of the *taille* dispute was dominated by their debates: it opened in 1595 with the decision of the king's council to hear the *taille* case and closed in 1602 with a new royal edict judging the controversy.

From 1595 to 1602 lawyers for both the third estate and the nobles sought out the edicts and precedents governing the question. They wrote long tracts and pamphlets for distribution to the public. They prepared the legal pleas that were presented before the Conseil d'état. This judicial and procedural stage of the conflict coincided with one of the major developments of sixteenth-century society, the renewed interest in law, especially Roman law. The period witnessed extensions of the legal approach to every subject of controversy. Lawyers wrote commentaries and treatises on witchcraft, on historical controversies such as the origins of France, and on contemporary problems such as tyrannicide.[1] The importance of legal arguments in every debate corresponded with the entry of judges, *avocats*, *procureurs*, *huissiers*, and legal officials into the social and economic elite of virtually every community.

Within this proliferation of legal studies the jurists of Dauphiné held a privileged position, since the University of Valence was one of the major centres of humanist law, at least until 1579. As early as the 1520s the city council had attempted regularly to attract an 'Italian doctor' or a 'famous' professor to enhance the prestige of the university.[2] With the nomination of Jean de Montluc as bishop of Valence and chancellor of the university in 1553, its humanist orientation was reinforced considerably.[3] From his position as bishop Montluc intervened before every level of government to increase the salaries allotted to university chairs and to recruit leading professors. Through such initiatives Antoine de Govea was attracted to Valence in 1554 and 1555; Francis Hotman taught at the faculty of law between 1562 and 1566, and the noted Jacques Cujas served as professor of civil law from 1557 to 1559 and again from 1567 to 1577.[4]

By his second term at Valence, Cujas had established the basis of a new methodology. It consisted of applying a historical approach to Roman law, that is, of going beyond the analysis and criticism of individual jurists to study the laws in their chronological context and to explain their works with reference to their contemporaries.[5] It was this approach that Cujas passed down to his students and colleagues. At Valence as at other universities where he taught, Cujas was surrounded by students and scholars who were to play important roles in the institutions of both France and Dauphiné. Numbered among these were Jacques-Auguste de Thou, one of the founders of the new school of historical criticism; Joseph Scalinger, among the most renowned of the learned humanists; Antoine Loysel, an author of legal treatises; Ennemond Rabot d'Illins, Guillaume Desportes, and Jean Truchon, future presidents of the parlement of Grenoble; Louis de Bretel, president of the parlement of Rouen; Soffrey de Calignon, later councillor to the French Crown's Conseil de finance; Jacques Colas, the *visénéchal* of Montélimar who participated in the 1579 revolt; Claude Delagrange, who prepared the third-estate case against the *taille* exemptions; and Claude Expilly, who defended the privileged orders in the same case.[6]

In a 1950 article Pierre Mesnard reproaches Cujas for not applying his discoveries in Roman law to the sixteenth-century context, but this was certainly not the case with his students.[7] In the 1595 stage of the *taille* controversy the spirit of Cujas's teaching was constantly present. With the 1595 edict the king allowed the third-estate case against the provincial *taille* structure to be submitted before the Conseil d'état; the lawyers for the third estate began earnest preparations to muster the strongest historical arguments possible, while the privileged orders sought the means to block the appeal through procedural wrangles.

At the meeting of the provincial estates following the 1595 decision, the nobles tried to force the third estate to reopen negotiations on the *taille* problem within the framework of provincial institutions. Noting that they would accept no arbitration that included judges from Dauphiné, the third estate refused.[8] At the Assembly of the Ten Cities following the Estates, the urban delegates decided to pursue their legal initiatives before the Conseil d'état. They selected Achilles Faure, Moyne Charbotel, and Gaspard Billionet to prepare the case, co-ordinate strategy, and locate the documents necessary to undertake the new appeal.[9]

One of the first actions of Faure, Charbotel, and Billionet was to consult a number of famous humanist lawyers in order to determine the most effective arguments for their appeal. Two questions were submitted to several legal experts: first, 'Should the nobles, clergy, councillors, and officials of the parlement, the Chambre des comptes, and other exempted groups contribute to the *tailles* imposed on their rural holdings?' and second, 'What is the procedure to be followed [to obtain such impositions]?'[10] The most detailed reply was written by René Chopin and Etienne Pasquier, along with *avocats* DuLaurens, Chauvelin, Thoard, and Buisson. Dated 26 May 1596, it noted that in terms of strict legality the precedent of *taille* exemptions for the nobility was practised almost everywhere in France to compensate for the nobles' contributions to the armies of the king. The lawyers noted that the case of the privileged orders was also reinforced by the two agreements of 22 March 1553 and 16 February 1554, in which the third estate itself had conceded exemptions to the nobility.[11] However, the legal approach developed by Cujas and other humanist lawyers argued that contemporary problems should be studied in their historical context, and it was this methodology that Chopin and Pasquier saw as the most promising aspect of the third-estate case: 'to judge the question according to its real merits, it is necessary to consider what has been the nature of the *taille* in Dauphiné from the beginning and in ancient times; ... If they are mixed [*tailles personnelles*], as they are considered to be in all of France, it is certain that nobles should be exempted ... But if they are patrimonial [*réelle*], there is no doubt that one can be considered exempt no matter what his quality or condition.'[12] The document went on to try to show that *tailles* were *réelle* in Dauphiné. It argued that just as Provence and Languedoc, Dauphiné was governed according to written legal codes. In such regions there was between nobles and *roturiers* no distinction possible that had not been proclaimed by law. On the contrary, Humbert II in the Statut delphinal had guaranteed exemption from regular taxation to all his subjects.

On the question of the 1553 and 1554 agreements, Chopin and Pasquier argued that it was possible to contest the legality of the acts, as neither of them had been voted before a full and legal assembly of the provincial estates. The 1553 agreement had been passed by numerous proxy votes and evidence showed that the procurations of the nobles contained neither the dates nor the year in which they were issued. Moreover, the 1554 document had been signed by only eleven representatives of the third estate. Many town representatives had not signed, and again most of the nobles had sent proxy votes.[13] Concerning the procedure to be followed by the third-estate leaders in their appeal, the Chopin-Pasquier document noted that they would have no chance to contest the exemption of judicial officials before the parlement of Grenoble. They should instead attack before the Conseil d'état or the king's court nobles and officials whose exemptions were most questionable. Another alternative would be to have the case heard by the parlement of Toulouse or of Aix, regions where the *tailles* were *réelle*. In any event, Chopin and Pasquier recommended, the whole case should be based upon the ancient property registers (*cadastres*), which showed that both nobles and officials had been subject to *tailles*.[14]

The Chopin-Pasquier memoir served as the basis for the initial presentation of the third-estate case before the Conseil d'état on 14 May 1597. Faure, Charbotel, and Billionet had been joined by Jean Bernard from Romans, and these four received legal advice from Claude Delagrange, *lieutenant particulier* in the court of St Marcellin, Jean Vincent, *avocat* from Crest, and Antoine Rambaud, *avocat* from Die. Each wrote *plaidoiries* to support the third-estate demands.[15] Aquin and Dufos, the lawyers for the nobility, replied that since the 1595 decision their clients had made numerous attempts to negotiate with the third estate, and there was no need for royal intervention at this stage.[16] The king in his decision accepted the arguments of the nobles' lawyers and asked for continuing efforts to reach a solution within the province.

Following the royal decision, the momentum of the Dauphiné delegation to Paris appears to have been interrupted, and town leaders began to criticize openly the work of their deputies. Charbotel claimed to have fallen ill, and on 15 June he asked to be replaced.[17] The first consul from Romans told his colleagues from Vienne that the delegation sent to Paris had made no progress on the case, and on 13 July he suggested that three new delegates with 'experience and training' should be sent to replace them.[18]

This discontent with the accomplishments of Faure, Charbotel, Billionet, and Bernard led finally to the convocation of a long-promised special assembly on the *taille* appeal. Meeting at St Marcellin from 11 to 15 October 1597, the consuls from the major towns, accompanied by a number of doctors of law and *avocats*, discussed methods for pursuing the *taille* case.[19] Charbotel, Faure, and Bernard defended the initiatives that they had taken in the 1597 appeal. Charbotel explained that they had acted in conformity with the directives of DuLaurens, one of the lawyers who had, along with Chopin and Pasquier, prepared the 1596 memoir. According to Charbotel the nobles had shown great versatility in blocking the appeals of the third estate, both before the king's council and before the governor of the province. The members of the assembly thanked the three delegates present at St Marcellin for their services and asked them 'to forget any subjects of discord between them,' an obvious reference to differences that seem to have arisen among Charbotel, Faure, Billionet, and Bernard, the third estate's four deputies.[20]

The St Marcellin meeting proceeded to revise and reinforce the Paris delegation and the local structures necessary to support it. The meeting proposed the selection of four syndics from different regions to co-ordinate communication between the deputies in Paris and the cities and towns in the province and to oversee the collection of the new funds that the assembly had voted. The towns accepted the proposition only when they were assured that the syndics could not intervene in their affairs. Martinon from Grenoble, Faure from Valence, Martin from Romans, and Sambein from Vienne were elected to the new positions.[21] In choosing its new Paris delegation, the assembly applied considerable pressure to acquire the participation of Claude Delagrange. After declining its initial overtures, Delagrange agreed to accept the case when the assembly consented to pay his full expenses, accord him a travel allowance, and compensate his heirs in the case of his death. Among the other deputies selected, Billionet and Bernard were returned to Paris and Antoine Rambaud and Jean Vincent were added to the official delegation.[22] Within this five-man deputation it was the trio of Delagrange, Rambaud, and Vincent that became the backbone of the third-estate case.

The new third-estate defenders represented the urban elite groups that were preoccupied with the increase in *taille* levies. Claude Delagrange was the only one who had actually studied under Cujas. His doctorate had been conferred by the University of Valence in 1572, with Cujas and Claude Rougier as sponsors. Delagrange's continuing interest in jurisprudence is demonstrated in the works he left behind. In 1581 he published a Latin commentary on a number of legal texts from the Valentinois and Viennois, and he appears to have been the author of a work on ancient usages and customs in the province of Dauphiné.[23] The great majority of the extant texts by Delagrange, however, date from his participation in the *taille* affair. It is clear from his commentaries, pleas, and rebuttals that he set the tone for the debate. The pamphlets of his colleagues imitated his arguments, and those of his opponents were restricted to replying to his attacks.[24]

The professional career of Claude Delagrange reflects the fusion of his reflections on jurisprudence and his actions in provincial affairs. In 1575 he purchased the office of *lieutenant particulier* in the *bailliage* of St Marcellin, and during his years of service in that position he was named to head several regional commissions.[25] In 1588 Delagrange was sent to the Estates General at Blois as one of the deputies from Dauphiné, and in 1595, well before being chosen by the assembly of St Marcellin, he had written a memoir supporting the third-estate contestation.[26]

Delagrange's background as a member of one of the most active families in the municipal affairs of St Marcellin can be reconstructed partially on the basis of *taille* rolls, scattered references to him and his family in the parish registers, and a few items in notarial minutes. These documents indicate that he followed the legal career of his father Maître Ennemond Delagrange, whose title indicates that he was probably an *avocat* or a notary.[27] Claude Delagrange was probably the oldest of the third-estate deputies. From the beginning of his Paris mission he was probably not well, for at the St Marcellin assembly he insisted upon the clause concerning compensation for his family in the case of his death. After his sustained legal activity in disputing the *taille* case, Delagrange died sometime in the year between the publication of the municipal *taille* rolls for March 1601 and March 1602. His financial position was very solid by the 1590s, and despite his expressed fears that a prolonged absence in Paris might compromise his 'affairs,' his position remained stable right up to his death.[28] At the time of the 1592 *taille* rolls, just after he had inherited the holdings of his father, Delagrange lived on the Grande Rue, among the notables of St Marcellin, and paid 3.4 times the average assessment. He was listed for 5 *écus* 8 *sous* when the average sum levied on taxpayers in the town was 1 *écu* 31 *sous*.[29] By 1599 Delagrange lived in La Porcherie district, a less exclusive area, but his assessment was still 3.5 times that of the average taxpayer, 3 *écus* 57 *sous* on a roll where the average payment was 1 *écu* 8 *sous*.[30]

Both of Delagrange's younger colleagues, Antoine Rambaud and Jean Vincent, came from similar social and economic backgrounds. Rambaud was involved from the very beginning in the new *taille* debate; his links with the community he served were described in the preceding chapter.

Like him Jean Vincent followed in the footsteps of his father, who was an *avocat* in the town of Crest. The Vincent family was well placed in the town. Jean Vincent's cousin was *visénéchal* of Crest and was ennobled by Henry III in 1584. His brother, Guy Vincent, became dean of the cathedral chapter of Die. Vincent himself obtained the judgeship of the seigniory of Autichamp in 1584.[31] Like Rambaud and Delagrange, Vincent seems to have been relatively wealthy. Crest does not possess *taille* rolls by which the exact evolution of his holdings may be judged, but he possessed at least one major rural holding in Divajeu. It was there that he died around 1636.[32]

Jean Vincent appears to have enjoyed a solid legal reputation within the circle of towns and cities of the province. He obtained his legal degree from the University of Valence in the period after the departure of Cujas.[33] In 1592 he was among the jurists invited by the consulate of Valence to examine Claude Frère's competence to continue as a lecturer at the university.[34] There is little evidence, however, that he pursued the legal research and scholarship so dear to Delagrange and Rambaud. The only texts that we possess from him are the two tracts that he wrote for the *taille* case.

Thus the three principal *avocats* charged with conducting the *taille* contestation for the third estate came from similar if not identical social and economic backgrounds. All three came from highly mobile families that had acceded to social and economic prominence in their respective towns through the legal profession. Just as the town consuls who selected them, they came from the wealthy tax-paying urban elite. They reflected this new social group's jealousy of the privileged orders, whose new acquisitions were not weighted down by *taille* assessments. Also, as was illustrated dramatically in 1579, the *taille* increases made the exercise of political power very delicate for the new elite that controlled the consulates of most towns. In this regard the defenders of the third estate and their urban colleagues had a genuine interest in reducing the weight of taxes upon themselves and upon the urban and rural poor.

Under the leadership of Delagrange, Rambaud, and Vincent, the initiatives of the third estate became far more methodical. The new offensive was characterized by attacks on three distinct fronts. First, propaganda: each of the three principal deputies composed pamphlets and tracts that were printed and distributed to the public, arguing the third estate's case and attacking its opponents. Second, towards the end of 1598 they decided to make another attempt to obtain information from the villages concerning the taxes they had paid, the lands that the nobles had acquired from their peasants, and the debts that they had accumulated. In the face of noble denials that *roturier* holdings had declined, these cahiers were intended to document the claims of the third estate. To avoid the methodological inconsistencies that had plagued a similar series of cahiers in 1596, the new defenders of the case sent out a document instructing village leaders on the data and criteria to be used in drawing up the new cahiers.[35] Finally, the three principal lawyers produced numerous legal pleas and rebuttals that were delivered at the different sessions of the Conseil d'état and thereafter printed for public distribution.

The privileged orders were indifferent neither to the organization of the new appeal by the third estate nor to the implications of the legal issues at stake. Up to 1595 the principal resistance to third-estate manoeuvres came from the Assembly of the Nobility, an organism that grouped nobles elected by their peers in each *bailliage*. Like the Assembly of the Ten Cities, this assembly met just before or after the meetings of the provincial Estates and organized the questions to be submitted by the nobles or the replies to be given to questions raised by other orders or by the king. This assembly, however, is not to be confused with the second estate's representation at the provincial Estates. The delegates to the Estates were often permanent. Certain seigneurs who held fiefs, baronies, or counties had the right to represent their holdings personally at every Estates meeting. The assemblies, however, were supposed to be composed of elected representatives, so not all of the noble delegates to the Estates could participate in their meetings.[36]

By 1595 this type of organization was judged too unwieldy to deal with the third-estate challenge and with the increasing number of legal questions that it presented for the second estate. At a special meeting of the Assembly of the Nobility in St Marcellin the nobles appear to have decided to organize a judicial service to counsel them on legal issues and in particular to organize their replies to the attacks of the third estate before the Conseil d'état. Although there is no documentary evidence of the date of the creation of what came to be known as the Council of the Nobility, Piémond and Chorier both mention that the St Marcellin meeting retained the services of *avocat* Jean Aquin and organized the reply of the nobles to the third estate.[37] The essential information on the composition and powers of this council comes from the registers of its deliberations between 1602 and 1622.[38]

During the period for which summaries of its deliberations exist, the council was composed almost exclusively of lawyers, generally the *avocats consistoriaux* or other ennobled jurists. From 1602 to 1607 attendance lists show that there were from four to ten members of the council and that of that number only one or two were not lawyers but were nobles delegated by the Assembly of the Nobility. This council acted as the permanent legal executive for the second estate, although in theory it was only to advise the general assembly of actions to be taken.[39] It appears probable that from 1595 to 1602 this council was made up of Aquin, Expilly, de la Croix, and Audeyer, the principal defenders of the privileged orders.[40]

It is very difficult to identify the exact contribution of each of the principal noble defenders, since the majority of the early pleas for the privileged orders are either unsigned or are texts of which our only evidence is their refutation by the lawyers for the third estate. In his reply to Jean Aquin's 1595 address to the king, Claude Delagrange reproached one of the nobles' lawyers for taking no responsibility for some of his own arguments. Delagrange noted that this was strange and charged that the Assembly of the Nobility had imposed certain arguments of the case upon their own lawyer.[41] After 1600, when Expilly became involved as one of the noble defenders, such slips appear to have been eliminated. The case for the nobility was constructed more solidly, and the lawyers signed and published their interventions and rebuttals.

The social backgrounds of the four principal noble defenders were not all that different from those of the lawyers who argued the third-estate cause. Unfortunately, it is impossible to assess their relative wealth, since the municipal *taille* rolls never carry an evaluation for nobles. All four traced their origins to obscure lines of minor nobility, but none of them owed his social prominence to his noble status. As with the third-estate lawyers, their legal expertise explained their social positions.

Avocat Jean Aquin was the first lawyer to be engaged by the nobility to organize its defence. He was selected at the Assembly of the Nobility in 1595, and he seems to have remained the principal spokesman for the privileged orders up to 1600.[42] Aquin was the natural son of a minor noble, Sebastian Aquin. He had been legitimized and therefore ennobled by royal letters in 1561.[43] Besides the reputation of his father, who had been *avocat* to the parlement, the influence of Jean Aquin was certainly enhanced by the position of his half-brother, Ansèlme, who was a canon at Notre Dame Cathedral in Grenoble and who served regularly upon the enlarged municipal council.[44] During the *taille* controversy Jean Aquin appears to have produced numerous unpublished pleas and one signed memoir arguing in favour of the *avocats consistoriaux*.[45]

Just as the third estate consulted Paris lawyers, the privileged orders, too, maintained contacts in the capital. They retained the services of *avocat* Dufos, a *conseiller d'état*.[46] A native of Toulouse, he had probably studied Roman law, and his texts were sprinkled with classical references. He was engaged to write legal briefs for the nobles from the time of the initial third-estate challenge in 1595, and he continued to serve the second estate up to the time of the royal edict of 1602.[47]

By 1599 the context of the legal controversy was enlarged. Still hoping to avoid rendering judgment, the king sent the *taille* issue back to the province, asking Lesdiguières and Méry de Vic, a *conseilleur d'état*, to try to negotiate a solution acceptable to both sides during the Estates of 1599.[48] In the wake of the failure of their mission the Conseil d'état accepted finally to hear and judge the dispute. There is evidence that Aquin and Dufos may not have presented the strongest case for the privileged orders at these sessions. In a series of published letters Antoine Rambaud noted that he found the lawyers of the nobility to be 'ignorant and incompetent,' and he characterized their arguments as 'pathetic, full of loopholes and loaded remarks.'[49] In order to strengthen their defence before the Conseil d'état the nobles and other exempted groups sought the aid of additional lawyers. It was perhaps in this context that they turned to Expilly, Audeyer, and de la Croix.

Besides Dufos, Claude Expilly was the only one of the noble defenders who had a real background in jurisprudence. Like Claude Delagrange he had studied under Cujas at the University of Bruges, in 1583. Upon arriving back in Grenoble, Expilly became *avocat* to the parlement. The social importance of the Expilly family was no more striking than that of the other lawyers for either the nobles or the third estate. Even the origins of his nobility are obscure. In the fawning biography of Expilly written by his nephew Boniel de Catilhon, the *avocat*'s father is described as one of the 'notables' of the town of Voiron. Rivoire de la Batie, in his *Armorial de Dauphiné*, found no trace of the Expilly family among the nobles of the province before the sixteenth century.[50] According to a list of ennoblements in the province compiled by Guy Allard, the Expilly family only received its title after 1582, and at that time their property and holdings were worth two thousand *écus*.[51]

Just as most of the successful provincial leaders at the end of the sixteenth century, Claude Expilly was particularly apt at political manoeuvre. Having espoused initially the cause of the Catholic League, he forsook the leaguers after their 1590 defeat in Grenoble and rallied to Lesdiguières, the former Huguenot leader whom Henry IV had named lieutenant-governor of the province. Abandoning temporarily his legal career, Expilly enrolled in Lesdiguières' army and participated in the victory of Pontchara in 1591. In succeeding years he became very close to the new lieutenant-governor and to Henry IV. He served them as president of the Conseil souverain of Chambery, avocat-général to the parlement of Grenoble, and as president of the latter parlement. His successive missions in the taille affair and in negotiating the boundaries between Dauphiné and Savoy and between Dauphiné and the Comtat Venaissin testify to his influence both in Dauphiné and at the royal court.[52]

The first evidence of Expilly's intervention in the taille controversy is a legal plea delivered on 5 July 1600 before the Conseil d'Etat.[53] In his biography Boniel de Catilhon argues that his uncle was single-handedly responsible for the eventual success of the nobles in opposing the third-estate challenge.[54] While this is an overstatement, it is clear that Expilly was the most competent of the nobles' lawyers.

Expilly was not the only new lawyer who was brought into the controversy during the period from 1600 to 1602. Both Audeyer and de la Croix also joined Aquin to write pleas and to locate evidence. Their specific goals were to defend the interests of the doctors of law, avocats consistoriaux, and officials of the parlement. This rash of tracts in favour of the nobles of the robe is evidence of their fear that they might be abandoned by the first and second estates, as the price of the old nobility's retaining its privileges. The parlement does not seem to have had total confidence in the Council of the Nobility, and its officials took the defence of their privileges into their own hands.

The two principal defenders of the officials were closely tied to the judicial orders of the province. Little is known of the family background of Jean-Claude Audeyer. In the first records we have of him, he was a councillor of the parlement, and from that position he appears to have engineered the upward social mobility of his family. His daughter Marguerite married the seigneur of Saillans, while his son, Jean Audeyer, became avocat to the parlement and seigneur of Montbel.[55] In 1626 his brother acceded to the position of first consul of Grenoble.[56]

The other major lawyer to argue in favour of the privileges of the nobles of the robe was Jean de la Croix, seigneur of Chevrières. Son of a famous magistrate who descended from a family of merchants of Romans, Jean de la Croix was named councillor of the parlement of Grenoble in 1578. Just as Expilly, he had supported the Catholic League prior to its 1590 defeat and afterwards rallied to Lesdiguières. His conversion was rewarded with a succession of important positions. From *surintendant* of finances in Dauphiné he acceded to the position of Keeper of the Seals of the *conseil* in Chambery, and in 1603, just after his interventions in the *taille* controversy, he became president of the parlement of Grenoble.[57]

In treating the backgrounds of the lawyers who defended both sides in the *taille* conflict, one is confronted with the problem of the consequences of upward social mobility in a society that had fixed social, economic, and political barriers between its component orders or estates. In professional, economic, and social terms the lawyers who defended both sides in the conflict constituted one social group, but in terms of legal rights, privileges, and future prospects their titles led the ennobled lawyers to form completely different political alliances than did their non-noble counterparts. Both noble and non-noble lawyers had attained enviable social positions on the strength of their legal competence, and the backgrounds of the defenders of the nobility differed little from those of the defenders of the third estate. Three of the four principal noble lawyers came from families that had received their titles within the last one or two generations, and the background of the fourth is obscure. At best they counted one more generation in the legal profession than their third-estate counterparts. One of the patterns that distinguishes the personal and professional ascent of Expilly and de la Croix is their political manoeuvring and their readiness to support Lesdiguières in his climb to power after 1590.

In the *taille* affair the relatively fluid dividing lines between similar social and professional patterns of ascent became one of the major sources of contention between those who held tax-exempt status and those who did not. The lawyers for the nobility were ardent defenders of the privileges and legal rights that they had just acquired. They argued against the more equitable fiscal arrangements that would have reduced their new privileges in order to aid the third estate. The ultimate example of this pattern of individualistic behaviour can be seen in the case of Ennemond Marchier, Antoine Rambaud's brother-in-law. After his ardent defence of the third estate before the king in 1595, Marchier's legal talents were recognized by the nobility, which requested his ennoblement in 1603 so that he could participate in the defence of its cause.[58] The title was granted in 1605, and he began serving his new social partners on the Council of the Nobility.[59]

The upward social mobility of most ennobled jurists, lawyers, and officials of the parlement was striking. From the time of their entry into the parlement in 1495, members of the Rabot family of Crest rose in rank from the level of town notary to that of first president of the parlement. In 1577 Ennemond Rabot married his son to the niece of the *surintendant des finances* of Henry III, and in 1601 his daughter married the son of Achille de Harlay, first president of the Parlement of Paris.[60] During the latter years of the sixteenth century Ennemond Rabot employed a full-time notary just to deal with the family's titles and holdings.[61] The same type of advancement marked the career of Artus Prunier, third president of the parlement of Grenoble. At his death in 1616 Lesdiguières remarked that Prunier was 'the richest magistrate in the kingdom.'[62]

Following the examples of the presidents, the principal councillors of the parlement were also deeply involved in acquiring rural holdings. The purchases of seigneurial domains in the Valentinois-Diois (see Appendix 2) demonstrate the speculation in real estate of Claude Frère and La Croix-Chevrières, future presidents of the parlement, as well as of Michel Thomé and Pierre de la Baume, councillors. It is evident that they all benefited considerably from their tax-exempt status.

It was precisely this status that was contested, and between 1600 and 1602 the lawyers for the third estate and for the nobility presented their respective arguments before the Conseil d'état. The case does not appear to have been an item of high priority, for Chorier indicates that the judges devoted only a few hours to hearings and seven official sessions to the dispute.[63] Nevertheless, the defenders of each side left a multitude of printed legal pleas and propaganda documents in which they argued their cases in detail and refuted the arguments of their opponents.

One of the earliest of these documents was *La juste plainte et remonstrance*, written for the third estate by Claude Delagrange. It appears to have served as the basis of the 1597 presentation before the Conseil d'état, and it was printed at Lyon in the same year. Both the form and content of this legal brief, argued logically and documented rigorously, were repeated by Delagrange, Rambaud, and Vincent in all their subsequent pamphlets. *La juste plainte* followed the advice of the 1596 consultation with Chopin and Pasquier. In order to contest the exemptions of the privileged orders, it traced the origins of the *tailles* in Dauphiné. The document argued that the ancient laws of the province had been 'violated' and that over the years the nobles and clergy had succeeded in obtaining exemptions from war costs and from other payments to which they had contributed originally. Delagrange noted that the people of Dauphiné had always been exempted from regular taxation. As far back as under the Roman Empire, the province had never paid tribute; it had been confederated with Rome, not conquered, and its people had held the same fiscal franchises as in Italy. These franchises had been guaranteed specifically in the 1341 Statut delphinal, whereby the dauphin Humbert II had accorded to everyone in the province 'franchise and immunity from all levies to support military halting places [étapes], hearth taxes [fouages], gifts, loans, collections, tailles, and extraordinary charges.' These exemptions had been reconfirmed regularly after the acquisition of the province by the kings of France.[64]

In a long section on the origins of the feux, or hearth registers, Delagrange tried to prove that these documents sought to evaluate the property held by all individuals and not only that of the tax-paying inhabitants. Aiming to demonstrate that tailles were réelle, based on all property in a village, and not personnelle, assessed in function of the holdings of tax-payers, he argued that from their beginnings the feux inspections or revisions evaluated the fiscal quota of each community in terms of the property held by each of its inhabitants. He admitted that he had had great difficulty researching and documenting this point because the privileged orders would not allow him access to the archives of the fourteenth- and fifteenth-century revisions des feux contained in the holdings of the Chambre des comptes and that he had pieced together the procedures of the feux investigations from documents in the community archives, notably from those in the region of the Baronnies.

For Delagrange these documents showed conclusively that the feux were not calculated from the number of inhabitants, since villagers who did not possess sufficient holdings or wealth to constitute a feu of their own were grouped together frequently with two or three other families to form a feu. In addition Delagrange noted that the 1461 révision showed that there were more than 13,000 feux in the province and that only 4,700 of them were attributed to the third estate. It was clear to him that the feux were listed on the basis of property holdings and that the nobles too had been evaluated. He even mentioned a discussion with an aged town notable who had consulted the archives of the Chambre des comptes in the past and who reported that there had been an ancient document that allotted payments to each of the three orders based upon the feux of 1461. The old man contended that this document had disappeared from the archives after the initial third-estate protests in 1545.[65]

If everyone in the province, members of the third estate as well as nobles, had been exempted originally from tailles and if the feux documents showed that the value of the property of both nobles and members of the third estate had a century before been evaluated for any eventual imposition, why had the third estate alone borne the full burden of taxes during the Wars of Religion? The pamphlet answers this question without conviction. Delagrange postulated that the privileged orders had escaped impositions towards the middle of the fifteenth century probably because of the negligence of the third estate and because the first and second estates controlled the provincial Estates. He noted that after the 1461 *revision des feux* the impositions to be charged to the privileged orders were so minuscule that the third estate may simply have agreed that it was not worthwhile to collect them. Meetings of village consuls may also have 'tolerated' de facto exemptions of noble holdings, 'not daring to contradict [the privileged inhabitants] of their village.' At the level of the provincial Estates, as each new imposition or *don gratuit* was discussed, the nobles and clergy had voted to attach the clause that 'clerics living clerically and nobles living nobly would be exempted from contributing to the levy.'[66]

Delagrange accused the privileged orders of bad faith in opposing the demand of the third estate that there be a return to the ancient customs and laws of the province. He cited numerous documents that 'proved' that nobles were considered to be subject to any tax levies necessary to the security of the province. He referred to, among others, a judgment rendered by the courts in 1510 in which the second estate had been ordered to contribute to the costs of lodging the royal army on its way through the province and to the 1537 Edict of Hesdin, which ordered the nobility to contribute to the expenses of sending an army into Italy.[67] Further, Delagrange attacked the argument that nobles deserved exemptions because of their services in the armies of the Crown. He dismissed this claim with contempt, describing their service as 'imaginary service' because the maximum aid the *arrière ban* could require was one hundred men-at-arms for forty days; as a result of the lengthy procedures necessary to raise the *ban*, the military crisis was usually over before the king received either men or money.[68] He added that during the Wars of Religion the great majority of the nobles from the province remained shut up in their castles, far from the battlefield.

Both the third estate and the nobility were conscious of the series of agreements and acts dating from 1554, 1556, and 1579 that recognized clearly the exemptions of the privileged orders. In 1596 the statement of Chopin and Pasquier had identified these precedents as the weakest links in the third-estate case. Delagrange tried to undermine the credibility of such precedents, but his reasoning was often inconclusive. Arguing the unlikely position that the 1554 transaction had been signed by thirteen individuals from the third estate who occupied no official position within their order, he held falsely that the 1556 decision had merely entrenched the 1554 document, without any additional consultation. He explained that the 1579 judgment had resulted from the influence that the leaders of the clergy and nobility exercised over the queen mother.[69] His reasoning was probably accurate in that case, but he neglected to mention the larger context of the popular revolts, which certainly alienated Catherine de Médicis from the third-estate leaders.

Finally, Delagrange turned to the series of bleak facts concerning the fiscal crisis in the rural communities of the province, noting that it was necessary to have a clear ruling that would stop the decline in the number of third-estate property holders caused by the acquisitions of the privileged orders and the newly exempted groups. Such rural holdings, when purchased by nobles, were not included in the *ban* and *arrière-ban* evaluations, claimed Delagrange, and the village lands acquired by townspeople were often exempted illegally. It was necessary for the king to produce a judgment similar to the series of edicts in Languedoc that had declared townspeople taxable for rural purchases and nobles and clergy subject to taxes for wartime expenses on all their rural acquisitions.

The basic argument of Delagrange's *La juste plainte* were repeated in the pamphlets written by Antoine Rambaud and Jean Vincent, although those pamphlets were often more exaggerated in tone and emphasis than the initial document had been. Both Vincent and Rambaud were more aggressive in claiming that the nobles had acquired their alleged exemptions by changing the fundamental laws of the province. Vincent did not hesitate to speak of their legal 'usurpation' and 'violations,' and concerning the basis of their new law, he claimed, 'it is violent, temporary, lacks documentation and is unfounded; for they only acquired it by force and through the injury and misfortune of the civil wars.'[70] After considering Roman and medieval precedents at even greater length than Delagrange, Rambaud concluded that neither the nobles nor anyone else in the province had special privileges. He argued that if the privileged orders were honest in their case, they would admit clearly that they wanted to tax the holdings of the third estate in order to 'take over their best land and houses, in brief, to keep them in the province just as slaves.'[71]

The other particular object of the verbal and written attacks by Rambaud and Vincent were the new nobles. Both went further than Delagrange in describing the damage done to the economic stability of the villages by the continuing acquisitions of the *anoblis*, the children of officials, the bastard sons of nobles, and the self-proclaimed nobles. 'Oh disorder! all these call themselves nobles,' Rambaud wrote. He added that these new social groups, with their attitudes of 'gain' and 'profit,' were ruining the 'virtue' of the nobility. He complained that numerous nobles worked or supervised work on their holdings, doing tasks that should be farmed out, while others engaged secretly in trade and commerce. Repeating the complaints against the new seigneurs whom the third estate had listed in its 1579 cahier, Rambaud asked the king to step in to force these newcomers to adhere to ancient tradition and laws.[72]

Vincent, for his part, posed the hypothetical question, 'How undignified is it, both of the nobility that they profess and of the rank and of the status that they want to hold, to see these great captains [of war], these pillars of the state, indifferent and without [enough] compassion for the ruin of the people and of the province to grant the aid that they should? Is this not a violation of the rights of the people, of the civil laws, and of natural piety?'[73] Attacking the nobles' illegitimate children and the offspring of officials, he accused them of having no right to the exemptions that they claimed. It was only by complicity with the courts that their so-called privileges were upheld. He argued that all these new nobles had rushed to buy up the lands and houses of the overtaxed peasants 'dirt cheap.'[74] They had even served as intermediaries by which certain townspeople acquired rural property under the cover of noble exemptions.[75] He, too, asked the king for a judgment that would tax nobles for their rural acquisitions and stipulate clearly that the illegitimate sons of nobles and the children of officials were not eligible for exemptions.

As could be expected, the rebuttals presented by the defenders of the privileged orders were vigorous. The earliest of the replies that can be identified is the anonymous *La verité des justes défenses de la noblesse du Dauphiné*, which is dated 1600, and the printed text of a plea delivered by Claude Expilly before the Conseil d'état on 10 July 1600.[76] Both demonstrate the attempt of the privileged orders to dismiss the attacks of the third estate as unreasonable, radical, and even revolutionary. Both begin their rebuttals by trying to portray the legal-contestation movement as an extension of the 1579 popular revolts.[77] Of the goals of the third-estate leaders, Expilly charged: 'under an appearance of compassion founded on ruin and calamity, [they want] to open the door to a popular state, establish equality among your subjects, and overthrow the ancient order and old customs observed in the province.'[78]

Neither Expilly nor the anonymous pamphleteer dwelt at any length on the historic question of whether all the people of the province had been exempted originally from all forms of taxation and when and how *tailles* were begun. Expilly admitted that it had been necessary to impose *tailles* in the province for warfare and other affairs, but he argued that the new taxes had been levied in conformity with the ancient customs of the province and with the decisions of the Estates.[79] Both of the nobles' pamphlets were more concerned to prove that their order had never contributed to *taille* impositions and that its exemptions had been confirmed by royal edicts in 1556 and 1579. Both added with great relish that even the official delegates of the third estate had recognized these exemptions in the 1554 transaction and in the text of the 1583 agreement on the town-country taxation dispute.[80] Both texts denied that the province had ever been a *taille réelle* region. They cited the fact that Grenoble had received a reduction in the number of its *feux* in 1440 to compensate for the number of officials from the court and parlement who had received exemptions. To them this proved that *tailles* were based on the social status of individual taxpayers and not on their holdings.[81] Challenging the third estate on this question, Expilly exclaimed, 'show me just one valid act where nobles are listed on a *taille* roll.'[82]

The nobles and officials were portrayed as having suffered just as much from the war years as the 'people' of the province. Expilly listed over twenty noble families that had died out or had suffered derogation during the previous forty years.[83] According to the anonymous author of *La verité*, the payments to such families from their peasants (*cens*) had declined; their fields had lain fallow, and they had had to pay to equip themselves and their soldiers to serve in the king's army.[84] But if the people were in such dire economic straits and the nobles had not profited from them, who had benefited from their losses? The reply from the nobles' defenders was conclusive. The culprits were the urban elite of the third estate.[85] To Expilly 'the towns were never as rich in capital and conveniences as they are today, such that if some of the villages are impoverished, their holdings have been transmitted into the hands of either their chatelains, clerks, or other officials (many of whom have become very rich), or the captains [of war] and *roturier* soldiers, or town merchants.'[86]

Both of the documents defending the cause of the nobles returned frequently to the charge that the third-estate demands were oriented towards establishing 'anarchy,' 'democracy,' or a 'popular state.' They took the third estate to task for its outspoken attacks upon the exemptions accorded to the children of officials or the illegitimate sons of nobles. Rather than debate the point, they cited these attacks as typical of the 'undignified' attitude of the third-estate lawyers, who, under the cover of the supposed abuses of *taille* exemptions, struck out at the king's officials and magistrates.[87] 'Wretched words, undignified to be heard and worthy of a hot iron,' said Expilly.[88] *La verité des justes défenses* went on to accuse the third-estate lawyers of accepting the case because of their 'envy' of the privileged orders and their desire to lower all the social groups of the province to the same condition.[89] The pamphlet noted in concluding that 'in 1579 [the third-estate] pretext to immunity and exemption, |Sire|, brought the government of your province of Dauphiné to the brink of its entire ruin' and that it was now up to the king to 'ensure that the [renewed] madness of the people does not end up in rage.'[90]

From the subsequent pamphlets, replies, and rebuttals of both sides, the evolution of the hearings on the case can be reconstituted. First, both the nobles and the courts appear to have been indifferent to the third-estate arguments concerning the historical origins of the *tailles*, and few of the later pamphlets argue that question at any length.[91] Second, each side repeated the arguments and recited the precedents that supported its case. Both argued generally that their opponents had falsified documents, misinterpreted evidence, or ignored the larger context of the proof they had presented. Each new document was presented with renewed vigour, but little new evidence.

In one of the rare new arguments presented by the third estate, Delagrange attempted to disprove the link that the privileged orders had established systematically between the *taille* contestation and the 1579 rebellion. Demanding that the nobles stop citing their role in crushing the popular revolts, he noted quite correctly that 'it was the third estate that slit the throat of the Captain [Paumier] ... who committed numerous abuses not only against the nobles but also against the most honourable and richest members of the third estate.' He added that in all the towns of the province the leaders of the third estate had either snuffed out the initial actions of the league movement or prevented its appearance.[92]

The most significant breakthrough apparent in the rebuttals is the identification of those who had profited from the war years. In their original arguments each side blamed the other for exploiting the limited resources of the rural villages, thus causing the misery of the peasants. As the hearings continued, the pamphlets became less emphatic. On the side of the nobles, the *Secondes escritures* recognized the profiteering of the officials and of the new nobles. It was not the fault of the old nobles, the pamphlet argued, but 'of an infinite number of persons from their order [the third estate], soldiers, merchants from the towns, artisans, men of professions, and such people, homebodies, whose opulence enabled some of them to become ennobled (it is up to the king to reply for them), others to take up public charges and offices in order to gain exemptions.'[93] While the pamphlet went on to note the excellent relations between old and new noble families that had intermarried and frequented the same circles, it is clear that the old nobles were not united on the necessity of defending the *anoblis*.[94] A 1602 text published in the name of the *anoblis* by P. Boissat further confirms the divisions within the nobility. Published after the 1602 decision, it thanked the king for maintaining the privileges of the new nobles despite the attacks they had suffered both from those who 'scorn us as newcomers' and from those who say 'there are enough nobles in Dauphiné and there is no need to create others.'[95]

Modifications were also apparent in the arguments of the third estate on the question of profiteers. The initial attacks on the order of the nobility and the totality of the exempted officials were toned down. Criticized by the nobles for undermining the king's justice with his outspoken declarations concerning officials, Rambaud retreated from his earlier position, claiming that he only meant to criticize those who had profited from their offices and not the whole group.[96] On the question of reducing the number of nobles in the province, Rambaud also moderated his initial stand, claiming that the third estate complained only of 'those who had infiltrated illegally into the true order of nobles.' They were the only ones he had asked be stripped of their titles and exemptions.[97] As to the third-estate profiteers, Delagrange conceded that some captains of war might have exploited their positions during the war years, but he hastened to add that they had to pay *tailles* on any new holdings they had acquired.[98]

In the same reply Delagrange denounced as exaggeration the claim by the lawyers for the nobles that the third estate was trying to subject the whole order of the nobility to *taille* payments when, in fact, the third estate wanted only to limit exemptions according to the traditional laws of the province. The third estate wanted nobles to pay *tailles* not upon their feudal lands but upon all the rural holdings that they had acquired from taxpayers within the last thirty years; it also wanted them to contribute to the levies collected for wartime expenses. Nor did the third estate ask that the exemptions for officials be abolished; according to Delagrange, it only wanted them to be limited to the number accorded in 1556, with their widows and children being excluded from *taille* exemptions.[99]

From the very beginning of the hearings the nobles argued that the final royal decision should not 'upset' the existing fiscal and social structures of the province but should punish those who had profited from the wartime taxation. As early as 1597 Claude Delagrange replied to this argument, saying, 'It will not cure the evil to try to implement some order or regulation [to punish] the extortion and impositions now that the poor third estate is already stripped of its holdings.'[100] Despite his appeal that the king go to the heart of the issue, the idea of an intermediary ruling reappeared regularly in the rebuttals and seems to have been one of the keys to the 1602 decision.[101]

A second key to understanding the eventual decision was the role played by the lieutenant-governor of the province, Lesdiguières. A close confidant of Henry IV, he intervened personally in favour of the privileged orders. After trying unsuccessfully to mediate the dispute in 1599, Lesdiguières wrote to Chancellor Bellièvre that the nobles of the province had made significant concessions to the third estate in the hope of reaching an agreement, 'but neither their offers, nor all the means which we [the mediators] employed, could move the people towards an equitable solution.' He noted that the third estate was now asking the Conseil d'état to accord a just hearing to the case in which that estate had now pitted itself against 'over three hundred years of possession.' Identifying himself clearly with the noble cause, Lesdiguières contended that 'on this judgment depends the peace of this province and its reliability in the king's service. It is from you, Sire, that they [the nobles] expect the retention of their rights.'[102] Such interventions by Lesdiguières had considerable effect at the royal court. This was recognized in the preamble to the 1632 decision to review the 1602 *taille* decision. It noted that the 1602 *arrêt* had been based on the 'necessities of the moment and the consideration for the late Constable Lesdiguières.'[103]

The judgment that was rendered on 15 April 1602 refused to 'upset' the principle that nobles 'living nobly' and 'clerics living clerically' were exempt from *tailles* for all their present and future holdings.[104] However, the document did rule that the bastard sons of nobles were not to benefit from exemptions, and it repeated the 1556 stipulation that the privileged orders were to pay their part of all common community expenses, such as repairing walls and roads, and the like. In a further concession to the third estate the edict struck out at the *anoblis*, who had been defended so poorly by the nobles. The *arrêt* provided that all ennoblements granted between 1578 and 1598 would be revoked and the interested parties would have to prove the validity of their title to the parlement. At the same time a commission was to undertake an examination of the validity of the new nobles created during the last forty years, and the fines levied on usurpers were to be applied to ease the debts of the rural communities. More important, no new noble could benefit from exemptions until he had paid an indemnity to the communities in which he held property. This tax was to be based on the value of the holdings that would be scratched from the *taille* rolls.

The third estate received even more concessions on the question of exemptions for officials, another of the groups identified as having profited from the war years. The decision confirmed the exemptions of those who held the major offices in the parlement and Chambre des comptes, as well as of the senior treasurer of France. It also pronounced in favour of all those who had served continuously in their offices during the last twenty years. In all these cases the children of officials were to retain exempt status. In the future, however, children whose fathers did not fit into one of the above categories would be subject to *tailles*. The most significant group added to the *taille* lists by the 1602 decision was the *avocats consistoriaux*, a group of senior lawyers of the parlement of Grenoble. This group, which the third estate had attacked back in 1553, was composed officially of twenty-one *avocats*, but the third estate argued that there were closer to forty individuals in the province claiming the status of an *avocat consistorial*, which up to then had conferred nobility and tax exemption.[105] Obviously, *avocats* who were nobles or who had been ennobled retained their tax-exemptions, but in the future senior *avocats* could no longer acceed to the ranks of the second estate through the nomination of their peers in the parlement; only the king could ennoble them. Others added to the *taille* lists included all *docteurs d'université* over and above four exempted positions, all *avocats* and *procureurs* in the *baillages* and *sénéchaussées*, the officials and treasurers of France other than the senior treasurer, the commissioners of war, and the *maîtres des eaux et forets*.

The judgment also made provisions for rectification of the basic third-estate land grievances. It allowed villages to tax their creditors for the sums of money that they had loaned to the community and gave them the right to list the holdings of nobles from Languedoc or Provence on their *taille* rolls. Back payments on village debts were suspended for the period from 1588 to 1597. The hope that these measures would give a certain financial stability to the rural communities is evident in the provision giving individuals four years and communities six years to repurchase the rural property that had been acquired by nobles and those benefiting from tax exemptions. Finally, a new revision of the *feux* in the province was to be organized within the six months that followed publication of the edict.

The 1602 edict has been presented often as a defeat for the third estate.[106] It is true that the lawyers for the privileged orders appear to have blocked the third-estate effort to convince the judges to treat the origin of *tailles* in the province, and they appear to have convinced the court to limit the edict to controlling the abuses of tax exemptions by new nobles and officials. Nevertheless, the clauses of the edict prescribing verification of the titles of all the new nobles created in the previous forty years, removing exemptions from the *avocats consistoriaux*, and decreeing a new inspection of *feux* quotas in the province constituted important concessions to the third estate. Because of these gains the meeting of the assembly of towns and villages following the 1602 judgment was far from morose. The delegates voted to continue pressure upon the king to clarify certain aspects of the decision and to be sure that other aspects of it would be executed.[107]

If we step back from the pamphlets and tracts presented during the case, however, we discover that the basic premises of the lawyers for both the third estate and the nobles did not entirely correspond with the reality of the situation. A series of tests comparing documents on the socio-economic evolution of the province with the arguments and pleas of both groups of lawyers reveal that both sides imposed their own interpretive framework. Both presented cases that argued and reinforced the social divisions between traditional estates or orders; each cast the other as exploiters and itself as exploited.

The third estate argued, for instance, that the land acquisitions of the nobles and exempt officials in the rural villages were responsible for the dramatic economic deterioration of the countryside.[108] Contending that one-third or more of the best land in every village had been acquired by individuals with tax-exempt status, third-estate lawyers argued that this evolution was different from that of the rest of France. They pointed with particular emphasis to Languedoc and Provence, where *tailles* were *réelle* and where all landholdings were listed in *cadastres*. There, they argued, the peasants had not been dispossessed of their best holdings, and the rural communities were still solvent.

TABLE 3
Acquisitions by tax-exempt inhabitants in fifteen villages according to the third-estate cahiers. Surfaces are represented in *seterées*, and the archival reference for the cahier is noted after the village; all refer to AC Vienne.

Village	Total tax-exempt holdings	Total village holdings	Percentage of tax exempt
Savasse (CC 42)	560.5	7,706.8	7
Eurre (CC 43)	1,580.5	4,222.25	37
Vaunaveys (CC 43)	1,346	2,700	50
Saou (CC 42)	2,472	7,416	33
St-Paul-3-Châteaux (CC 42)	726	2,384	30
Montéléger (CC 42)	2,795	3,800	73.5
Mirabel-en-Diois (CC 42)	524	1,677	31
La Garde-Adhémar (CC 43)	733	4,398	17
Loriol (CC 43)	1,001	7,407	13.5
St-Gervais (CC 43)	710	4,260	16.6
Etoile (CC 42)	3,519	5,598	63
Domène (CC 42)	447	927	48
Le Touvet (CC 42)	1,600	2,500	64
Livron (CC 43)	1,238	12,380	1
St Antoine (CC 44)	2,037	2,718	75

How accurate was this claim? One of the most revealing measures of the truth of third-estate reasoning is to be found in the series of village cahiers.[109] It was upon these documents that the third-estate lawyers supposedly based their statistics on property evolution. In fact, however, these documents do not always bear out the third-estate arguments. First, the question is difficult to judge from the data in the cahiers. Despite the 1598 attempt to standardize the categories of information that communities were to furnish, the data included in the 152 documents submitted are too irregular to permit a serial treatment. Only around one hundred villages replied with statistics to the question concerning the acquisition of their holdings by nobles and officials. Some of them listed the name of the purchaser and the date and size of each transaction; others listed only the size of the village holdings that members of the privileged orders had acquired. Most neglected to note the total surface of the village, which made it impossible to judge the percentage held by the new owners.

The second problem encountered in drawing generalizations from these documents is the variety of replies. Table 3 lists a geographical distribution of fifteen communities that replied with the most complete cahiers. It demonstrates a considerable gap between the town of Livron, where nobles and exempted groups owned only 1 per cent of the village holdings, and Montéléger, where they held 75.5 per cent. This irregular pattern of property acquisition was still characteristic of Dauphiné a century later, as Bernard Bonnin has shown in his study of the 1698 *revision des feux*.[110]

Table 3 indicates that the problem of noble or tax-exempt buyers was most acute in communities that were close to cities or towns: Domène and Le Touvet were on the outskirts of Grenoble; Etoile, Montéléger, Eurre, and Vaunaveys surrounded Valence, and St Antoine was near Vienne. The more southern villages and even the communities surrounding Montélimar did not claim generally that such purchases accounted for more than 30 per cent of their holdings. The argument that villages surrounding cities were most affected by the phenomenon of outside purchasers can be seen in both the third-estate pamphlets and the nobles' argument in the *Secondes escritures*. Both groups saw the newly exempted town elite as responsible for the increase in rural investments, but the nobles claimed that the purchasers were bourgeois, while the third estate held that they were the ennobled governors, captains of war, and town officials. The third-estate claim that the problem of rural acquisitions was widespread in the province is undermined by the limited response of the villages to their leaders' request for information. The villages that bothered to draw up cahiers were probably the ones where the issue of outside purchasers was most serious. The majority of the cahiers came from the plains along the Rhône Valley, the Baronnies, and the plains around Valence; few came from the northern areas of the province or even from the Graisivaudan around Grenoble, and none came from the mountain region. For the villages that did reply it is clear that the situation was very uneven; in certain villages there were practically no outside property owners, while in others outside ownership by exempted groups constituted an enormous problem.

The third-estate comparison between property acquisition in Dauphiné and in the rest of France was even more distorted. In reality the proportion of village land held by the privileged orders in Dauphiné was small when compared with such holdings in other regions. Jean Jacquart has analysed the *terriers* of seven seigniories in the Ile-de-France, a *taille personnelle* region, comparing them for the periods prior to the Wars of Religion and during the wars. The comparison demonstrates that before the wars peasants owned only between 20.65 per cent and 54.71 per cent of the cultivated lands in the area, an average of only

36.8 per cent of the holdings in the seigniories studied.[111] Jacquart proceeds to show that their holdings were reduced even further during the wars, particularly in the villages surrounding important towns and cities where bourgeois officials and *rentiers* made important acquisitions.[112] Even in Languedoc, *pays de taille réelle*, so often cited as an example by the third estate, the decline of peasant holdings was just as evident. In his study of Lattes, just outside Montpellier, Le Roy Ladurie has demonstrated that the nobles of the robe, the officials of the financial and judicial courts, had made numerous purchases between 1547 and 1677. In the midst of the movement to constitute large domains the peasant share of village property sank from over 40 per cent in 1547 to under 10 per cent by 1677.[113] It is clear that even if the third estate was accurate in its claim that the privileged orders owned over a third of the village holdings in Dauphiné, that percentage was still not critical when placed within the context of the kingdom.

On the question of who had profited from the war years, the lawyers for both the third estate and for the privileged orders imposed their own readings of the socio-economic evolution. Each group denied systematically that members of its order had been involved in rural speculation, but the village cahiers show both sides to be wrong. From the replies of communities to the question concerning the amounts of their debts and the names of their creditors, it becomes clear that moneylenders were just as plentiful within the ranks of the third estate as within the privileged orders (see Graph 5). Most villages replied to the question concerning their debts with a simple reference to the amount that they owed, and only twenty of them identified their creditors and the date and amount of each transaction, as the third-estate lawyers had requested. As in the case of property acquisitions, the majority of the best cahiers were submitted either from the villages along the Rhône Valley between Valence and Montélimar or from the Diois and the Baronnies. From the submissions of the seven villages represented in Graph 5, a certain pattern of investment can be identified. The third estate and the military class accounted for the majority of the loans accorded to the villages of Savasse, Gigors, La Garde Adhémar, and Vaunaveys. The nobles were more attracted to investments in the debts of the larger towns because the military governors or garrison officials, who were often nobles, had considerable influence over the budgets of these towns. Their exorbitant financial demands increased town debts, placing them in a position both to embezzle the funds that were furnished to them by municipal officials and to invest in the debts that their own demands

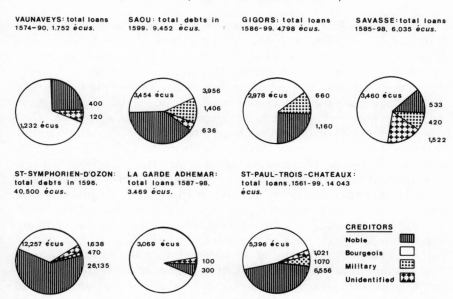

VAUNAVEYS: total loans 1574–90, 1.752 écus.

SAOU: total debts in 1599, 9,452 écus.

GIGORS: total loans 1586–99, 4,798 écus.

SAVASSE: total loans 1585–98, 6,035 écus.

ST-SYMPHORIEN-D'OZON: total debts in 1596, 40,500 écus.

LA GARDE ADHEMAR: total loans 1587–98, 3,469 écus.

ST-PAUL-TROIS-CHATEAUX: total loans, 1561–99, 14 043 écus.

CREDITORS
Noble
Bourgeois
Military
Unidentified

Graph 5 Holdings of different social groups in the debts of the villages along the Rhône Valley
Source: Third-estate cahiers, AM Vienne, CC 42, 43

created.[114] It is clear, however, that neither nobles nor bourgeois were beyond profiting from the misery of the rural communities.

A third example of the distortion created by the lawyers for both sides lies in their presentations of the effects of the new ennoblements. According to the third estate the new titles granted during the war years had increased out of all proportion the number of those benefiting from tax exemptions.[115] With the exception of the *Secondes escritures*, the pamphlets and pleas of the lawyers for the privileged orders denied that the number of nobles had increased. They cited the families that had died out or suffered derogation, arguing that the number of nobles had even declined during the period in question.[116]

Was there really a significant increase in the number of nobles in Dauphiné, and was the province different in this regard from the rest of the kingdom? The most useful source for replying to these questions is the *actes d'anoblissement* registered by the parlement of Grenoble. In Dauphiné as elsewhere in France there were several ways of acquiring a noble title: by letter, by holding an office conferring nobility, by knighting on the battlefield, by petition, or by acquiring a noble fief and living 'nobly' during a period of twenty years. To be valid legally, all these avenues to nobility had to be recognized by an official act registered in the parlement.[117] For the period from 1578 to 1620 acts can be found that conferred nobility upon fifty-five individuals. In her thesis on the question Christiane Masson-Fauchier has identified another nineteen who claimed nobility on the basis of letters of confirmation or other official sources (see Appendix A). It is true that Expilly identified twenty families that had lost their titles during the war years, but this still amounted to a net addition of fifty-four new noble lines.[118] The nobility certainly had not declined, as many of the nobles' lawyers claimed, but neither had it increased dramatically, as the lawyers for the third estate charged. The increase in new titles did, of course, aggravate the tendency of the privileged orders to acquire tax-exempt holdings. Twenty-four of the seventy-four new nobles already possessed seigniories before acquiring their titles, and in all cases they obtained tax-exemptions for these holdings.

The situation concerning new nobles in Dauphiné should not be detached from the larger context of the kingdom. The number of ennoblements in Dauphiné represented a minor addition of new titles when compared to the *élection* of Bayeux. There, the regular inquiries that were conducted to weed out phoney nobles have been studied by James B. Wood. They reveal that 250 nobles were created between 1540 and 1598.[119] Once again, when placed within the context of the whole kingdom, the real evolution of the social groups in Dauphiné does not appear to be as erratic as the lawyers' presentations claimed.

The legal pleas, pamphlets, and rebuttals of both sides developed two diametrically opposed explanations of social and economic evolution in the province during the Wars of Religion. Both of these explanations were traditionalist in the sense that they conformed rigorously to the institutional framework of the province and the kingdom and reinforced the system of estates of orders. The lawyers for the third estate argued that their whole order was 'miserable' and 'exploited,' ignoring the well-heeled urban elite, which had benefited just as much as the nobles from the plight of the poor peasants. On the other side, most of the documents from the privileged orders defended with vigour the new nobles, officials, and questionable members of the second estate. They argued that a noble was a noble and there was no distinction to be made between old and new nobles. With the exception of the *Secondes escritures* these documents denied the clear evidence of the numerous new and enriched nobles and officials who had joined the privileged orders. The lawyers for the nobles continued to insist that none of the nobility had profited from the economic decline of the peasants.

The arguments of neither side contained the distinctions and nuances that characterized the real social evolution of the province. The terms of reference of the lawyers for both the third estate and the nobles seem to have corresponded to the ideological orientation that the leaders of each group wanted to impose upon the conflict. Just as in the 1570s the role of the assemblies of both social groups was crucial to the organization and presentation of the case. The third-estate leaders changed their Paris delegates in 1597, after Faure, Charbotel, and Billionet failed to obtain a proper hearing before the king. They reinforced the structures of consultation of their order at the assembly of St Marcellin and made every effort to maintain contacts between the consuls of the cities and towns and the new Paris delegation. It was clear that the urban elite controlled the presentation of the third-estate case. For their part, the nobles set up the Council of the Nobility to co-ordinate their pleas before the king and in 1599 added new lawyers to their defence, apparently because of dissatisfaction with Aquin's efforts. The case for the privileged orders seems to have been directed by the new nobles and particularly by the nobles of the robe, who dominated the Council of the Nobility. In fact the debates seem to have confronted the elite of the third estate with new nobles and officials who had only recently acquired their titles.

On a superficial level the *taille* conflict of the 1590s demonstrates a clear dichotomy that would appear to reinforce the Mousnier thesis that the essential division between social groups in late sixteenth-century France occurred along the lines of orders. The courtroom rhetoric of the two sides indicates a confrontation of two monolithic orders, the miserable third estate and the earnest, hard-working nobility. The vast majority of each of the social groups probably corresponded to this tableau, but the members of the urban elite, who were most evident in the *taille* dispute, did not. The urban notables who reanimated the dispute and the third-estate lawyers who presented their pleas before the Conseil d'état had little in common with the miserable people. And the case for the nobility was directed by the ennobled officials and *avocats consistoriaux*, who were considered to be on the borderline of nobility by their new social partners.[120]

But which way was this urban elite moving in the evolving social framework? This is a question of considerable importance to the long-term debate over the social base of the evolving absolutist state. According to Mousnier the most capable and talented elements of the third-estate elite gravitated continually towards the nobility of the robe and the new venial offices that the king created and sold. This new group ended up by imposing its own bourgeois values upon the new absolutist kingdom. Boris Prochnev, by contrast, holds that the new nobles passed a class barrier with their ennoblement. From their new positions they acquired property holdings and a considerable stake in the feudal mode of production. They became integrated into the system, and they reinforced it with their talent and capital. Alexandra Lublinskaya also considers that the new nobles belonged to a new class, but she argues that they continued to fulfil a double role: those who sought out offices and property became integrated into the renewed feudal system; however, a second group remained active in communal and entrepreneurial ventures, and they continued to infuse bourgeois values into the bureaucratic functioning of the kingdom.

Beneath the superficial rhetoric of the courtroom, the social evolution of the urban elite during the *taille* dispute does not demonstrate any clear-cut class division between the nobles and the third-estate elite. The urban leaders of the dispute were clearly different from the vast majority of the third estate. They could be distinguished in terms of their economic situation as well as in terms of their future perspectives. They imposed a unity and a coherence upon the rhetoric of the *taille* debate that did not necessarily correspond to actual social conditions. The economic activities of the members of this elite who had passed over to the nobility appear to be simply a carry-over from the diversified activities of the third-estate elite.

Statistically, the sampling with which we have to work is very limited since, relative to other areas of the kingdom, Dauphiné produced so few new nobles. Nevertheless, the activities of both the new nobles and the third-estate elite differed very little. Both groups delved into bourgeois financial speculation on rural debts, as the third-estate cahiers demonstrate. At the same time both groups invested in feudal landholdings: Claude Frère, Jean de la Croix, seigneur de Chevrière, and Michel Thomé were very present in property speculation in the Valentinois, but as the acts of ennoblement demonstrate, many of the new nobles had already acquired their rural holdings while still members of the third estate. It appears, therefore, that the social evolution of the bourgeois elite of

Dauphiné towards the second estate does not fit neatly into the framework of any of the classic theses on social evolution.

In the Porchnev-Mousnier-Lublinskaya debate too much attention has been focused upon orders or classes: the passage of the bourgeois elite into the category of the nobility has drawn attention away from the common occupations, interests, and perspectives on social and economic mobility on both sides of the class or orders barrier. This similarity is far more evident between the third-estate urban elite and the new nobles or nobles of the robe than between either the third-estate elite and the rest of the third estate, or the new nobles and the rest of the nobility. This observation is buttressed by the legal manoeuvres of the *taille* debate. After all, was the nobility not ready to sacrifice the new nobles, *avocats consistoriaux*, and certain officials in order to retain its exemptions? And was the third estate not faced with a continual cleavage between the interests of its urban and rural elements? As Denis Richet has argued, did the bourgeoisie in the third estate not form a common grouping with those who had been recently ennobled, bought offices, or become nobles of the robe? From this perspective it certainly appears that those who passed across the social barrier retained the same economic and social values as before. Mousnier has argued that they went after offices and bourgeois economic opportunity, and it is clear that they did. Porchnev holds that they bought into domains and feudal landholdings, and they certainly did. But they had been investing in both those sectors before becoming nobles: their behaviour did not alter; only their economic perspectives changed. As nobles they benefited from *taille* exemptions, and that issue was the essence of the challenge from their non-noble counterparts in the *taille* debate.

5

Towards Royal Intervention: Third-Estate Initiatives and Noble Resistance

In the period extending from 1602 to the early 1620s the third estate and the privileged orders continued to debate the *taille* question and the application of the 1602 judgment. On the third-estate side the new *commis* of the villages, Claude Brosse, pressed the Crown for the application of certain sections of the new judgment, clarifications of other sections, and extensions of some of the concessions made to the 'poor people.' He presented cahier after cahier pointing out the difficulties of executing existing royal edicts, and demanding new and clearer judgments. On the nobles' side resistance was the watchword. This was understandable because the most striking change from the earlier period was the increasing number of royal decisions that favoured the position of the third estate. In the deliberations of the second estate the nobles regularly expressed their dismay at the new decisions. They worried that the privileges and influence of their order were being whittled away. Relying upon records of these deliberations, historians have frequently portrayed the second estate as a group in full economic and social decline in the face of the new and dynamic alliance between the Crown and the third estate.

In fact, after 1602 it was the increasing role played by the Crown that constituted the most important element of change in the *taille* dispute. After the 1602 edict it became evident that the royal court was more disposed to step into what had previously been considered a provincial quarrel. This new interventionist policy was not limited to Dauphiné. Numerous historians have demonstrated that under Henry IV royal commissioners were sent regularly into all the provinces to look into fiscal abuses, and their missions are often seen as having paved the way for the creation of royal intendants.[1] For these missions Henry IV used special *maîtres de requête*, men like Jacques de Montholon, who was a *conseilleur d'état*, or Méry de Vic, Pomponne de Bellièvre, and Jean de Thumery, seigneur of Boissize, who were all connected with the Parlement of Paris.[2] In the case of Dauphiné, Méry de Vic was one of the regular visitors. He had been sent into the province in 1599 to try to resolve the *taille* question within the framework of the provincial Estates, and in 1601 he was named to a new royal commission obtained by Brosse to inquire into rural debts.[3] Through this commission the uninterrupted presence of royal commissioners in Dauphiné was extended up to the mid-1620s. They constituted an important source of information for the Crown concerning the *taille* affair.

Throughout the period the man most in evidence was Claude Brosse. He appeared regularly before the king, the Conseil d'état, and the provincial Estates to plead the cause of his constituents. The new *commis* of the villages appears to have been elected sometime between 1598, when the post was held by Raymond Chaliat, and November of 1601, when Brosse was sent to Paris to join the third-estate delegation in arguing the *taille* case.[4] Sent back to Paris after the 1602 decision, he was responsible for drafting at least twelve cahiers of grievance presented before the institutions of the province or before the king between 1603 and 1639.

Brosse's social origins and economic status are almost impossible to verify. He was referred to as the châtelain of Anjou, and the Estates-General in 1614 listed him as the seigneur of Serizin, but it does not appear that Brosse was a noble. Baptism records are one of the only documentary sources for Brosse's native village of Anjou. Begun in 1583, they contain several mentions of Claude Brosse as godfather, but he was never qualified as a noble. Furthermore, André Lacroix located a document prepared in 1768 for the consuls of the village, and it clearly identifies Brosse as a *roturier*.[5] Just as had the other defenders of the third estate, Brosse and his family appear to have occupied a position of social esteem in their village and region. The uncle or grandfather of Claude Brosse had been a royal notary, and the title of châtelain of Anjou, the village representative of the marquis of Saluces, seems to have been acquired by the Brosse family in 1576.[6]

Brosse acted as the principal spokesman for the villages and after 1610 for the whole third estate. Except for a short period in the 1620s when he was replaced as *commis*, he represented the rural communities at virtually every meeting of the provincial Estates, and in 1614 he was one of the delegates from Dauphiné to the Estates-General of the kingdom. His interventions between 1602 and 1628 were directed towards two major goals: first, reducing the weight of rural debts, and second, finding alternative fiscal solutions to *taille* levies.

From the time of his election Brosse concentrated upon the question of rural debts. It had been specifically mentioned in the 1602 judgment that the rulings on the sums owed by the villages had been demanded by their *commis*. In the judgment Brosse acquired Crown consent for the villages to tax their creditors for the investments they had made in property loans, a reference to a type of share-cropping contract called the *rente bâtarde*. Under these contracts, in return for a simple loan to enable a peasant to meet his *taille* obligations, creditors obtained rights to a share in any future sale of his property and rights to the first fruits of his harvest.[7] The imposition of tax levies upon this type of contract became one of the most difficult challenges in applying the 1602 decision. In another clause of the judgment Brosse acquired Crown consent for the cancellation of one-third of the back payments due on loans or *rentes* negotiated by the peasants from 1588 to 1597. During this period the wars had made agricultural development almost impossible, and the debts of the rural communities had increased dramatically. The problem of implementing the tax readjustments and deciding which loans were to be repaid was left to the new commission charged with re-evaluating the *feux*.

Immediately after the 1602 judgment Brosse and Antoine Rambaud were delegated by the assembly of the towns and rural communities of the province to continue their pressure upon the royal court in order to obtain further concessions. They prepared a cahier asking for 'clarifications' of twenty-three points in the judgment. The king replied to the cahier on 28 April 1603, but he accorded few new concessions. His reply extended the time period during which individuals or communities could repurchase their former holdings, and it fixed the interest rates on rural loans at a maximum of 5 per cent for the following four years and at 6.25 per cent thereafter.[9] Nevertheless, the new concessions had little effect upon the difficulties encountered in re-evaluating village debts or in applying the articles relating to the *rente bâtarde*.

Brosse continued his demands for a clearer mandate for the debt commission. At the provincial Estates of 1603 he submitted a cahier containing thirty-one articles, the majority of which concerned rural debts. The meeting concluded that the whole problem was related to the revision of the *feux* quotas and that it should be left to the *commis du pays* to consult representatives from the three orders and the *commis* of the villages and to propose the most expedient method of re-evaluating the quotas.[10] The *commis du pays*, however, merely evaded the question. At the following meeting of the Estates it was noted that they had ruled simply that all communities should pay one-sixth of the principal and interest due on their debts each year for the next six years. They made no provision for revising the *feux* or for redistributing taxes between rich towns and poor villages. As for collecting taxes from *rentiers*, or holders of share-cropping contracts, the villages even lost ground. The *commis*, together with the *commissaires* of the king, ruled that such individuals should be taxed by their place of residence and not by the locality where they had invested in the parcels.[11]

The rulings of the *commis du pays* did little to resolve the problem of village debts or the inexact *taille* quotas. Subsequent discussion and proposals on the question demonstrate that the village demands were opposed not only by the nobles but by the consuls of the major towns. In a meeting with the consuls of six of the ten recognized cities on 29 October 1603, Brosse protested that they were holding up a new revision of the *feux* in the province by their opposition to the king's edict reducing interest rates on village debts.[12] In January 1604 Brosse went before the royal court to explain the problem, but the king asked him to retire, noting that the 1603 clarifications had specified that in the future all problems between the three orders should be resolved before the provincial Estates.[13] At the same time the king asked the Estates to see to it that rural debts were reduced. He ordered the sieur de St Julien, second president of the Grenoble parlement and *procureur général* of the province, to create two *commis* in each *bailliage* and *sénéchaussée*. They were to hear the complaints of the village syndics on the problem of reducing debts and to make recommendations on ways to expedite the review procedure.[14]

When the Estates met at Valence in 1604, Brosse submitted a new cahier containing twenty-one articles. It protested against the resistance of both the towns and the nobles to the 1602 judgment and to the 1603 clarifications. In the résumé of their deliberations, however, the Estates merely reaffirmed the 1603 rulings of the *commis du pays*, adding that the principle of interest rates *au dernier vingt* (5 per cent) should be respected.[15] The 1604 session was reconvened in February 1605, and the towns again resisted any change. The three orders separated without adopting any measures of relief for the rural communities.[16]

Following the refusal of the Estates to act concerning village grievances, the Conseil d'état heard Brosse's complaint in September of 1605.[17]

An important element in the council's decision to hear the case was the fact that Brosse's arguments concerning the difficulties of revising village debts had been confirmed in a letter from the royal commissioners for the revision of the *feux* quotas in Dauphiné. In August of 1605 they complained that the commission did not have sufficient powers to proceed with the revisions.[18] By 14 September 1605 the first of a series of royal edicts on the debt question was issued. It accorded more time to the commissioners to study the problem. But the king ordered, until the final report was issued, all peasants who had been imprisoned for debt should be released, creditors should no longer be allowed to institute legal actions against individuals or communities for debt, and judges and *huissiers* could no longer act upon any such decisions taken in the past.[19]

During the hearings of the commission numerous meetings of rural villages and delegates from the *bailliages* were held to discuss the proposals to be submitted.[20] The delegates eventually prepared a report containing twenty-seven suggestions for facilitating the review of their debts. On 3 May 1606 their document was submitted to the syndic of the village creditors for his reactions. This exchange, along with numerous legal precedents, was sent to the Conseil d'état, which heard both the sieur de Villiers in the name of the creditors and Brosse in the name of the villages. On 5 August 1606 the Crown issued a significant new edict that ordered the verification and reduction of village debts by commissioners to be named by the king.

The new commission initiated direct royal intervention in the province. It was composed of Méry de Vic, councillor of the Parlement of Paris, along with important provincial figures like Claude Frère, the sieur de St Julien, Jean-Baptiste de Simiane, Jean-Baptiste de Ponnat, and Soffrey de Calignon, all from the parlement of Grenoble.[21] Even before their nomination, detailed instructions for the new commissioners were published. They specified that within a month of the arrival of the commissioners in each *bailliage*, the villages that had difficulties in reducing the amount of their debts should write to the commission seeking aid. The commissioners were authorized to judge without appeal any amount of less than two hundred *livres*. Their judgment on any higher amount could be appealed to a group of at least seven debt commissioners in the presence of commissioners from the king's council. Beyond them the judgment could only be appealed to the Conseil d'état.[22]

The commission was to have the right to judge all rural debts incurred since 1580 in accordance with the numerous edicts permitting the reduction of debts. First, the principal of each village debt was to be reduced to take account of inflation. Thereafter the commissioners were to establish whether interest could be charged, and in no case could it be higher than 5 per cent. Taxes and other fiscal obligations of the village could be deducted from the debt, and since back payments had been cancelled for certain years, any instalments that had been paid during those years could also be deducted. Finally, to permit the remaining debts to be paid off as rapidly as possible, the document ordered that in the future villages should make annual payments of one hundred écus on their debts. Village syndics were given the right to include in the special levies raised to pay the hundred écus, holdings that had been exempted since the debt had been created, so that many nobles and exempted officials were required to contribute.[23]

Complaints from the villages concerning the biases of the commissioners from Dauphiné eventually brought changes in the composition of the commission and the nomination of new men from outside the province. In 1608 Nicolas le Provost and the sieur de Ronceau, conseillers d'état, were appointed, along with Robert Aubery, as maîtres des requêtes.[24] The powers given to these men by the king constituted an unprecedented intervention in the affairs of the province, but an intervention that oddly enough went uncontested. The lack of open contestation may have been a result of the contradictory position of the nobility on the question of rural debts. Its leaders continued to insist publicly, as in the late 1590s, that the nobles had not invested in rural property or debts. In the assemblies of the second estate the issue was rarely mentioned, and in a letter to Sillery, garde des sceaux, just after the 1605 arrêt, Claude Expilly noted that the nobility felt that a resolution of the debt question would pacify the province: 'The creditors [of the villages], who are mostly bourgeois gentlemen and merchants from the cities, were stunned [by the edict]. They are trying to get the nobles to join them in the protests that they are preparing to make to the king, but they [the nobles] will not listen to them for most of them have no interest in this arrêt.'[25] Nevertheless, a close examination of the legal protests in village after village against the rulings of the debt commissioners contradicts the impression given by Expilly. The nobles' role as important rural creditors is evident from the condemnations of members of the second estate in virtually every village where the commissioners' judgments have survived.[26] Their interest in the debt question was also confirmed in a 1614 legal plea by the same Claude Expilly. By that time he argued that it was insulting and degrading for the debt-verification procedures even to be applied to the investments of the nobles and court officials.[27]

The main resistance of the nobles and urban elite to resolving the debt question was essentially carried out at the local level. Letters from the commissioners to the royal chancery in Paris in 1610, 1612, 1614, and 1620 noted the difficulties encountered when efforts were made to force village creditors to open their books for verification.[28] In 1610 Melchior de Fillon, president of the commission, wrote that usurious loans had made the financial situation of most of the villages worse than it had been during the Wars of Religion.[29] In 1620 Commissioners Aubery, Nicolas le Provost, and Monsieur de Faran were still having problems with creditors. They decided that if those who held rural debts refused to open their books to permit inspection of the terms of the debt, they would simply invalidate the contract. The commissioners also mentioned in the letter that they still had five to six thousand *écus* of debts to verify in their first *bailliage* before they could move on to hear grievances from the initial verifications in the other *bailliages* and *sénéchaussées*.[30] From these letters it is clear that the progress of the commission was held back considerably by the complexity of the various debt contracts, the resistance of creditors, and the piecemeal extensions of legal rulings by the Conseil d'état. After fourteen years of work by the debts commission Claude Brosse presented a new cahier to the king in 1620. It protested the fact that the commissioners were still having trouble interpreting such legal contracts as the *rente batarde*, that the peasants were still being imprisoned for debt, and that creditors were still using numerous legal loopholes to escape taxation.[31] The concrete results of the commission hearings seem to have been very limited.

The coalition of interest between bourgeois and noble investors in rural debts that was evident in the resistance to the debt commission again belies the rhetoric of the legal submissions in the *taille* dispute. The common interests of the two groups can be seen in the investments in rural debts, in the judgments rendered by the debt commission, and in the subtle undermining of the work of the commission. These common interests demonstrate the artificial nature of dividing lines conceived according to class or order. Once again it becomes apparent that there was a bourgeois spirit, a 'fourth estate,' to use Denis Richet's expression, that defied the structures of class or order and incorporated both the third-estate elite as well as a good number of the nobles of the robe and the captains of war who had acquired noble titles. All of them worked together to sabotage the inquiries of the debt commission.

If the nobles did not publicly oppose the Brosse initiatives on the debt question, the same cannot be said of their resistance to his second major goal, the introduction of indirect taxes to replace direct *taille* levies. At the time of the 1602 judgment the Crown had conceded revenues from certain indirect taxes to provide fiscal relief to the debt-ridden third estate. The decision had accorded the third estate 450,000 *écus*, which were to be taken from the revenues of the salt farm, together with either an imposition of 2 1/2 per cent on all 'foreign' salt imported into the province or a levy upon specific goods, to be determined by future negotiations.[32] The privileged orders, however, decided to block the transfer of such revenues. They argued that the designated impositions amounted to indirect taxes levied upon them in order to reduce the *tailles* demanded of the third estate. They maintained that they already furnished their part of provincial revenues through the *arrière ban* and that the 1602 judgment had confirmed their exemption from all other impositions or contributions. At the 1603 Estates the nobles opposed third-estate efforts to implement the clauses giving them indirect tax revenues, and they went even further. They succeeded in passing legislation to eliminate many of the existing indirect taxes, to close the *douane* (customs station) in Vienne, to lift the recently imposed tax on livestock imported into the province, and to leave the management of the provincial salt farm to the *procureur du pays*.[33]

When the documents containing these proposals were transmitted to the royal court, the question seems to have been raised why the third estate had not been accorded either the revenue from the salt farm or those from another tax. At the meeting of the Council of the Nobility in September 1603 it was noted that someone should be sent to court immediately to 'oppose the bad impression [of us] given to the king and members of his council by the third estate concerning that which occurred during the last Estates.'[34] The sieur de Passage, one of the old nobles who assisted regularly at the sessions of the Council of the Nobility, was sent. On 10 June 1604 it was reported back to the nobles that their lawyer had succeeded in getting the whole question of indirect taxes transferred back to the provincial Estates.[35]

The cahiers presented by Claude Brosse to the Estates of 1604 and 1605 returned to the question. They singled out the nobles for their resistance to third-estate claims to a portion of the indirect taxes levied in the province. Articles seven and eight of the 1604 document referred specifically to previous proposals for taxing imported wine. They argued that the revenues from such a tax should, together with the reduction in rural debts, go to reduce the fiscal burdens of the village communities. The officials of the Estates appear to have rejected the proposal, arguing that letters patent issued by the king in 1602 had forbidden the importation of wine into the province.[36] Nevertheless, in February 1605 Brosse expanded upon his demands in a new cahier containing eleven articles. It was submitted to the Estates at Valence. Article three asked that the letters patent of 16 April 1602 be verified. He argued that they had clearly made provision for a tax on imported wine. The document also noted that following the suppression of indirect taxes by the 1603 Estates, the wine tax remained one of the only possible sources of revenue for the third estate.[37]

The nobles' deliberations clearly reveal that they were uneasy in opposing the wine tax. Immediately after the 1605 Estates they sent delegates to the court who argued that the tax had been rejected because of a split in the third-estate delegation and not because of noble opposition. According to them, the urban representatives held that a tax on wine would be detrimental to the poor people.[38] The old split between the bourgeois elite of the major cities and the rest of the third estate probably did compromise the wine tax in 1605. A year later, however, the breach seems to have been healed, and again pressure was applied to the second estate. It was noted in the deliberations of the Council of the Nobility that the towns and villages had resolved their disagreements. Antoine Rambaud, representing the ten cities, had gone to the court to support the Brosse request for a tax on all imported wine. The members of the Conseil d'état asked the nobles if they had anything to say on the question, adding that their judgment could not be delayed much longer. The nobles were short of funds and wrote to the sieur de Bompar, who was at court, asking him to intervene for them. To document their case they dispatched legal memoranda drawn up by lawyers Pelloux and Robert, arguing against indirect taxes.

On 27 June 1606 a general assembly of all the nobles of the province discussed the issue and resolved that if such a tax were granted, it should be levied only on the third estate. The new wine tax was to be used exclusively to reduce third-estate *taille* levies or the debts resulting from such levies. In addition the 1602 judgment had recognized the exemption of the privileged orders from all such *tailles* and impositions. The nobles went on to complain to the king about the expense of sending delegates to the court, noting that the 1603 clarification had specified that all such issues should be settled in the provincial Estates.[39] In July and August 1606 the Council of the Nobility wrote to the duke of Saulne and to Sully to explain their position. They even asked Lesdiguières to speak to the king about the proposed wine tax.[40]

By August 1606 the king appears to have bowed to the pressure applied by the second estate. The case was again sent back to the province for further study in the Estates, where, it was noted, all such issues should be settled. The résumé of the Estates meeting for that year records that Brosse was re-elected as syndic of the villages and that he once again attacked the second estate on wine-tax issue. Confronted by the nobles' objections, Rambaud and Brosse stated that they were simply trying to resolve the question of rural debts without reducing the 'privileges and exemptions' of the privileged orders. They asked the nobles if their order could propose a more adequate solution.[41] The meeting broke up without any decision having been reached, and the issue was again returned to the king. It was bounced back and forth between the Estates and the royal court until 1609, when the Assembly of the Nobility was informed that it should send a delegation to the king to prevent him from signing an edict to create the new tax.[42] A four-man delegation composed of the major nobles of the province was sent to the court. Henry IV received them and promised to do nothing to reduce their privileges. He agreed to suspend the wine tax on the condition that the three orders hold a conference to find solid ground for reconciliation. He particularly insisted that if the nobles wanted to avoid the wine tax, another means for relieving the people had to be found.[43]

To prepare the assembly that was to lead to the 'reconciliation and union of the three orders of the province,' the *commis du pays* asked each of the three estates to hold meetings in their *bailliages* to draw up cahiers of grievance. Thereafter, each order was to meet to prepare a unified cahier that was to be presented to the meeting of the provincial Estates scheduled for 22 December 1609.[44] The meeting was to be presided over by the duke of Créqui, the son-in-law of Lesdiguières, who had succeeded his father-in-law as governor of the province at the same time that Lesdiguières became constable of France. Both the third estate and the privileged orders were very hesitant to involve themselves in serious discussions, and it was only through Créqui's force of persuasion that any agreement was reached.

Rambaud, representing the third-estate delegation, arrived at the assembly with the cahier of his order, but he refused to negotiate. He claimed that the third estate had received mandates from its regional meetings to draw up and present cahiers containing demands that were minimal but also, therefore, non-negotiable. The meeting decided to create a subcommittee that would study the documents article by article, but the nobles protested, saying that the third estate was clinging to each word of its resolutions. Créqui brought the orders together, reminding them that it was the will of the king that they negotiate. Thereafter, the third estate replied that it could accept the wording of most of the nobles' articles.[45]

As for the negotiators for the second estate, the deliberations of the Assembly of the Nobility reveal that the rapidity of the negotiating process took them by surprise. From 29 December to 3 January the nobles of the robe repeated that the negotiations should be slowed down so that they could ascertain that no article was prejudicial to the traditional privileges and *franchises* of their order. The most difficult problem for them was how to adopt a position on the question of 'relieving the people' without committing themselves to contributing to the eventual relief. On the twenty-ninth Sieur Robert, one of the nobles' lawyers, noted that the desires of the king and the pressure of Créqui had caused the second estate to enter into wholesale compromises without its having studied the consequences of the articles voted. After consulting the members of the parlement on the articles negotiated, he reported back to the assembly that in legal terms the expression of 'commiseration' on the part of the privileged orders for the requests of the poor rural communities could bind them to furnishing relief. Robert noted, however, that the nobles could not back out of the negotiating process without being accused of bad faith.[46]

On 31 December, when the meeting returned to the question of proposing aid to the people, the third estate again refused to change any of its resolutions, and the nobles used this excuse to break off negotiations. Again Créqui stepped in and ordered both sides to meet with him in Lesdiguière's house. In the presence of the king's *conseillers d'état* he met with the first and second orders and assured them that none of their privileges would be compromised. Thereafter, in a meeting with the delegates of the third estate, he repeated that it was the king's will that the three orders agree to a compromise through which a 'pacification' of the province could lead to relief for the 'misery of the people.' He insisted that questions of semantics should not stop negotiations and noted that he would transmit to the king the names of any individuals whose 'fixed opinions' on the question further held up the talks.[47]

In the article concerning relief of the poor, the nobles wanted simply to make a general reference to 'aid for the people' (*soulagement*), without specifying who should supply the aid. Rambaud protested that the third-estate delegates did not have a mandate to accept such a change in their proposed articles, but Créqui replied that the royal councillors had decided otherwise and that the nobles' alteration offended neither side.[48] Such quarrels continued, but by 14 January the three estates had agreed to a general declaration of the 'union of the three orders.'

At the Estates a year later Rambaud and Brosse arrived with a new cahier asking for the application of the article in the 'union' that concerned the controversial question of the aid to be given to the people. The third estate proposed, as a means of implementing the article, that revenues from the provincial salt farm be applied not just to rural debts but also to reducing the extraordinary *taille* levies.[49] The salt farm was one of the principal sources of provincial revenue to be managed by the Estates. During the sixteenth century the third estate had frequently asked that its revenue be applied to paying wartime expenses and to maintaining garrisons, *étapes*, or fortifications, but their requests had never been granted.

The privileged orders immediately protested that such use of the revenues from the salt farm constituted an indirect tax imposed upon all the inhabitants of the province in order to reduce *taille* levies that the third estate alone should pay. They noted that this was just another 'trick' (*artifice*) of the third estate to get around the 1602 decision and to tax the privileged orders. At the meeting of their delegation the nobles and clergy proposed a whole series of alternatives to the third-estate proposition. They asked that the king apply the revenues from his domain lands to reduce village debts or that the revenues from the salt farm be applied to rural debts alone, as the king had ruled in 1602. They were even ready to vote for a tax on imported wine, to be applied to rural debts. They noted, however, that they would never accept the application of salt-farm revenue to the reduction of *taille* levies without receiving compensation.[50]

In the presence of Lesdiguières, Rambaud and Brosse both insisted that this was an initial test of the seriousness of the 1610 agreement. The nobles argued that the third-estate demands went far beyond the intentions of the article demanding relief for the poor. Finally, a compromise was reached by which the great majority of the revenues from the salt farm were allotted to the third estate for five years, but only to be applied to rural debts and not to reduce extraordinary levies.[51] In addition, the privileged orders were provided compensation for their contributions to the salt farm. They were awarded an eighth of the annual revenues from the farm. In terms of the 1611 receipts, this meant that the nobles and clergy would receive about five thousand *écus* and the third estate about forty thousand.[52] Despite these concessions the privileged orders were not entirely satisfied with the amount of the revenues awarded to them nor with the loss of the right to dispose of the totality of the annual revenues from the salt farm, revenues that had generally been channelled into projects that benefited members of their orders.

It is evident from the negotiations concerning indirect taxes that it became increasingly difficult for the nobles to convince the Crown of the merits of their position. The financial needs of the monarchy increased as military initiatives against the Huguenots and great nobles were begun after 1616. Indirect taxes were an appealing alternative to direct *taille* levies, which generally incurred the wrath of the peasantry and aggravated the rural-debt problem.

At the provincial Estates of 1616 the third estate asked that the Crown impose a 2 per cent tax on salt collected through the salt farm instead of imposing a new general levy to support both a quarter of the cost of a new company of soldiers raised in the province and to pay a month's salary for the regiment of the count of Saulx. Representing the nobles and clergy, the abbot of Boscodon met with Lesdiguières and argued that the third-estate proposition was contrary to the 1606 edict. Lesdiguières told Boscodon that although he did not know what the king intended to do, he considered himself a member of 'our order' and would work for the conservation of 'our rights.' In discussions with some of Lesdiguières's aides after the meeting, however, Boscodon learned that despite what he had been told, the third estate had already convinced the king of the enormous weight of its tax burden and that the king had decided in order to cover new expenses, to levy a tax of forty *sous* on each *minot* of salt imported into Dauphiné.[53] Despite Lesdiguières, however, the privileged orders again succeeded in preventing the new increase.

In 1619 it was decided at an Assembly of the Nobility and Clergy that they could no longer depend upon Lesdiguières to defend their position on indirect taxes, and the count of Saix was sent to argue their case before the king. The new negotiations changed nothing, and in 1621 still another delegation had to be sent to oppose a new cahier presented to the king by Claude Brosse. The 1621 cahier requested that revenues from the salt farm continue to be applied to levies and that portions of the revenues of the customs station (*douane*) in Vienne also be used to reduce the continually increasing tax levies. The nobles repeated their arguments against such taxation, and they protested that they were no longer even receiving their allocation of the revenues.[54]

By 1620 it had become clear that the nobility was losing ground on the question and that its relations with both Lesdiguières and with the royal court were becoming increasingly strained. By 1622 the initiatives for increasing indirect tax levies were coming not from the third estate but from the king himself. Louis XIII finally ordered that the basic tax levied on salt be doubled, going from twenty *sous* a *minot* to forty. At the Estates of that year the privileged orders opposed the new tax, asking the king to return to the traditional levies, the *decimes* paid by the clergy and the *bans* and *arrières-bans* charged to the nobles. At the assembly of the privileged orders held during the Estates it was noted that Lesdiguières was 'very displeased' with their opposition, but the meeting continued to insist that the new forms of taxation were contrary to the 1602 edict, and it was decided to protest once again to the king.[55] The rhetoric of these deliberations became increasingly radical as the second estate became increasingly isolated.

Up to the early 1620s Claude Brosse had been the instigator of attacks directed on the one hand against village creditors, the enriched urban elite, and the nobility, and on the other against the privileged orders, which refused to contribute proportionately to the expenses of the province. By striking out against virtually all of the privileged groups, Brosse appears at first glance to have been a sort of Robin Hood acting alone to defend the indebted peasantry, the poorest and most oppressed social group in the province. André Lacroix, Charles Laurens, and even Le Roy Ladurie have all contributed to this profile of Brosse as the 'intrepid defender,' the 'saviour,' and the authentic rural spokesman of the people of Dauphiné.[56] Although the vigour and competence of Brosse's initiatives cannot be denied, he was not as isolated as the historians of the province have often implied. From the time of his earliest negotiations with the royal court Brosse seems to have been supported and encouraged by the king and his ministers. Indeed, Brosse's actions to resolve the *taille* question fit a pattern that coincided with the objectives of the Crown.

Nicholas Chorier wrote that in 1604 Chancellor Bellièvre saw Brosse as 'a man who sacrificed himself to the public interest, to the hatred of the powerful.'[57] Brosse appears to have been well considered by both Henry IV and Louis XIII. His interventions were clearly mentioned in the 1602 edict and in the 1603 clarification. In 1606, after he had obtained the edict setting up the commission to verify village debts and had requested the imposition on wine imported into the province, the Conseil d'état accorded him its protection for the next two years and granted him immunity from any legal actions taken against him.[58] Two years later the *conseil* renewed its protection and granted Brosse the right to carry a pistol to defend himself as long as he pursued the revision of village debts, given 'the hatred and animosity that has spread through the body of the province because of the rulings.'[59] A second decision of the Conseil d'état ordered the *receveur général* of the province to make provision for collecting the thirty thousand *livres* that village assemblies in Loriol, the *bailliage* of the Montagnes, and the Graisivaudan had voted to pay Brosse in 1606.[60]

The third-estate cause seems to have become highly personalized under the leadership of Brosse. The cities of the province always had difficulty dealing with him, as was evident in their hesitation over the wine tax and their opposition to the debt commission. As village *commis* he attended the meetings of the assemblies of the ten cities, meetings that became enlarged into *assemblées du pays*. At these meetings his initiatives were discussed and debated before being presented to the provincial Estates. There is little sign, however, of the grass-roots consultations that had marked the preparation of the third-estate cahiers in the 1570s. Most village archives contain only notices of a series of meetings in 1605, when the first steps towards the establishment of the debt commission were announced.[61]

The documentary gaps in local archives make it difficult to trace the relations of Brosse with his constituents, but it is clear that by 1617–18 the communities were less and less satisfied with his actions. Their dissatisfaction was evident in the face of his regular demands for additional remuneration. A meeting of the village syndics on 17 June 1617 delayed consideration of a request by Brosse for a lifetime annuity in return for his services.[62] At an assembly of the *commis du pays* a year later he asked for the payment of an annual grant of fifteen hundred *livres*, which he claimed that the conseil du roi had accorded him on 4 December 1617. No payment was made by the *commis du pays*, which noted that it had received no confirmation from the king concerning such a grant.[63]

Another indication of the disenchantment of the villages with their *commis* is that he was voted out of his position in the 1620s. It is not clear why, or when he was replaced. Certainly, the villages were not pleased with the demands made by Brosse in 1621, when he requested thirty thousand *écus* plus continuation of his annual pension of fifteen hundred *livres*.[64] This may have led to the selection of a new *commis*. As to the date when he lost his position, a document issued by the *commis des villages* late in 1621 was signed by Monsieur Bezançon, but he might have been only a temporary replacement.[65] It is certain that Brosse was no longer *commis* in 1624. In May of that year a disputed election led to the appointment of Jacques Amat, châtelain of Upaix, to the position.[66] The decision in favour of Amat notes that he had been legally chosen by electoral procedures that had begun on 11 May 1624, when the Conseil du roi gave permission to village representatives to assemble before judges or *commis* in one of the towns of each *bailliage* in order to elect representatives who would be sent to the Estates to choose the new *commis des villages*. The elected representatives favored Amat, but on 13 August the *procureur du pays* called a special assembly composed of six representatives from the clergy and nobility. They ruled that the election of Amat was null and void, and they chose Brosse to replace him.[67]

The towns immediately appealed the case to the king, and in the deliberations of the Romans consulate it was noted that Brosse had been chosen by the privileged orders 'better to silence the poor third estate and to stop the pursuit of its valid grievances.'[68] The king retained Amat in the position, but there seems to have been an attempt by Brosse to obtain further compensation for his services. The consulate of Montélimar wrote to the consuls of La Garde Adhémar on 20 July 1624, asking them to join a movement to oppose a new levy of twenty thousand *livres* that had been granted to Claude Brosse.[69]

A second possible explanation for the opposition to Brosse revolves around his rapid acceptance of a number of Crown initiatives to raise money in the province. In 1627, in one of the more controversial of these measures, Louis XIII proposed the creation of a number of new Crown officials. Brosse was back in his position as *commis*, although it is not clear whether or not he had been elected to the position. He carried out a nominal consultation of the villages concerning the creation of the new tax-exempt officials proposed for the *cour des aides* and the office of the treasury. Despite village opposition he then consented to the creation of thirty-five or thirty-six new positions. The third estate immediately protested that its *commis* had been bought off with the promise that his own position would become hereditary, carrying an annual pension of sixteen hundred *livres* and the services of two aides.[70]

By 1628 the village protests against Brosse's collaboration with the Crown were coming together with the long-simmering discontent of the provincial elite concerning his attacks upon their fiscal exemptions and investments. This new coalition of interests led to a series of legal initiatives against the village syndic. The offensive came in the wake of the major royal interventions of 1628, in which *élections financières*, or tax districts, had been established and the provincial Estates suspended. By these measures the Crown had assumed direct control over the imposition, levying, and collection of *tailles* in the province, and intendants were sent in to supervise financial operations.

The legal action against Brosse came in the midst of this coup. Its origins went back to accusations on the part of the villages that he had attempted to extort remuneration from them, but the collaboration of the urban elite and the privileged orders is evident.[71] Complaints had been made to the king concerning Brosse's continual claims for payment. As early as the meeting of the *assemblée du pays* in March 1628 it was noted that legal charges had been brought against him.[72] These charges appear to have led to his arrest on 7 January 1631 and his trial on 21 January. The documents in the case show that Sieur Jacques Putod, a councillor of the king, acted on the charge that Brosse illegally claimed and received fifteen thousand *livres* in remuneration for his services from Félix Basset, president of the Estates in 1627. It was argued that this payment had been made in error, and the trial was directed to recover the payment. Brosse was fined six thousand *livres*, payable prior to his release, plus restitution of the fifteen thousand *livres*.[73]

Brosse appears to have remained in prison until 6 March 1631, and during that time the king's council intervened twice. First, on 30 January it ordered the seizure of all the papers of the *commis* of the villages, including an inventory drawn up by Putod. The grand provost of France was asked to draw up a new inventory of all the documents. After studying the papers and the acts of the Brosse trial, the council intervened again on 6 March to liberate Brosse. It declared the judgment of the Grenoble court null and void and ordered the *procureur général* Musy and the *conseiller rapporteur* Putod to be relieved of their functions.[74] Once again the direct Crown intervention demonstrates the links between the initiatives of Brosse and the interests of the king.

The demands of Claude Brosse appear to have pleased the Crown from the very beginning of his implication in the *taille* controversy. His third-estate colleagues Delagrange, Rambaud, and Vincent were closely linked to the new urban elite. Their cahiers and pamphlets asked that the *taille personnelle* system be abandoned, a radical change that would have benefited the whole third estate but would have been of particular usefulness to the enriched merchant and professional groups of the towns. In contrast, Brosse singled out the problems that were most acute for the poorest communities in the province: debts, new tax levies, and the revision of the *feux* quotas. In pursuing these demands the *commis des villagers* alienated both the third-estate elite, which had considerable interest in the rural debts, and the privileged orders, which opposed both the reductions in debts and the attempt to tax them through indirect fiscal measures. The successes achieved by Brosse in obtaining the commission for the verification of rural debts, the use of indirect taxes to reduce *taille* levies, and eventually the establishment of the *taille réelle* system were made possible by his own persistence and by the support of the Crown.[75]

The second major explanation of Brosse's success revolves around what numerous historians have called the crisis, or the deteriorating position, of the nobility. The defensive attitude of the nobles is clear in the minutes of their assemblies. These documents record an increasing fear that the arguments of the third estate were gaining adherents in the royal court, that the resistance of the nobles was misunderstood, and that the nobles had to have recourse to excuses in order to defend their rights. All these fears were confirmed by the Crown intervention in 1606 to create the debts commission, in 1609 and 1611 when the king forced the privileged orders to yield revenues from the salt farm to reduce the rural debts, and in the 1620s when indirect taxes were imposed upon the nobles and clergy by the Crown. It is obvious that the privileged orders sensed that they were losing the unlimited support of the Crown.

In the historical controversy over the crisis of the nobility in sixteenth-century France, Dauphiné has often served as an example. It has been pointed to by those who see a major decline in the number of old families, an accumulation of debts by the surviving families, and the introduction into the second estate of numerous members of the economic and professional bourgeois elite. A century ago Mariéjol linked the attack upon provincial privileges with the decline of the second estate.[76] More recently Davis Bitton has cited third-estate attacks upon the nobles in Dauphiné made during the *taille* confrontation from 1595 to 1602. He has used their rhetoric to demonstrate the breakdown of the old hierarchical mentality and the vehemence of opposition to the privileges of the second estate.[77] Evidence of the dissatisfaction of the old nobles in Dauphiné with Crown interventions in the province has led Boris Porchnev to argue that in the long series of peasant revolts that shook the province in the 1630s, the old feudal order often allied itself with the peasants against the bourgeoisie and the Crown.[78] Pierre Deyon, too, has noted that the reversal in the nobles' *taille* status in Dauphiné in 1634 came on the heels of a general offensive against the second estate throughout the kingdom.[79]

While Dauphiné has been cited as one of the prime examples of an area where the old nobility was in difficulty, the whole theory of the crisis of the nobility has been challenged by other recent historical work.[80] William Weary has shown that, contrary to the argument that old noble families were destined to inevitable decline, the house of La Trémoille, in the west and centre of France, actually increased its fortunes. The seigneurs of La Trémoille adjusted to the economic necessities of the time by more closely administering and managing their estates. Similarly, they adjusted to the new political designs of the absolutist regime by acquiring important and lucrative offices sold by the Crown.[81] Russell Major's 1981 article on the Albret family provides another example of an old family that suffered neither decline nor debts as a result of the wars.[82]

On a more global level, James B. Wood has studied the nobility in the *élection* of Bayeux using periodic nobiliar *recherches*, or inquiries designed to weed out false nobles who were claiming noble status and exemptions.[83] On the basis of his study Wood argues that it is true that there had been an unprecedented number of new nobles created during the period from 1540 to 1598 and that the great majority of the *anoblis* had judicial, professional, or financial backgrounds.[84] However, this influx was in no way related to a decline in the old families of the *élection*. Wood's research does not at all confirm the pessimistic evaluations of earlier studies. The number of old noble lines did decline by at least fifty per cent for the period studied, but Wood has shown that this decline was not any more dramatic than in any previous century. In addition he finds that despite the decline in the number of noble lines, the demographic increase in the number of nuclear noble families almost permitted the old nobility to maintain its numbers by procreation alone.[85] As to the financial decline of the old families, Wood has shown that there were more bankruptcies among the new nobles than the old and far more property acquisitions by the *noblesse de race*.[86] According to Wood there was definitely no general crisis for the old families during the period 1463–1666.

Given these attacks upon the crisis theory in other parts of France, does a close examination of the second estate in Dauphiné really confirm the hypothesis that the social, economic, and political position of the nobility was declining? Several important holdings in the archives of

Dauphiné permit a partial analysis of the problem. The nobles' position on the continuing *taille* quarrel can be followed with considerable precision in the series of deliberations of the Council and Assembly of the Nobility that have been preserved for the period from 1602 to 1622.[87] Changes in the social structure of the nobility can be demonstrated from the acts of *anoblissement* registered in the parlement of Grenoble.[88] The question of the economic decline of the old families can be partially answered by data on the changes in ownership of the major seigniories of the province available through the seventeenth-century Inventaire Marcellier.[89]

The deliberations of the nobles' assemblies from 1602 to the early 1620s demonstrate the regular reappearance of different aspects of the *taille* dispute. Meetings were dominated by discussions of strategy and tactics in the continuing confrontation with the third estate. However, the tone of these debates is indicative of a group that felt its position weakening progressively. One of the principal preoccupations of the second estate was to re-establish the noble status of a number of lawyers and jurists who had been eliminated from its ranks. The nobles congratulated their representatives at the royal court for obtaining the maintenance of second-estate *franchises* and privileges in the 1602 edict, but they deplored the loss of exemptions and noble status for the twenty-one *avocats consistoriaux*. The Assembly of the Nobility voted to send Sieur Ferrand, secretary of the meeting and of the Council of the Nobility, to the royal court with a request that the king maintain the 'rights and privileges' of the *avocats*.[90] At the subsequent council meeting the question was raised again, but this time it was more clearly linked to second-estate interests. The council noted that at a time when the nobles were faced with numerous legal challenges from the third estate, the elimination of the *avocats consistoriaux* from their ranks weakened the whole order of the nobility and deprived them of an important source of legal aid. Noting that Aquin, Pelloux, and Robert, the most important noble lawyers, were old and frequently indisposed, the meeting asked for the ennoblement of Sieur Marchier, a man 'who has always shown such affection for [our] order.'[91] On 11 July 1602 the council repeated the request and asked that *avocats* Fine and Flory be granted letters of ennoblement as well.[92]

The Crown appears to have granted letters to the candidates proposed by the second estate, but this did not solve the nobles' problems. Their new defenders seem to have become less involved in defending the nobles' cause than Robert, Pelloux, or Aquin had been. Although the letters of ennoblement for Marchier cannot be found, he seems to have been ennobled in 1605, and he started attending meetings of the council in 1607[93] The letters for Flory are also absent from the registers of the parlement, but he began attending council meetings in 1609.[94] Fine received letters of ennoblement in 1606; however, he appears never to have been very active in the council or in the assembly.[95] The lack of zeal of all the newly ennobled lawyers was pointedly underlined at a meeting of the council in 1615. Du Mottet, representative of the old nobles, noted that since the establishment of the council, the 'gentlemen of the robe' who had so greatly assisted their order were almost all dead. Aquin, Pelloux, and Roune had all passed away, and Robert had just died. Regretting that the second estate had been deprived of necessary counsel and advice during the negotiation of the 1610 union between the orders, he appealed to the lawyers who had been ennobled recently to come to the aid of their order. Specifying Marchier, Flory, and Reynaud, he asked them 'to take the time' to assist more regularly at the council meetings.[96]

A signal indication of the progressive weakening of noble institutions in the period from 1602 to the 1620s was the inability of the nobles to continue to operate their institutions as separate bodies independent of the clergy. To prevent the third estate from being accorded the revenues from the salt farm, the tax-exempt groups were told at the 1610 Estates to arrive at the 1611 meeting with alternative methods of reducing the debts of the rural communities. To present a more solid front in the ensuing discussions, the nobles integrated their assembly and council with the representative institutions of the clergy. The positive effects of the fusion were never really apparent, and in 1611 the third estate obtained the revenues from the salt farm despite the new alliance. From that time on, however, the representative assemblies of the two privileged orders remained integrated. It is clear that the purpose of this integration was not simply to strengthen the institutions of the privileged orders but also to bolster up institutions that were no longer capable of functioning independently.

The weakness of those institutions is further evident in the dramatic decline in the number of meetings of the Council of the Nobility during the period for which deliberations are available (see Table 4). From 1602 to 1606 the council met an average of 5.5 times a year, but after 1606 the number of its meetings dropped to an average of only 1.6 a year. This decline had important consequences for the nobles' legal positions on the wine tax, the salt farm, the 'union' of the three orders, and so

TABLE 4
Number of annual meetings of the
Council of the Nobility

1602	9	1611	0
1603	2	1612	2
1604	5	1613	0
1606	6	1614	0
1607	4	1616	2
1608	1	1617	1
1609	3	1618	4

Source: Registre des Assemblées de la
noblesse, 1602–22, AD Isère, 1 J 175

on. The council was the principal source of legal advice for the second estate, and the decline in the number of its meetings was directly reflected in the quality of the nobles' strategy and interventions in the *taille* debate after 1606. The nobles blamed the decline on the disappearance of some of the council's most active members and the difficulty of recruiting new members. Aquin, the principal lawyer for the second estate during the 1590 *taille* controversy, appeared for the last time in the attendance lists of the 1604 council meeting. Imbert Pelloux, a lawyer who was ennobled for the aid that he had given to the 'projects' of Henry IV,[97] had been another active collaborator in the legal defence of the nobles. He attended the meetings of the council regularly up to 9 September 1609, and he was brought in as a special adviser to the nobles during the 1610 negotiations on the union of the three orders.[98] He died in 1613.[99] Robert, the most assiduous of the noble advisers, died on 5 March 1615. The replacement of these aged legal counselors by new defenders was rendered difficult by the 1602 edict eliminating the noble status of the *avocats consistoriaux*, who until then had been the principal new legal recruits for the second estate. The assemblies of the nobility were increasingly uneasy over the lack of regular legal advice available to their order, and they attributed their setbacks in 1606, 1610, and 1622 to this state of affairs.

It is not at all clear, however, that the apparent decline in the legal apparatus of the second estate was indicative of a general demographic or economic crisis among the old nobles. It has already been noted that Expilly named twenty noble lines that had either died out or lost their titles during the war years.[100] Going even further, Guy Allard contended that the provincial nobility declined dramatically during the period between the 1523–4 *ban* muster and that of 1684. Of the 431 noble lines present on the 1523–role, only 204 were among the 434 lines that appeared on the *ban* rolls for 1684.[101] While this data appears to confirm the crisis theory, in fact this decline of 47 per cent during a period of 161 years was less than the average decline of noble lines in other areas of France. Both Edouard Perroy and James Wood have shown that on average 50 per cent of the noble lines disappeared during any given century.[102] It is not at all clear that the old noble lines in Dauphiné were in the late sixteenth century any more exposed to the economic difficulties of their time than was the nobility of any other period.[103]

It is not clear either that the old established families were obliged to sell off their holdings, or that the new nobles who joined the ranks of the second estate had amassed great fortunes.[104] To test the first hypothesis concerning the evolution of noble holdings during the period, I selected one region of Dauphiné, the *sénéchaussée* of Valentinois. There I examined the titles listed for the 193 seigniories that were included in the five volumes of the Inventaire Marcellier that cover the *sénéchaussée*. The Inventaire Marcellier is a thirty-five volume manuscript listing of the seigniorial archives held by the Grenoble Chambre des comptes. Begun in 1696 by François Marcellier, the inventory was completed in 1710.[105] The documents are inventoried by *bailliage* or *sénéchaussée* and are listed alphabetically by seigniory. The inventory is of considerable importance since the archives of the Chambre des comptes were dispersed and most were destroyed during the French Revolution. In addition to listing the documents concerning each seigniory, the *inventaire* transcribes extensive sections of each register; thus, it provides extensive information on sixteenth-century holdings in each seigniory. It includes the relevant excerpts from the report of the commission on the *dénombrement*, or enumeration, carried out between 1540 and 1542, of all seigneurial titles in the province. Acts of homage, sales of seigniories, or procedures for the transfer (*aliénation* and *réunion*) of lands to and from the Crown domains are listed. To check and complete the titles listed in the inventory, I consulted seven of the eight volumes of the inventory compiled by André Lacroix of family and village archives located in the department of the Drôme, the region that formerly constituted the *sénéchaussée* of Valentinois. I also checked the inventory against Lacroix's works on the Montélimar and Nyons regions and Joseph Braun-Durand's *Dictionnaire topographique*, with its lists of the principal seigneurial families for each community in the Drôme.[106] This search enabled me to trace 113 seigniories where the owner or co-owners could be verified at least for periods before and after the Wars of Religion. Thirty-eight of these holdings remained in the hands of the same family between 1540 and 1600. Forty-three of them were sold once, twenty-one twice, and twelve changed hands three or more times (see Appendix B). This turnover rate was higher than that of Bayeux, where about half the seigniories changed hands during the same period.[107]

Traditional historians of Dauphiné have noted that the nobles most engaged as captains of war or as military governors were the most active buyers.[108] René de la Tour, seigneur of Governet and military governor of Die, acquired the seigniories of Aix, Barry-en-Verchères, Quint-Pontaix, and Cornillon. Hector de Forest, seigneur of Blacons-Mirabel and governor of Orange, purchased Upie and Sauzet. Louis de Blain, seigneur of Poët-Célard and governor of Montélimar, bought La Batie Rolland and Saou and added Châteauneuf-de-Mazenc to his holdings in 1616. Finally, Claude de Lattier, seigneur of Charpey and lieutenant to the royalist commander La Violette, acquired Orcinas, Rochefort Samson, and Vassieux. The prices paid for a domain represented a substantial sum of between four thousand and ten thousand *livres*. Such purchases by military leaders indicate that certain minor nobles profited considerably from the war years.

The same is true of the purchases of the *parlementaires* and the nobles of the robe. Numerous *conseillers* to the parlement were active buyers in the Valentinois-Diois. Michel Thomé acquired a part of the seigniory of Barcelone in 1583; Pierre de la Baume bought La Rochette in 1606; Claude Frère purchased Barbières in 1606 and Rochefort Samson in 1623; Jean de la Croix Chevrières obtained Pisançon in 1595. Ennemond Rabot, first president of the parlement, held Upie up to 1593, when he sold it to Hector de la Forest. The attraction of the judicial elite towards rural domains shows that they were anxious to become assimilated into the old feudal, landowning elite. Compared to the acquisitions of the military men, *parlementaire* buying in the Valentinois-Diois remained modest, but it can be presumed that nobles of the robe were far more involved in property speculation around Grenoble.

Despite the many examples of military or judicial figures engaged in acquiring seigniories, they were marginal when compared with the old noble families, who dominated both the buying and selling. In 1540 the Eurre family line alone possessed fifteen of the 113 seigniories, and by the end of the Wars of Religion the family had alienated or transferred three of its holdings. The Montoison-Clermont line controlled nine seigniorial titles in 1540 and seven in 1600. During the same period the

Vesc line lost the seigniory of Pennes, thus declining to five seigniories, and the Adhémar family added Beaufort to its four traditional holdings. The old noble families did not pursue aggressive acquisition policies during the Wars of Religion. The Marcellin inventory indicates that almost all of them lost seigniories, which indicates a certain economic decline. Yet the decline or changes in the estates of the established families hardly indicate their ruin. The marginal acquisitions made by those who served in the religious wars or in the judicial elite did not upset significantly the hierarchical structure of the property holdings in the region. The same old families dominated the landholding structure of the Valentinois both before and after the wars.

The case of the new families entering the ranks of the nobility opens up a more complex problem. Druout and Romier considered that it was very common practice for enriched non-nobles to purchase a noble fief and thereby acquire a title and tax exemption. It is clear, however, that a very limited number benefited from such ennoblements in Dauphiné.[109] In the acts concerning the 113 seigniories of the Valentinois contained in the Inventaire Marcellier, only three cases of major purchases by non-nobles were found. In the first case Pierre Chapuyer, bourgeois from Montélimar, purchased half of the seigniory of Roussas in 1561 for 1,500 *livres*.[110] In 1580 Achilles Lambert, a bourgeois from Valence, acquired a minor portion of the seigniory of Saillans for 1,008 *livres*. This purchase, made from the bishop of Die, was confirmed by the Chambre des comptes.[111] The other act concerned the holdings of Vassieu, where Jacques Muret, an *avocat* from Montélimar, purchased the rights to a shared seigniory in 1604. In that case the Chambre des comptes refused to register the sale, declaring the 'incapacité' of Muret to hold the fief.[112]

It seems, however, that purchases by non-nobles were more frequent than is indicated by the acts quoted in the *inventaire* or in the official family papers. The acts of *anoblissement* registered by the parlement of Grenoble demonstrate that a good number of the candidates for ennoblement already possessed fiefs before acquiring their titles. This was the case for twenty-four of the seventy-four individuals who presented letters of ennoblement for registration by the parlement.[113] Nevertheless, that Dauphiné absorbed officially only seventy-four new nobles during the period from 1578 to 1620, an average of less than two a year, reduced the impact of such newcomers upon the social structure.

In addition, it does not appear that the great majority of the new nobles possessed sizeable amounts of land after 1602. From that date

TABLE 5
Indemnities paid by anoblis, 1578–1620

Reasons for ennoblement	Indemnities assessed				
	49 écus or less	50–99 écus	100–199 écus	200–299 écus	300 écus +
Service as royal officials	0	3	1	1	2
Armed service	7	3	6	1	5
Special distinction	3	1	2	0	2
Unknown	2	2	3	1	0

on, the beneficiaries of new titles were obliged to declare the value of their holdings and to pay an indemnity of one-tenth of that amount to compensate the communities for the fact that their holdings were to become tax exempt. This provision of the 1602 judgment allows an approximate evaluation of the landholdings of the new nobles. The evaluation remains approximate because the declared value of the property was chronically underestimated and the amount actually assessed seems to have varied according to the power and patronage of the candidate in question.[114] Out of the seventy-four ennoblements, the amounts paid by forty-five of the candidates can be traced through acts of *anoblissement*, through accompanying letters, or through a seventeenth-century role of *anoblis* compiled by Guy Allard.[115] The average indemnity paid by the forty-five nobles was 171.6 *écus*, but there were considerable differences in the amounts assessed (see Table 5). Louis Villeneuve, a Grenoble doctor honoured for his services to those affected by the plague, paid an indemnity of 15 *écus*, indicating property holdings valued at only 150 *écus*, while Jean de Villard from Gap, who had served thirty-eight years as a captain in the Huguenot armies under Lesdiguières, was charged 1,500 *écus*, indicating property holdings valued at 15,000 *écus*.[116] In general, evaluations of the holdings of the new nobles were closer to the evaluation of Villeneuve than to that of Villard. The wealth of the new arrivals was certainly not sufficient to upset the economic dominance of the old families.

The economic evolution of the old nobility of the province appears to argue a certain stagnation, but the position of the old nobles does not appear to have been challenged by enriched *anoblis*, as the advocates of the crisis theory argue. In fact, more than economic problems, the social and professional composition of the order would seem to be the key to explaining the fears expressed by the Council of the Nobility between

1602 and 1615. In Dauphiné access to the nobility and to its economic benefits was progressively closed to the most dynamic social groups. Because of Crown interventions in 1548 and 1602, the opportunities of the new urban elite or of the new legal and juridical experts to enter the second estate were steadily reduced. In Bayeux there were considerably more new nobles who joined the second estate during the period in question than in Dauphiné, but even more important is it that the social composition of the new additions was very different. In Bayeux two-thirds of the *anoblis* came from the ranks of the provincial officials, from the legal professions, or from the sovereign law courts.[117] In Dauphiné, however, the military dominance of the second estate continued and was reinforced. Acts of *anoblissement* are available for fifty-five of the *anoblis*. Of these, thirty-two were honoured for their military service, and seven can be identified as having gained nobility through their services as provincial officials, three through the parlement, two through the Chambre des Comptes, four as judges, four as special negotiators, and two as doctors of law and professors at the University of Valence (see Appendix 1).

The importance of military affairs as a reason for ennoblement can be seen in the cases of three of the military *anoblis* who had studied or practised law before taking up arms. The act for Jacques Bellefin notes that 'having left the legal studies to which he had devoted himself in his youth ... , he did not practise any other profession than that of arms, on foot or horseback, earning his living from warfare.'[118] Arnaud de Four and Pierre de la Motte, both *docteurs-en-droit*, were ennobled for their military service and not for their official functions. The same was true of Jean de Bein, who was cited for his bravery on the field of battle rather for his pioneering work in civil engineering.[119]

These *anoblissements* demonstrate that for the son of a bourgeois family in Dauphiné, the easiest access to the rank of noble was through a military career. The traditional association of noble honour and military service appears to have remained the dominant ideology of the second estate in Dauphiné, while nobles in areas like Bayeux were rapidly assimilating official and legal groups into their order. The lack of the more dynamic social groups in the ranks of the nobility of Dauphiné was probably partly responsible for the general indifference of the order to the third-estate initiatives.[120] It is not the crisis of the old nobles nor the influx of new families that explains the difficult legal position of the second estate; it is the lack of competent trained jurists.

It was precisely this situation that the Council of the Nobility denounced so frequently. The members of the council realized that the 1602 judgment had deprived the whole order of the legal aid that the *avocats consistoriaux* had furnished until then. Prior to 1602 twenty-one senior lawyers in the parlement of Grenoble had been granted the title of *avocat consistorial*, thereby acquiring noble status and tax exemptions. The 1602 royal edict abolished noble status and tax exemptions for the majority of the twenty-one (the lawyers for the third estate claimed that the number was actually closer to thirty-nine or forty).[121] To be deprived of such a large number of experienced advisers constituted a considerable blow for the nobles. Their attempts to reduce the effect of the cut-back by requesting special ennoblements for *avocats* who they hoped would help their order did not succeed. Most of the new nobles of the robe never became ardent defenders of the nobility, and by 1615 they had to be asked specifically to assit from time to time at the council meetings. It becomes apparent that in Dauphiné the weakness of the nobility in the face of the initiatives of Brosse and of the Crown was more a qualitative than a quantitative issue.

It is obvious that the actions of Brosse and of the Crown did not restore the economic and social stability of the rural population, nor did they lead to the disintegration of the dominant privileged groups in the province. The period from 1602 to 1628 witnessed the initial steps taken by the Crown to respond to the long-term grievances voiced by the third estate of Dauphiné. Evidence from other areas of France suggests that the redistribution of *taille* levies was one of the general goals of the Crown. Several commissions had been created under Charles IX and Henry III to study such reform.[122] In 1598 a new commission for the *régalement* of the *tailles* was given the specific mandate to 'remedy the excessive disparities in the assessments of our *tailles* and to provide for the infinite abuses that are committed, to the ruin of our weakest and least powerful.'[123] Again in 1623 a commission was sent into the provinces to try to redistribute *tailles* so as to increase levies on the rich and lower them for the poor.[124] The third-estate demand in Dauphiné corresponded closely to the reforms envisaged by the Crown, and the cahiers presented by Claude Brosse provided a discreet means for the Crown to realize its objectives, even as they replied to the expectations of the third estate.

The nobles constituted the principal source of resistance to the objectives of both the rural element of the third estate and the Crown. They bore the brunt of the pressure from Brosse, the royal advisers, and the king himself from 1602 to the 1620s. In the face of these pres-

sures the nobles stubbornly repelled all attempts to reduce their privileges, and juridically they maintained their position. The wine-tax project
was sent back to the province in 1606 and was abandoned in 1609. The
privileged orders received compensation for the salt-farm revenues that
were accorded to the third estate in 1611. The nobles resisted by every
means the attempts of the debts commissioners to inspect their accounts
and to verify village debts. Such rearguard, uncompromising resistance
to conceding any aid to the impoverished villages was received poorly
by the Crown. As early as 1609, during the discussions over the wine
tax, it became evident that the king wanted some concession from the
privileged orders. Again, during the negotiation of the 1610 agreement
among the three orders, the royal commissioners, Lesdiguières, and
Créqui all demanded some symbolic concessions. That the privileged
orders refused to co-operatie appears to explain the deteriorating relations between the Council and Assembly of the Nobility and the Crown.
During the period in question the privileged orders lost none of their
privileges, but they sacrificed very precious allies.

The all-out resistance of the nobles to any change in their privileges
seems to indicate both economic and social weaknesses within the second
estate. While it is excessive to speak of a general crisis, there are indications that the property holdings of the old established families in the
Valentinois-Diois region stagnated or even declined. Anoblis in the region
had purchased numerous scattered titles, but still none of them came
close to challenging the old families, who, even in decline, dominated
economic and social structures. In fact it may be this dominance of the
old families, the traditionalist criteria for ennoblement, and the lack of
new legal and professional talent in the ranks of the nobility that explain
the lack of judgment and innovation in the arguments of the second
estate during the *taille* debate. The lack of significant social evolution
and professional competence within the nobility appears to have limited
their capacity to reply constructively to new third-estate attacks.

6

The Fiscal and Social Foundations for Crown Intervention

The repeated cahiers of Claude Brosse and the creation of the royal commission on rural debts constituted initial steps towards trying to obtain a gradual revision of the provincial fiscal system. After 1628, however, this method was abandoned in favour of a series of more direct and unilateral Crown actions. In 1626 Antoine d'Aguesseau was sent to Grenoble as intendant of the army.[1] In March 1628 ten financial *élections* or districts were established in Dauphiné, permitting future *tailles* to be imposed directly upon the province. The following June the provincial Estates were suspended and replaced by a reduced and emasculated version of the *assemblée du pays*. The powers of the parlement were also reduced by the creation of a bureau of the *trésoriers de France* in Grenoble and ten years later by the establishment of *présidial* courts in Valence and Gap and of a *cour des aides* in Vienne.[2] On the fiscal front, Intendant Talon was sent into the province in 1634 to direct the implementation of an edict ordering the establishment of *cadastres* and of a *taille réelle* system. Contested by the nobility, the new fiscal arrangements were finally imposed by royal edict on 24 October 1639.[3]

Legal opposition to the new royal interventions and the series of revolts that shook the province in the 1630s and 1640s lead to one essential question. Why did the Crown abandon the gradual process of revising debts and introducing indirect taxes in favour of the more drastic measures? A reply can be found in an examination of the financial situation of the province and its repercussions on the social structure during the period from 1620 to 1639.

The financial condition of Dauphiné in the 1620s had become difficult. After remaining at relatively low levels from 1600 to 1610, *tailles* had begun to inch their way up again as the kingdom became more and more involved in military operations against the great nobles, the Huguenots, and the Hapsburgs. By the 1620s the curve of *taille* levies, expressed in *quartals* of wheat, had taken a definite upward turn (see Graph 6).[4] Peaks of 256, 164, 159, and 203 *quartals* were attained between 1621 and 1627. The new levels remained inferior to those of the 1590s, but they still constituted a definite turn of the fiscal screw.

These increases in direct taxes occurred despite numerous efforts to seek alternative means to meet royal *taille* requests and to alleviate the overwhelming financial demands upon the rural villages. To accomplish this double goal indirect taxes were increased, and by the 1620s revenues from the tax on salt importation were being used regularly to reduce *taille* levies.[5] Another important expedient was the creation and sale of Crown offices. Between 1615 and 1629, 210 new official nominations were registered in the parlement of Grenoble. One 1623 edict alone created posts for seventy *procureurs* in the parlement. Just one of these positions, acquired in 1624 by Jean Pascal, produced 1,320 *livres* for the royal coffers.[6] A number of new *trésoriers généraux* of France were also named in 1623. Among them, Michel Antoine paid the handsome price of 33,000 *livres* for his nomination.[7] While office selling was important for its social and political implications, the fiscal receipts obtained from this practice provided alternative revenues to *tailles*, particularly in the 1620s, when sporadic civil wars resulted in increased fiscal demands.

A series of armed disturbances marked the 1620s in Dauphiné. Besides the chaos wreaked by localized Huguenot bands, which were organized around the sieur de La Tour Montauban, the province witnessed a serious peasant rising during the winter of 1625–6, a rising in which both the Huguenot and the *taille* problems played a part. According to a 1626 report prepared by the parlement, the disturbance seems to have been motivated not only by increasing *taille* demands but by the return of military impositions and levies to support *étapes* for royal armies either stationed in Dauphiné or sent across the province into northern Italy or the Valtelline.[8] From 1623 to the signing of the treaty of Monçon in May 1626, France sent a number of regiments towards the Valtelline or Genoa. As these forces crossed Dauphiné, they confiscated the grain supplies of villages, demanded forced loans from local syndics, and presented *taille* mandates that the communities were forced to honour. In a memoir to Lieutenant-Governor Créqui the syndics of Mirabel complained of the 'excesses' committed by five companies in the regiment of Captain Ferrières. The soldiers beat their consuls, ravaged the gardens of the village, held peasants for ransom, and mistreated the owners of

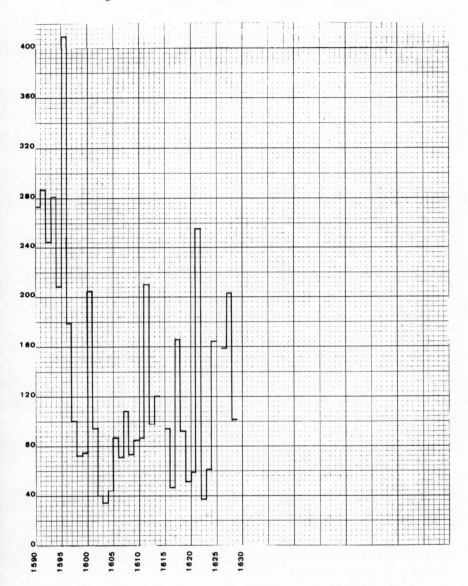

Graph 6 Official *taille* levies in Dauphiné from 1590 to 1628, expressed in *quartals* of wheat

TABLE 6
Official *taille* levies and local impositions collected at La Garde Adhémar, 1614–1627, in
livres

Year	Official levies	Total amounts imposed	Loans negotiated
1614	421.8	1,825	
1615	376.6	468	
1616	192.2	254	
1617	670.2	289	389
1618	409.2	1,418	
1619	269.8	643	
1620	343.4	872	
1621	1,043.4		
1622	171	1,336	
1623	350.6	969	300
1624	703.2	1,627	
1625		438	618
1626	604.6	1,421	420
1627	815.2	930	

the houses where they were lodged.[9] This context exacerbated the already serious problem of the fiscal and debt burden of both the rural
villages and the peasants who inhabited them. For this reason Claude
Brosse in 1628 lodged a new complaint against the renewal of the practice
of imprisoning villagers for debt.[10]

The taxes that rural communities were obliged to levy reflect this
return to undisciplined impositions and blackmail payments. This can
be demonstrated from an analysis of taxation in the village of La Garde
Adhémar (see Table 6). A comparison of the level of official *taille* demands with the level of taxes that were really imposed upon the villagers
reveals the amounts that were paid out to soldiers with mandates for
military impositions, or demands for contributions (*octrois*) for town fortifications, and for the maintenance of garrisons and *étapes*.[11] Year after
year, just as during the years of the Wars of Religion, the taxes levied
by the village were higher, often substantially higher, than the official
Crown levies. In addition, in 1617, 1623, 1625, and 1626 the village
officials had to negotiate loans in order to cover community fiscal needs,
another practice reminiscent of the sixteenth-century wars. It is evident
that this situation led to a deterioration of the already fragile rural
economy and played a large part in fostering the 1626 rising.

The disturbance in 1625–6 appears to have been localized in Huguenot villages around the Baronnies, for the report from the parlement spoke of attacks upon Le Poët and Isson. Also, in a résumé of the deliberations of the Assembly of the Ten Cities that year, it was mentioned that the peasants were in rebellion very close to the château of Mollans.[12] The fear that the rebellion would spread was ever present. The city council of Romans established armed patrols and ordered that the bridges along the Isère be closed to all traffic.[13] At the same time the report from the parlement asked permission for the province to levy a tax of thirty-six *livres* on each *feu* in order to hire soldiers to put down the rebels. The popular armies appear to have remained active until March, for on the eighth of that month the consuls of Nyons agreed to the creation of six or seven military squadrons to ward off robbers and to prevent 'the entries and departures of the rebels.'[14] In an assembly of notables held in late October 1627 the nobles made it clear that they had put down the rising with the aid of the other orders and without receiving any assistance, either financial or military, from outside the province.[15]

The correspondence between Lesdiguières and the royal intendant in Dauphiné and the officials of the royal chancellery in Paris refers frequently to the military operations that were at the base of these economic and social difficulties. Virtually all the surviving letters treat military affairs and the efforts to eliminate the operations of brigands and irregular Huguenot forces both in Dauphiné and in the neighbouring provinces. Lesdiguières, the former Huguenot leader, played a key role as a royal intermediary, negotiating with his old co-religionists and eventually directing military operations against them. The arrival of Intendant d'Aguesseau in the province in 1626 provided the king and his council with considerable information on these activities.

Lesdiguières had taken the Huguenot fortresses of Pouzin and Baix-sur-Baix in March of 1622, and thereafter he led troops into Piedmont. In 1625 a new round of fighting began with the Huguenots, and by the middle of 1626 Lesdiguières was still trying to crush their resistance.[16] In the correspondence with the court, allusions are made to all of these manoeuvres, but discussions centred around organizing the destruction of the château of Pouzin. On 13 August 1626 d'Aguesseau reported on the expenditures that the operation made necessary. He noted that the reimbursement for the 1622 sieges had not yet arrived.[17] Between 13 April and 14 September eight letters to the king or to d'Herbault, councillor to the King, concerned the progressive razing of Pouzin and where the money was to be found for the demolition.[18] A letter of 26 August noted that the province had been forced to pay the full price of the operation but that reimbursement was expected.[19] In the last letter, on 14 September 1626, d'Aguesseau noted that he had gone down to Avignon and had inspected the work at Pouzin. He was satisfied with the demolition but added that the château of Baix-sur-Baix should also be razed, since brigands had installed their headquarters there. The most important news in his letter, however, concerned Lesdiguières. D'Aguesseau wrote that the constable had been ill for the last twenty-one days and as a result it was not possible to discuss affairs with him. At the conclusion of the letter d'Aguesseau added that the constable's fever continued.[20] Lesdiguières died four days later, on 18 September 1626.

The death of Lesdiguières after thirty-seven years at the head of his province signalled a fundamental change for Dauphiné. His death combined with the increasing fiscal needs of the Crown may well have influenced the royal decision to issue orders for the establishment of financial *élections* in the province. Such financial *élections*, or districts allowed the Crown to impose *tailles* directly upon a region without having to receive prior approval from a representative assembly. The amount of any new levy was simply apportioned out to *élections* according to an established formula. The new structures were imposed on Dauphiné in an edict proclaimed on 14 March 1628, but an *assemblée générale* of the three orders held in Grenoble in October 1627 already seems to have been informed of the king's intentions.[21] Similar edicts established *élections* in Burgundy, Languedoc, and Provence between 1628 and 1630, but the latter three provinces avoided the new structures. For considerable sums of money they bought back the 'privilege' of having Estates debate and approve *taille* levies, but Dauphiné did not.[22]

The inability of the three orders in Dauphiné to present a common front against the desires of the monarchy stemmed from their divisions over the *taille* question, divisions that have already been touched upon and that will be discussed in more detail in the next section. What is clear, however, is that the move by the Crown in 1628 was occasioned by essentially fiscal motives. Yves-Marie Bercé has shown that the Crown preferred *élections* as a goal for long-term reform[23] but that the need for short-term financing left the door open for any of the provinces to buy back their privileges. Financial motives are also evident in the 1634 and 1639 decisions to alter the fiscal assessment system of the province, making the whole of Dauphiné a *pays de taille réelle*. These actions once again followed the Crown's long-term preferences to redistribute taxes in order to relieve the overburdened third estate.[24] As early as 1631 Intendant d'Agenson wrote to Cardinal Richelieu that it was necessary to find some way of relieving Dauphiné of the exorbitant expenses caused by the levying of troops in the province and by the quartering of outside armies that passed through.[25] In an even more detailed letter one of the *créatures* of the cardinal, Claude Frère, first president of the parlement of Grenoble, wrote,

For the last eight years the province has been overburdened by troops. In the last two years all those who went into or returned from Italy passed through, and several regiments and garrisons are still here, [Monsieurs de] Champaigne, Normandie and Sault, and others. We are now preparing to set up the *étape* for the troops that return from Italy, [but] it is impossible to supply the *étape* for the regiments that will be quartered here, for the people don't even have enough bread for themselves, let alone for the troops. Many of them live only on wild herbs and roots. Every day we find dead bodies in the countryside because of malnutrition. There are also many in the cities, and those who live here do not hesitate to leave their houses and find refuge in the fortresses and mountains when they hear of the coming of soldiers.[26]

The Crown reply was certainly not that anticipated by Claude Frère, who had been involved in an earlier confrontation with the third estate over his right to tax-exempt status. On 21 December 1632 the Conseil d'état issued an *arrêt* or edict asking the privileged orders to reply to the recent charges by Brosse that they had taken advantage of their privileges and of the exemptions that the 1602 judgment had confirmed. The new order stated that the 1602 decision had been motivated by the 'affairs' of the time and by the consideration that the king held for the late Constable Lesdiguères. However, it noted, Brosse now argued that the articles of the decision, which had been intended to reduce the debts and the oppression of the poor people, had never been respected. According to Brosse, the exemptions and *franchises* confirmed for the privileged orders in 1602 had reduced the village communities to 'extreme misery.' Since 1628, he noted, the number of holdings acquired by tax-exempt individuals had increased dramatically, partly because of the excessive number of ennoblements, another practice that the 1602 document had promised to eliminate.[27] Besides using the new Brosse charges to justify a review of the 1602 decision, the *arrêt* makes clear reference to the reports of the debt commissioners concerning the difficulty of applying the judgments on rural debts.

Following the 1632 decision to review the *taille* controversy, the king authorized the first and second estates to hold an assembly in Grenoble, in the presence of the lieutenant-governor, to draw up their reply. Their cahiers along with those of the third estate were examined in hearings before the Conseil d'état on 14 and 16 February and on 24 July 1633. A new *requête* was issued on 4 July, ordering all groups wishing to submit statements on the question to present them within eight days to Intendant Talon. On this occasion the third estate produced a new series of village cahiers in which individual communities reported on the continuing progress of land purchases by the exempted groups.[28] At the same time a new series of legal pleas and printed statements debated the case for each side. They reviewed the legal arguments and precedents concerning the *taille* in Dauphiné but added little to the debates that had taken place between 1595 and 1602.[29] All the new documents were meticulously listed and summarized by Talon and presented to the Conseil d'état.[30]

Louis XIII issued a new edict based on the Talon report on 31 May 1634. The new document reversed the traditional *taille* system of the majority of the province and ordered the implementation of the principal characteristics of the *taille réelle*. All existing *roturier* lands were to be listed in *cadastres*, and they were to serve as the basis for all future levies of *tailles*, *taillons*, garrison duties, military impositions, and all other taxes. In addition, the definition of *roturier* lands was to be extended. All ecclesiastical holdings or donations acquired after 1556 were to be considered *roturier* and taxable. As for the nobles, those who had received their titles before 1539 were to remain exempt for the holdings they had acquired prior to 1 January 1628. All officials or nobles whose letters of nobility had been confirmed prior to 1602 were to remain exempt for all the possessions they held on that date. Finally, all ennoblements accorded after 1602 were revoked. These provisions established a new division of taxable and non-taxable landholdings in the province. They were to be completed by a new revision of the *feux* quotas for each village.[31]

The 1634 judgment raised a storm of protest. The king immediately sent Talon into Dauphiné with assurances that the *règlements* according to which the edict would be applied would contain certain changes that would please everyone.[32] Summarizing his mandate, Talon wrote to the cardinal that he was responsible, first for 'assuring the fiscal basis of *taille* levies' in the province, and second for providing tax relief for the people. He explained to the cardinal that he had translated his mission to the nobles and clergy: 'I told them that the *réalité* of *tailles* was absolutely necessary both for the financial security of the king and for the common good of the province.'[33] It appears that, just as in 1628, fiscal issues rather than social or political motives constituted the principal reasons for the new intervention.

At the beginning of June 1635 the intendant met with the privileged orders in Grenoble. In a letter to Chancellor Séguier he reported that he had told them that with the decline in taxable holdings caused by the land purchases of nobles and officials, *taille* returns from Dauphiné had declined steadily. He noted that the assembly had finally accepted the need to install the *taille réelle* system but that it had asked for a series of changes.[34] Talon transmitted a copy of the twenty-three resolutions adopted, along with his own comments in marginal notes. The fiscal preoccupation of the royal government was evident in the notes. Talon wrote that the assembly's demands that exemptions be extended on new acquisitions up to 1634 would considerably diminish *taille* returns. Talon also rejected the nobles' demand that the *taille* reform respect the principle that once a community defined a holding as *roturier* or noble, its status should not change. In fact this basic precept of the *taille réelle* had not been observed in the 1634 edict. The edict stated that noble purchasers would have to respect the category under which the holding they acquired was listed in *cadastres*, be it exempt or taxable. Further, if an exempted possession was acquired by a *roturier*, he would have to pay *tailles* on it. This loophole provided the Crown with the means actually to reduce the number of exempted holdings in the province. Talon argued that if the king backtracked on this clause, it would be very difficult to return to the goal of the 4,750 taxable *feux* that had been enumerated in the *revision des feux* of 1461.[35]

In a separate document describing the general tone of his encounters with the privileged orders Talon wrote that his work continued to be opposed by the Council of the Nobility. In particular, he was opposed by four newly ennobled council lawyers who were threatened with losing their titles: 'What is extraordinary is that four men of their social position can decide among themselves all affairs concerning the nobility, send delegates to the court whenever they wish, order levies in the province through *arrière bans* without royal permission, and form a general opposition in the province to the imposition of royal tailles.'[36] These comments of Talon's seem to have provoked a royal order on 15 May 1635 to disband the council.

The documents left by those opposed to Talon's negotiation indicate far less acceptance of the principle of the *taille réelle* than the intendant

implied there was. One of the most detailed of these documents constituted an all-out attack upon both the 1634 decree and the attitude of
the intendant. Written ten years later, in 1644, to describe the process
by which the 1634 judgment was adopted, it argued that the only documents that had been used in the preparation of the edict were those
that had been prepared for the 1602 hearings. It asserted that the Conseil
d'état actually refused to accept any new documents.[37] This was obviously
false, for lists of the pieces of evidence drawn up by Talon show a number
of documents written precisely for the 1633 hearings.[38] The memoir of
1644 also contested the use of a 1461 document on the revision of the
feux, a document that supposedly proved that *tailles* in the province had
traditionally been *réelles*.[39] Again this was false, for the official judgment
made no mention of such a document, nor did it list the 1461 *feux* revision
among the pieces of evidence studied by the council.[40] The 1461 *taille*
documents were used to determine what should constitute the number
of *feux* assessed to the province. After the 1634 judgment was rendered,
Talon fixed the goal of reimposing *tailles* in Dauphiné at the 4,750 *feux*
that had been evaluated in 1461. The nobles protested that a new evaluation should determine the actual state of the *feux*, but according to
the memoir, Talon remained intransigent on the question.

Talon's intransigence certainly aggravated the strained relations between the Crown and the nobility. In a common document the nobles
and officials complained to the king of his 'vanity' and 'rigidity.' They
noted that after listening to them, receiving their grievances, and promising to improve several aspects of the edict, he had left the province
ordering that the document be applied in its totality.[41] The rhetoric and
personal attack used by the nobility in their campaign against Talon
convey some sense of the undercurrent of determined resistance that
marked their opposition to the new edict during the 1630s. This resistance led eventually to the outbreak of armed opposition in the 1640s.
Boris Porchnev has noted the widespread attacks against tax collectors
in that period; he singles out the case of the seigneur of La Salle, who
led his peasants against the taxmen in 1645.[42] It is obvious that Talon
became the immediate scapegoat, an excuse for all-out resistance on the
part of the nobility to the 1634 edict.

The organized resistance of the nobility to the 1634 decree forced a
new series of negotiations and a number of revisions in the text. On 9
January 1636, 25 May 1637, and 6 April 1639, new edicts were issued
that backpedalled on one question after another. In the 1634 document
clerics had only been given the right to retain exemptions for the pos-

sessions that they held prior to 1556, but in 1636 this date was pushed ahead to 1628, the date that had been established for the nobles. By April 1639 the Crown had retreated on the question of revoking ennoblements granted since 1602. New nobles could retain their titles, but they would not acquire *taille* exemptions. As for those who had served in the armies of the province, it was agreed that if a noble had acquired his title before 1602 and had served in the king's armies for at least ten years, he would have the right to exemptions for all the holdings he had acquired before 1628, just as did the old nobles. Those ennobled after 1602 who lost exemptions for their *roturier* lands were to be granted a reduction of one-quarter of the assessment of each holding. Finally, annual indemnities were to be granted to officials whose holdings became taxable.[43]

These concessions came as replies to the constant pressure of the privileged orders upon the Crown and its commissioners. The minor modifications suggested by Talon and contained in the 1636 *arrêt* were poorly received. The nobles openly accused the intendant of siding with the third estate in trying to apply the edict.[44] Their opposition led to a second conciliation attempt, ordered by Richelieu in 1637 This time Talon was dropped and replaced by Monsieur De Ligres, who was to try to bring the two sides together without sacrificing the principles of the 1634 decree. The nobles noted that they were impressed by their meeting with the new *commissaire*. He had listened to their arguments, and they hoped that he would recommend a satisfactory ruling.[45] The resulting edict still did not satisfy them, however, and in 1638 still another intendant, Hélie Laisné, was sent to meet them. The mandate issued to Laisné in April 1638 had been discussed thoroughly within the royal government. Sublet des Noyers, *secrétaire d'état* for war and a native of Dauphiné drew up the new commission, and its wording was commented upon in detail by Bullion, *surintendant des finances*, who had been an intendant in Lesdiguières's army in 1620.[46] Once the mandate was issued, Laisné met with thirty-five syndics of the principal orders and negotiated two sets of cahiers. The results of these discussions were submitted to an assembly of 245 representatives of the principal noble families of the province in November 1638. They approved the transactions and signed a petition asking the royal government to stop persecuting them and to recognize their rights.[47] These documents appear to have served as the basis for the final edict.

The final document on the *taille* case was issued on 24 October 1639. It established the full principle of the *taille réelle*. In the future all property held prior to 1635 by nobles, clerics, or those ennobled before 1602 was to be exempt from *tailles*. Such property was to be entered into *cadastres* as a tax-free noble possession, and it was to remain tax-free even if purchased by a non-noble. This represented a retreat from the previous position of the Crown, for it froze the noble-*roturier* fiscal distribution according to its actual division in 1635.[48] The earlier edicts had used 1628 as a fiscal starting-point, but they had been aimed at recovering tax-free lands for tax collection, since each noble holding acquired by a non-noble was to revert to taxable status.[49] For the Crown the change meant that any hope of returning rapidly to the 4,750 taxable *feux* contained in the 1461 revision was impossible.

The treatment of the other exempted groups was uneven. The officers of the parlement and of the Chambre des comptes and the *trésoriers de France* who had acquired their positions prior to 1602 were given the right to exemptions on all property that they had acquired prior to 1635, just as were the nobles. As for the officials who had acquired their positions after 1602, they obtained nothing new. All their *roturier* acquisitions became taxable, but they received an annual indemnity reducing their taxes on those lands by a quarter. The *anoblis* actually lost ground. None of their ennoblements was to be revoked, but they lost the indemnity of a one-third tax reduction on their assessments, which had been granted in the 1636 text. This setback may have been owing to the radical opposition of the *anoblis* in the Council of the Nobility and to the opinion formed by Talon that it was possible to break up the union between the old nobles and the new nobles and officials.[50]

The nobles had accused the urban elite of being the principal beneficiaries of the new fiscal arrangements, and Brosse had even been accused of being their lackey.[51] To silence this criticism, the edict of October 1639 instituted a new tax on goods, materials, commercial activity, loans, and investments of the third estate in the province. The new tax was to be fixed at one-eighth of the levy demanded of cities and one-tenth of that demanded of the villagers. Finally, to reduce second-estate complaints against the consulates, nobles were guaranteed participation and a more important voice in the deliberations of the towns and communities of the province.[52]

When compared to the 1634 edict, the October 1639 document represents a significant retreat for the Crown, and the final decision was well received by the officials of both the parlement and the Chambre des comptes. They wrote to Richelieu to express their satisfaction and the hope that the new edict would be implemented by competent and 'well-chosen' commissioners.[53] There are no similar letters from the nobility, and their 1644 memoir contesting the establishment of the *taille réelle*, along with their continual opposition to a new *feux* evaluation, indicates that the second estate had still not digested the change in the fiscal system.[54]

As to the initial question of why the Crown abandoned its gradual method of revising rural debts in favour of more drastic measures, there are three elements to a reply. On the fiscal side there were the complaints that were lodged regularly between 1611 and 1620 by the royal commissioners for rural debts. All their letters noted the difficulty of forcing creditors to reveal the terms of their loans, and all of them pointed to the slow progress of the commissioners' work. At a higher level there were also the recommendations of the royal commissions on *taille* reform that were sent into numerous provinces in 1598 and 1623. They had generally suggested that the Crown assure more equitable *taille* distribution. Finally and perhaps most important, there was an urgent need for considerably higher tax levies by the 1620s, owing to the renewed warfare.

These issues seem to have dominated considerations regarding both the edict of 1628 and the series of decrees between 1634 and 1639. It is probable that in 1628 Dauphiné could have bought back the right to have *tailles* voted and distributed by its provincial Estates, just as did Languedoc, Burgundy, and Provence, but the three orders in the province could not agree to such action. The adoption of the principle of the *taille réelle* in 1634 seems to have been directed at increasing Crown revenues. This is confirmed by the exchanges between Talon and Richelieu. 'Assuring the fiscal basis of *taille* levies' and at the same time relieving the financial burden of the people were the mandates given to Talon. His evaluations of the demands of the exempted groups reflects this mandate. He estimated the financial implications of each of their counter-proposals, and his goal was to return the province to the 1461 division of landholdings between *roturiers* and nobles. This would have permitted the Crown to re-establish the allotment of 4,750 *feux* as the fiscal basis for *tailles* in Dauphiné. The opposition of the privileged orders was too great for Talon to attain the latter objective, and the Crown had to be satisfied with freezing the prevailing land and tax situation.

The fiscal objectives of these interventions are clear, but it has often been argued that these Crown initiatives to implement increasingly absolutist institutions were based upon a series of social mutations. For Mousnier, Porchnev, and Lublinskaya the interventions that permitted the establishment of the new structures were carried out with the support of the 'bourgeoisie.' Mousnier holds that this social group built up its own social and financial hierarchy through the positions sold by the Crown, and finished by imposing itself and its policies upon the king.[55] Porchnev contends that the accession of the new bourgeoisie to offices and to nobility was aided by Crown policies. He notes that, while they sided initially with the peasants and *menu peuple* in the popular revolts that shook the country in the 1630s and 1640s, the members of the new bourgeoisie realized that such participation jeopardized their investments in official positions and in property. According to Porchnev, this realization led them to take their place within a vast new feudal coalition of Crown, nobles, and bourgeoisie.[56] Alexandra Lublinskaya has refined the Porchnev thesis by looking more closely at the minor officials and the commerical and professional bourgeoisie. She sees them as having been aided by the Crown at every step. They were favoured by royal legislation, by new tax farms, and by their incorporation into the upper echelons of government through the creation and sale of offices.[57]

All of these theses argue that a permanent social coalition or alliance was formed between different groups or classes. This alliance permitted the institutions that governed France to be changed and replaced by structures that reflected the new philosophical theories of absolutism. To what extent did Dauphiné witness such a social mutation prior to the implantation of *élections*, *taille réelle* structures, and *presidial* courts? To what extent can the new royal initiatives be explained by such a social evolution?

It is clear that the Crown was interested in increasing its revenues from Dauphiné without provoking the protests and contestation that had marked *taille* increases in the 1540s, the 1570s, and the 1590s. Inquiries in other provinces had concluded that direct intervention through *élections* and reform of the tax-distribution structures were the best means of accomplishing these goals.[58] *Elections* gave the king the right to intervene directly in procedures of *taille* distribution, and they permitted him to impose *tailles* direcly upon his subjects without his having to defend the levies before provincial Estates. The urban elite and the rural communities were similarly anxious to obtain significant fiscal reforms. The overtaxed villages wanted to stabilize or increase the number of holdings listed on their *taille* rolls, the same holdings that exempted groups continued to purchase and subtract from village taxation. The socially mobile urban elite wanted to extend its investment opportunities and to reduce the fiscal barriers between itself and its tax-exempt neighbours

and colleagues. The interests of all three of these groups, Crown, peasants, and urban elite, were served by the initiatives taken during the
period from 1628 to 1639.

However, the lack of organized opposition to Crown intervention in
1628 seems to have been determined more by social divisions resulting
from the *taille* dispute than by any positive support for the Crown from
the different social groups. This is evident from the records of a series
of meetings held prior to the 1628 intervention. A special assembly of
representatives of the nobles, the ten cities, and the *commis* of the villages
met in Grenoble between 20 October and 2 November 1627 to discuss
the new Crown proposals. It concluded with a fragile agreement between
the orders to oppose the establishment of the 'nouveautés' in the province
and to send a delegation to the king to argue the case. The heart of the
agreement was a twofold decision. The nobles refused to concede any
of their fiscal privileges or to permit any new tax on salt to be applied
to *taille* levies. For their part, the third estate rejected any move that
would result in higher taxation. The differing and even contradictory
interests of the two groups were reinforced when each of them met
separately and sent its own representatives to the royal court.[59]

Less than five months later, the same month that the edict was issued
creating the new *élections*, the common front broke down. A second
assembly of the three orders was held in Grenoble, and the issue of
common opposition to the new edicts was raised once again. During the
discussion M Borin, consul from Vienne, stated that the third estate
would not support any new measures to block the *nouveautés* until 'the
messieurs of the first two orders had decided to consent to having the
lands that they had acquired from the third estate since 1598 listed in
cadastres and to contribute to *tailles* for the holdings acquired ... '[60] The
town delegates argued that the third estate remained opposed to the
nouveautés and to the creation of all new offices that would become an
additional financial drain upon its contributions. They called upon the
avocats of the Council of the Nobility to accept their conditions and to
join with them to avoid the 'consequences of the edict, which would be
so detrimental to each of the orders.'[61] Faced with the refusal of the
privileged orders to give up their fiscal benefits, the third estate refused
to join in a common front to oppose *élections*.

The abolition of the provincial Estates also went unprotested because
of conflicts that had grown up during the *taille* controversy. The third-
estate leaders had always been opposed to the Estates' structure, a structure dominated by the first and second orders and by the executive

committee, the *commis du pays*. Since the 1550s every major third-estate proposal for revising fiscal policy had been rejected or postponed indefinitely by the provincial Estates. In this context it is not surprising that the third estate did not oppose the suspension of the Estates. Indeed, Claude Brosse noted that he had been promised that the Estates would be abolished a month before the edict of suspension, and he considered their abolition to be a major victory.[62] In other provinces the leaders of the third estate were at the forefront of the movement to maintain provincial Estates, but in Dauphiné the cleavages reinforced by the *taille* dispute led them to conclude that they had nothing to gain within the existing Estates' structure.

The structure and system of representation proposed by the king to replace the old Estates did in fact represent a considerable victory for the third estate. The king replaced the Estates with a new institution called the *assemblée du pays*, which corrected several of the third estate's traditional complaints. The bishop of Grenoble continued to preside over the new assembly, but the number of delegates from the three orders was reduced to twenty-four ordinary and fifteen extraordinary representatives. The proportion of these delegates granted to the privileged orders was far smaller than in the old Estates. Among the ordinary representatives were to be included the *procureur du pays*, ten great nobles (the four barons and six nobles possessing a fief), two clerics, and eleven delegates from the third estate (consuls from the ten towns and the syndic of the villages). Besides these ordinary representatives, there were to be six additional nobles chosen at large and nine village delegates, among whom were to be at least five royal *châtelains*. Under this system the third estate could send between fifteen and twenty delegates to the assembly, depending on whether the *châtelains* were nobles or not. The nobles and clergy, for their part, were to be represented by between twenty and twenty-five delegates, again depending on the status of the *châtelains*.[63] The role given to the third estate in the new structure placed it almost on a par with the combined forces of the first two estates, a far cry from its marginal representation in the old Estates. Of course, in terms of power the new institution was far removed from the old Estates. Gone was its decision-making role in economic affairs and its ability to control tax levies or to bargain tax approval for greater administrative powers. The new *assemblée* played only a consultative role.

Further evidence of Crown intervention in favour of third-estate options arises from the incidents surrounding the arrest and imprisonment of Claude Brosse. Arrested on 7 January 1631, he was released by royal order on 6 March, and the charges against him were declared to be null and void. The *procureur général* Musy was at least temporarily relieved of his functions, and the same Musy later published a tract defending Crown officials against the charges by Brosse that they had profited from their *taille* exemptions to buy up rural lands.[64]

Events between 1632 and 1639 demonstrate that the king and his agents had become convinced that if they wanted to increase levies, there was no alternative to changing the *taille* system. The implementation of the changes, however, was far less unilateral than has often been suggested. From 1634 to 1639 the king and his agents negotiated, offered compromises, and sought to break up the united front of their opposition. When Intendant Talon was accused of collaborating too closely with the third-estate leaders and was the object of an inquiry by the provincial Estates, the king set up a royal inquiry into Talon's conduct.[65] Despite the rejection of the charges against Talon, the king changed his negotiator.[66] The new negotiators, De Ligres and Laisné, were more diplomatic than Talon had been, and they conceded a number of revisions demanded by the different groups within the privileged orders. It even appears that Brosse became engaged in the negotiating process, for in 1637 the Romans consulate criticized the village syndic for meeting 'in secret' with the representatives of the privileged orders to try to reach agreement on the different questions at issue.[67] The eventual decision to tax the commercial profits of the town bourgeoisie may have resulted from these meetings. In such negotiations and revisions the Crown maintained its determination to impose the *taille réelle* but retreated on a number of clauses concerning its application. By 1639 it had even received the open support of the officials of the parlement and the Chambre des comptes for the new measures.

The imposition of the new structures in Dauphiné was certainly not accomplished in the way described by Mariéjol in his portrait of the installation of absolutist institutions. The old intermediary officials were not 'stripped' of their authority. The 'excessive powers' of the old nobles were not removed in favour of Crown-controlled structures staffed by more docile nominees. Nor is there any evidence of the great feudal-absolutist coalition, proposed by Porchnev, among the bourgeoisie, the nobles, and the Crown. There was little protest from Mousnier's *parlementaires* as their future right to exemptions was removed and as new offices and jurisdictions were created. The officials of the parlement even supported the 1639 *taille* edict. And if the 1628 to 1639 decisions seem to favour Lublinskaya's 'commercial bourgeoisie,' the members of this group had not been favoured by the edicts of 1548, 1556, 1579, or even by the new taxes imposed on them by the 1639 decree. Rather than collaborating with the Crown, they continued their traditional resistance to royal interference in their fiscal and economic affairs.[68]

Rather than finding the evolution of a whole new absolutist power base built upon philosophical principles and a new social order, what we see in Dauphiné is an alliance of interests. The royal interventions between 1628 and 1639 were carried out principally for fiscal motives. *Taille* levies during the 1620 conflicts with the Huguenots reflected a new escalation of tax demands. The already indebted rural villages were too overburdened to pay the new taxes, and yet the Crown felt that Dauphiné was still not contributing enough. This is the context that seems best to explain the mandate given to Talon to reform the fiscal system. In effect, by adopting the *taille réelle* system and therefore extending the base of taxation in the province, the Crown could both reduce the weight of taxes upon the rural communities and the poorest sectors of the third estate and at the same time increase the general levy demanded of Dauphiné. The recent *anoblis* and officials who lost their exemptions paid the price of the new transaction.

In proceeding with its new fiscal objectives, the Crown aligned itself with the urban elite, the non-noble legal class, the new officials, and the rural communities led by Brosse. This group had everything to gain from a change in the *taille* system. The alliance drew together those who suffered most dramatically from the effects of the tax levies and those whose personal economic ascension was merely slowed down by the prevailing *taille* system. Their unity of interest in the *taille* controversy concealed numerous social and economic divisions, divisions that had been carefully exploited by the privileged orders to defeat previous demands for *taille* reform. In the 1630s, however, the situation was different. This time the monarchy needed to increase its tax levies significantly. With the death of Lesdiguières it became possible for the king to implement the *taille* reform favoured both by his advisers and by the third estate.

Epilogue

Between 1628 and 1639 Crown interventions in Dauphiné did not signify either the final destruction of provincial privileges or the end of the *taille* conflict. During the remainder of the seventeenth century, however, the king stepped in regularly to stabilize and institutionalize the political, economic, and social evolution of his increasingly absolutist policy.

On the institutional front, the parlement of Grenoble remained an important obstacle to the numerous Crown initiatives, and there was also resistance from the representative bodies that survived in the province after the suppression of the Estates. The authority and jurisdiction of the parlement had been substantially reduced by the establishment of new, competing sovereign courts, such as the *élections* set up in 1628, the *présidial* courts created in Valence in 1639 and at Gap in 1641, and the *cour des aides* in Vienne, which was founded in 1638. Such initiatives, together with the 1639 elimination of tax exemptions for new members of the high court, stimulated considerable protest from the *parlementaires* between 1641 and 1645.[1] Crown officials claimed that this protest movement used illegal assemblies to exploit the general discontent of the nobles and the third estate in the province. This accusation followed a series of urban rebellions and rural unrest in 1641 and 1642.[2] By 1645 there were few reports of any illegal activities by the *parlementaires*, and they were surprisingly calm during the Fronde rebellion of 1648–9 that affected most regions of France. Nevertheless, throughout the remainder of the ancien régime the *parlementaires* remained the backbone of provincial resistance to Crown initiatives.[3]

As for the representative institutions of the province, they continued to exist on several levels even after the suspension of the Estates. At the highest level, the structure of the old *assemblée du pays* became the new representative institution regrouping the three orders. The assembly lost most of the decision-making power of the old Estates but retained a consultative role. It met regularly, debating and frequently protesting major royal initiatives. After the Fronde and the organization of illegal meetings in 1661, the royal chancellery informed Intendant Saron-Campigny: 'We order you to see to it that no assemblies are held for any reason and under any pretext without our express permission.'[4] Assemblies continued to be authorized up to 1664 for specific reasons, but they frequently got out of control and raised new protests against taxes and officials.

As for other institutions in the province, both the Assembly of the Ten Cities and the Assembly of the Nobility continued to meet. The Assembly of the Ten Cities returned to the function it had performed prior to the *taille* affair. The *commis* of the villages and the consuls from the minor towns and villages were no longer invited to its meetings, and the sessions were limited to questions affecting the major cities. Among the exceptions to this rule were the animated debates over *taille* increases in 1641–2 and the mobilization of town and village forces against the *étapes* imposed in 1655.[5] The pressure exercised by the assembly in those instances seems to have brought action. Its protests led eventually to efforts to reduce the fiscal load imposed upon the third estate of the province.[6] Such pressure was not appreciated by the Crown, however, and after the suspension of the *assemblée du pays* in 1664, meetings of the towns became rare. They appear to have been convened for the last time in 1673.[7]

The nobility did not remain inactive either. Despite the supression of the Council of the Nobility in 1635 and royal orders forbidding meetings of the second estate in 1636 and 1637,[8] assemblies of the privileged orders were permitted once again in the 1640s, and they generally met prior to the *assemblée du pays*. There are no records of these meetings except for a manuscript cahier entitled 'Délibérations de la noblesse (1605–1658),' which contains not deliberations but acts and edicts that concerned the nobility.[9] Among the most pressing demands of these sessions was that the Crown restore the provincial Estates. In 1649, 1651, and 1661, the nobles tried to force the recall of the Estates.[10] Another of the regular subjects of discussion seems to have been how to resist the implementation of different aspects of the 1639 edict. The opposition of the nobles appears to have led to the regular repetition of directives concerning rural debts and the inclusion of the privileged orders on *taille* rolls.[11]

The numerous local and regional assemblies that had been used so effectively throughout the *taille* controversy continued on into the seventeenth century, and some went right up to the French Revolution. It is clear from the 1655 debate over the *étapes* that local meetings had been held to propose action by the *assemblée du pays*.[12] In the Briançon region of the *bailliage* of the Montagnes a representative assembly convened regular meetings of delegates from the surrounding communities up to the end of the ancien régime, and these assemblies maintained numerous fiscal privileges for the inhabitants of the region.[13] Similar representative organizations existed in the Embrun and Gap regions of the *bailliage*, and they continued meeting well after 1628.[14] There were even periodic assemblies of representatives from the three regions alternately at Gap, Briançon, and Embrun. Such meetings were controlled closely, and they could be convened only with permission of the parlement or the governor; nevertheless, they continued to be held up to the middle of the seventeenth century.[15]

Bernard Bonnin has argued that such local assemblies, presided over by *châtelains* or syndics, demonstrate the vigorous activity of local government even under the increasingly absolutist system.[16] Certainly, the assemblies continued, but they were merely a shadow of the local institutions that had grown up and multiplied during the period from 1540–1640. The rash of spontaneous meetings held between 1560 and 1590 had produced cahiers and sent deputies to regional assemblies to debate important new legislative or military policies. After the 1650s such initiatives gave way to meetings geared to the administration of *bailliages*, *sénéchaussés* or towns. Structures that competed with its new absolutist policies were tolerated by the Crown but also regarded as at best superfluous and at worst suspect. Whenever possible, they were suppressed. The royal interventions between 1628 and 1639 had been dictated primarily by fiscal considerations, but by the middle of the seventeenth century the control and suppression of provincial institutions was more and more clearly politically inspired. Fiscal reforms opened the doors to the political changes that came to characterize absolutism.

It took almost thirty years to impose the juridical authority of the absolutist structures over the traditional institutions of Dauphiné, and the *taille* question was no more rapidly solved. The 1639 edict had decreed that a general revision of the *feux* in the province should be undertaken within six months. Given the opposition of the nobles to the new edicts, the localized risings against taxes, and the legal resistance of the *parlementaires*, no action was taken on the revision until 28 October

1658, when Louis XIV ordered commissioners to undertake a new *feux* inquiry. The preamble to his 1658 letters patent noted that 'periods of disorder caused by the war' had made it impossible for the Crown to act earlier on the *feux* revision.[17]

The 1658 letters were registered in the parlement and Chambre des comptes only on 17 June 1659. Commissioners were designated and visits were begun. Registers in the Archives départementales de l'Isère provide documentary evidence of the commissioners' inquiries in the Viennois, Valentinois, and Graisivaudan.[18] In 1660, however, the revision process was stopped by the king. The major explanation for the suspension seems to be that the local working documents, the *cadastres*, or land registers, had not been prepared in the great majority of villages. Without such documents the task of preparing new *feux* quotas was enormous. New *cadastres* had not been drawn up because there were fundamental objections to carrying out a new *feux* revision, objections that came from both the privileged orders and the village communities.

The officials, nobles, and clergy resisted both the *feux* revision and the orders aimed at reducing rural debts throughout the seventeenth century. The parlement was generally at the centre of the resistance, which explains the difficulty encountered by the lieutenant-governor in enforcing royal edicts and the vehement reaction of the king's officials to the parlement.[19] In 1679 Colbert wrote to his intendant concerning the court's opposition to new levies, saying, 'As regards the comments that the parlement might make, they merit neither to be sent nor to be replied to, for you know that the protests of the parlement are no longer in season. They are so old that no one remembers them, and it is better that way.'[20] Colbert's view and the continuing difficulties with the parlement seem to have led to its reorganization by Intendant Bouchu in 1698.[21]

The privileged orders were not the only group that resisted the full implementation of the *taille réelle* system. Bernard Bonnin has demonstrated that village communities were frequently reluctant to commission the preparation of new *cadastres* or the revision of old ones. The cost of preparing such documents was considerable. It entailed engaging surveyors to measure the village land parcels, experts to classify the parcels in the categories stipulated for the *feux* revision, notaries to write up the new register, and judicial fees to have the register recognized and ratified by the parlement. Bonnin notes that, in addition to the financial burden, the communities often feared that all the 'outsiders' who came into the villages for these operations would make mistakes or deliberately misinterpret their situation such that they would end up paying higher *tailles* than before the revision.[22]

The question of revising the *feux* was very complex, and when Inten-. dant d'Herbigny broached the question of reducing *feux* quotas in 1680, Colbert replied: 'Take care ... it is never well to touch the old *cadastres*, for it is an enormous job; it is impossible that, in carrying it out, many errors will not be committed; it is best only to weed out the errors committed since the last *cadastres* were drawn up.'[23] Colbert did tell d'Herbigny that if he was interested in studying the dossiers on the *taille* problem, he could eventually undertake the revision.[24] He never did, however, and it was only two decades later, in 1697, that Intendant Bouchu was commissioned to carry out the *révision des feux*.

As to the evolution of property holdings in Dauphiné between the 1639 edict and the new feux inquiry, statistics are contradictory. Bernard Bonnin implies that the 1658 revision was abandoned because the tax-exempt holdings of the privileged groups had increased.[25] André Lacroix also believed that tax-exempt holdings in the province remained considerable. He noted that this was the principal reason for the suspension of the 1658 inquiry.[26] While the number of exempted holdings remained high, it is not clear that they increased after 1639. The evidence that I have located indicates that the number of exempted landholdings had been stabilized and probably had declined after the 1639 edict. Communities were slow in drawing up new *cadastres*, and it took the rest of the century to produce the documents from which we might draw an adequate picture of the directions of property movement. Nevertheless, a partial profile can be derived from eighteen *cadastres* listed in the inventory published by André Lacroix of communal archives in the Drôme. These documents were drawn up during the period extending from 1639 to the beginning of Bouchu's revision in 1697 (see Table 7). They reveal a fundamental unevenness in property distribution from one community to another; in villages such as Veaunes, Mureils, or Charnes the tax-exempt holdings were considerable, while in Duprès, St-Laurent-en-Royans, or Baix there were few noble possessions.

A comparison of the data in Table 7 with the property distribution revealed in the third-estate cahiers of the 1590s (see chapter 4, Table 3) shows that exempted groups generally owned smaller percentages of village property than they had half a century before. Details of this property evolution can be directly compared for two villages during the periods for which the sources are available. Both Châteauneuf-de-Mazenc and Mollans experienced sizeable declines in tax-exempt landholdings.

TABLE 7

Proportions of non-taxable landholdings in the villages that prepared *cadastres* between 1639 and 1698

Village and date of *cadastre*	Total holdings	Total tax-exempt holdings	% exempted holdings
Aix-en-Diois (1650)	1,528	594	38.8
Mollans (1666)	2,554	402	15.7
Châteauneuf-de-Mazenc (17th c)	7,099	2,429	34.2
Baix/Batie-de-Baix (1653)	1,488.5	210.5	14
Autichamps (1698)	2,549.25	599.25	23.5
Chabrillan (1634)	6,307	1,697	26.9
Montmaur (1634)	1,650	341	20.6
Sainte-Croix (1658)	2,778	808	29
Miscou (1663)	1,179	350	29.6
St-Laurent-en-Royans (1639)	1,798	179	10
Veaunes (1656)	1,020	455	44.6
Ratières (1666)	3,393	763	22.5
Mureils (1645)	1,064	596	56
Charmes (1644)	3,193	1,347	42
Bathernay (1642)	1,027	330	32
Des Près (1663)	1,136	21	1.8
Chantemerle (1671)	2,654	685	25.8
Jonchères (1673)	1,888	691	36.5

Source: André Lacroix, *Inventaire sommaire des archives départementales antérieur à 1790, Drôme*, vols. III–VIII

The privileged orders owned 3,597 *sétiers* in Chateauneuf-de-Mazenc according to the 1599 cahiers, and by the time of the seventeenth-century *cadastres* their holdings had declined to 2,429 *sétiers*.[27] At Mollans in the Baronnies the same tendency was evident. In 1599 the privleged orders were listed as holding one-third of the village lands, but by the 1666 *cadastre* they owned only 15.7 per cent of the total holdings.[28] This apparent reduction in exempted holdings seems to be corroborated by the fact that third-estate complaints concerning the rural holdings of the privileged orders virtually ceased after 1639, and the village communities showed little interest in drawing up new *cadastres*.

A further indication of the complexity of the evolution of the rural land market is furnished by a study of urban land purchases in the *département* of the Isère during the seventeenth century. Daniel Gaudissard and Jean-Paul Pascal have demonstrated that the patterns of property acquisition by the urban merchant elite, *parlementaires*, officials, and legal groups are most pronounced around Grenoble and Vienne,[29] but even in those cases many communities do not follow the general trend. Allevard shows a clear pattern of urban acquisition, but in Laval, Coublevie, and Voreppe patterns are far less evident. Frequently, the problem in tracing this evolution is the instability of the legal boundaries of the communities. In effect, the land surface owned by the Grenoble elite in Voreppe declined as the village limits became larger and larger. But this decline conceals the fact that important urban families extended their control and management techniques over some of the best land in the village.[30] Gerard Delille has demonstrated the same tendency in the nearby village of Vourey.[31] In general the economic predominance of the urban elite over the nearby villages continued and became accentuated after 1639. The difference from the old noble acquisitions made under the *taille personnelle* is that the members of the urban elite paid taxes on their new possessions and their purchases did not upset the fiscal-apportionment system of the villages.

The fiscal, political, and social evolution of Dauphiné from 1540 to 1640 was influenced by a number of general tendencies that were common to every region of France. At the same time the dynamic of the provincial *taille* controversy altered or accelerated many of the national economic and social trends. Thus, the fiscal implications of the *taille* conflict are the real key to understanding transformations in the political, institutional, and social structures of Dauphiné. Historians of the *Annales* school, together with Immanuel Wallerstein, Alexandra Lublinskaya, and Yves-Marie Bercé, have noted that everywhere in France there was a causal relationship between *taille* increases applied 'from above' and the initial destabilization of fiscal structures 'down below.'[32] L. Scott Van Doren has conclusively demonstrated this relationship for Dauphiné.[33] In effect, Crown intervention in Dauphiné began with increasing tax demands. In the 1540s, 1570s, 1590s, and 1620s the turn of the fiscal screws again and again demonstrated the inadequacy of the taxation structure of the province to meet the king's demands. The Crown stepped in unilaterally to alter the procedures for levying the *taille* in the 1540s by creating the *taille extraordinaire* and in the 1570s by giving the *commis du pays* the right to add to already approved levies.

These initiatives merely added to the tax burden of the third estate. It was impossible to lighten the third estate's load without reducing the fiscal privileges held by the groups belonging to the dominant social orders of the province. These privileged orders benefited from tax exemptions accorded during the late Middle Ages, but they maintained and extended those exemptions through their control of the political institutions of the province. Their social, fiscal, and political powers were embodied in provincial institutions, but with every new royal tax demand, new pressure for change was brought to bear upon the whole structure.

The contestation movement in Dauphiné resulted from the pressures of the *taille* system upon the third estate, and it lasted for over a century. Both the objectives and the leaders of the movement changed from one period to another. In the 1540s the overtaxed rural communities applied pressure to the Estates to distribute *tailles* in a more equitable manner. Their attack was aimed particularly at the de facto exemptions received by the urban elite for rural purchases and against the manoeuvres of the towns to shift part of their tax load back to the villages. The 1548 decision of Henry II to eliminate the fiscal loopholes from which townspeople had benefited was a first step towards satisfying rural demands. At the same time the decision constituted an initial destabilization of the social privileges held by groups participating in provincial institutions.

From 1548 to the 1620s the third estate formulated its demands more coherently, and it continued to achieve important successes in its struggle to obtain a more equitable taxation system. By the 1570s the town elite had joined with the rural notables to establish a new philosophical basis for the third-estate attacks. Rather than making piecemeal requests, the new contestation movement pursued global demands that the tax system itself be revised and that the province become a *pays de taille réelle*, but the 1579 popular rising divided and discredited the movement. During the 1590s the urban group returned to the offensive. Again the Crown refused to change the *taille* structure, but the *avocats consistoriaux* were in turn scratched from the list of exempted groups. However, it was the 1606 decision by Henry IV to create a royal commission for the verification of rural debts that constituted the most important new initiative. With this decision, the Crown sent royal inspectors into the province to look into third-estate protests against the effects of *taille* exemptions. The commission visited the villages of the province, inspected their accounts and reported back to the king regularly during a period of over fifteen years. After 1606 the number of royal interventions and appointments in the province increased. Royal commissioners were present at the negotiation of the 'agreement between the three orders' in 1610 and at the Estates of 1611. They pressured the latter meeting to apply the revenues of the provincial salt farm to rural debts. Fiscal problems 'down below' continually forced the Crown to take new initiatives, each of which reduced the traditional powers of the provincial elite and of the provincial institutions.

Historians have frequently noted the link between taxes and contestation in other areas of France in the seventeenth century, but it is evident that the fiscal-protest movement in Dauphiné was organized earlier and that it led to more serious confrontations than in most provinces. Why? The *taille personnelle* system cannot have been the main cause, for Dauphiné was not alone in possessing such a system. Indeed, most of the northern provinces of France imposed taxes through *taille personnelle* assessments. The demands for a change in the fiscal system of Dauphiné seem to have been more pressing than elsewhere because of its proximity to Provence and Languedoc, which possessed the more equitable *taille réelle*. Even within Dauphiné the *bailliage of the Montagnes* possessed the *taille réelle* system. The evident advantages of the *taille réelle* assessements for all of the component groups of the third estate made it one of the key demands of the movement for fiscal reform.

A second factor that explains the accelerated progress of fiscal reform in Dauphiné was the existence of a multitude of local political institutions that maintained pressure upon provincial institutions and upon the Crown for over a century. In contrast to the political structures of most other provinces and in particular contrast to those of the northern provinces, the Estates structure of Dauphiné was extended by assemblies of the ten cities, *assemblés du pays*, assemblies of the nobility, councils of the nobility, and a wide array of local, village, *bailliage*, and district meetings. These structures enabled each of the protagonists in the *taille* case to communicate with their supporters at the grass-roots level, to establish objectives for their movement, and to maintain a certain momentum in the contestation.

In terms of its political institutions, just as in the fiscal sphere, Dauphiné was influenced by currents that affected every region of the kingdom and by specific tendencies that were related to the *taille* challenge. In discussions of institutional change, one of the most most keenly contested issues has been the initiatives of the French Crown and its officials, initiatives aimed at abolishing local and provincial institutions and replacing them with men and structures imposed upon the province by the Crown. Historians have frequently traced initial royal interventions to show how they led to the imposition of political absolutism in France. Historians such as Mariejol, Pagés, Zeller, and Major have argued that Crown structures became more organized and more interventionist in the course of the sixteenth century.[34] The changes imposed in Dauphiné during that period, however, suggest that the king had little desire to alter provincial political strucutres and even less success in his attempts to do so. When changes were made, such as in the Edict of Abbeville and in the *taille* transformations in the 1540s and 1570s, they made little difference to the institutional independence of the province.

The first significant step towards Crown intervention in the province or in the *taille* dispute occurred with the 1606 appointment of the royal commission on rural debts, during the term of Sully as minister of finance. J.R. Major has argued that Sully was one of the ministers most determined to reduce the independence of provincial institutions.[35] It is not at all clear, however, that the 1606 commission signified the intention of Sully to intervene politically in Dauphiné. The establishment of the commission seems to have been more the result of the previous sixty years of *taille* contestation than of Crown political designs. Sully was always very cautious in his interventions in Dauphiné. He resisted third-estate pressures up to 1606; even after that he let the wine-tax project drop in 1609, and his commissioners granted the nobles compensation for the salt tax accorded to the third estate in 1611.

When placed within its historical context, however, the 1606 decision constitutes a turning-point. The Crown interventions between 1628 and 1639 resulted from the difficulties met by the commission in carrying out its mandate. They correspond to the institutional preferences of royal commissions on fiscal reform and of the Crown ministers inclined toward absolutism. It is clear, however, that the success of the Crown in installing *élections* and the *taille réelle* system and in suppressing the Dauphiné Estates owed more to the conflicts that divided the social orders in Dauphiné than to any theoretical plans by Sully or any other minister for establishing political absolutism in the province. The *taille* question created the social conflicts that opened the door to royal intervention.

The social divisions that were so important in the *taille* dispute led to groupings and alliances very different from those proposed by Porchnev, Mousnier, or Lublinskaya.[36] Since the *taille* dispute was essentially a juridical debate, each side in the century-long conflict corresponded more to juridical and institutional categories of society than to socio-economic or Marxist breakdowns. The protagonists were determined by their membership in one of the three traditional orders represented in provincial institutions. Therefore, the third estate combined the often divergent interests of the rural villages, the small towns, and the four largest cities as well as of such diverse groups as ploughmen, peasants, agricultural workers, artisans, merchants, professional men, and the nu-

merous categories of legal professions. The privileged orders, for their part, grouped the often irreconcilable interests of the old noble families and the clerical hierarchy with the recent *anoblis*, the nobles of the robe, officials of the parlement and Chambre des comptes, Crown officials, *docteurs d'université*, and various other tax-exempt individuals.

The groups that combined within either the third-estate coalition or that of the privileged orders were often adversaries in other provinces because of their differing economic situations and future perspectives. In Dauphiné, however, the almost constant protest movement imposed a certain fragile solidarity on each of the larger coalitions. On the side of the third estate the contestation was directed first by rural villages, then by the urban elite and the *commis* of the villages. Each in succession used propaganda, pamphlets, cahiers, and mobilization efforts to impose both concrete objectives and a certain solidarity upon its movement. The reaction of the privileged orders was defensive. Like the third estate, their movement was characterized by legal pleas, position papers, and propaganda tracts. These documents were intended to reply to third-estate attacks, to reinforce the often fragile internal solidarity of the groups that made up the privileged orders, and to justify the first and second estates' historical rights and privileges before the Crown. It is obvious that the two sides were formed more as a function of their *taille* interests than of their general socio-economic positions.

In Dauphiné as elsewhere in France, there were signs of constant social and economic mutation within each of the two larger coalitions. There were rural-urban disputes, differences between the major towns, and confrontations between the new and old noble families. Two of these evolutions were of significance to the eventual Crown intervention. The first was the upward mobility of the town elites. The economic perspectives of townspeople in Dauphiné were limited by the continually increasing *taille* levies and in particular by the effect on those levies of the tax exemptions of the first and second estates. Nevertheless, the *taille* rolls of the major towns towards the end of the sixteenth century demonstrate that in Dauphiné and elsewhere numerous merchants, Crown officials, lawyers, and *procureurs* had prospered and advanced. Some of these enriched groups were eventually ennobled, but the great majority were not. It was this non-ennobled, well-heeled elite that provided the greatest impetus for change. Elsewhere its members were among the principal defenders of provincial rights, but in Dauphiné they spearheaded the *taille* contestation against the other major social groups in the province. Town leaders co-operated with rural protesters in the

1570s. They took over the leadership of the movement after the town-country agreement of 1583 and especially after the new *taille* increases of the 1590s.

The old nobility was affected by the second major social evolution. The old families appear to have remained stable or perhaps to have suffered minor losses in economic and social terms. The seigniories held by the old nobles in the Valentinois-Diois secured for them a dominant position over any of the newcomers, but it is clear that during the period of the Wars of Religion they lost more domains than they acquired. The few ennoblements accorded in the province did not significantly improve the legal and bureaucratic competence of the second estate, for the great majority of the new titles were granted for military prowess. Its traditional social composition and lack of new legal recruits made the nobility of Dauphiné different from that of many other provinces that have been studied. In Bayeux, Normandy, and even in Provence the emergence of numerous ennobled *parlementaires* transformed the nobility. It was perhaps this lack of social evolution that handicapped the nobility of Dauphiné in its struggle against the urban elite and eventually against the Crown.

When we examine the century prior to the Crown interventions between 1628 and 1639, it becomes evident that local and provincial conflicts in Dauphiné were far more important than national priorities in explaining the eventual reduction of provincial 'liberties.' The *taille* affair played a central role in creating the dissidence and in determining the divisions that opened the way for royal action. Stimulated by Crown fiscal policies, the *taille* protests in Dauphiné went far beyond tax protests in other parts of France. The leaders of the third estate organized their contestation around an *issue*: the replacement of the *taille personnelle* by the *taille réelle*. By exploiting this question they mobilized and rechannelled the traditional social and political grievances of the tax-paying group into a protest movement contesting those who held tax exemptions. This confrontation weakened and eventually paralysed provincial institutions.

As early as 1552 the provincial Estates had been warned that if the three orders in the province did not agree on *taille* reform, the problem could bring the intervention of outside forces and undermine the independent laws and customs of Dauphiné.[37] By the end of the seventeenth century the social, political, and fiscal divisons created by the *taille* controversy had led to the royal initiatives of 1628 to 1639, and they in

turn brought the installation of increasingly absolutist governing structures in the province.

Seigneurial Holdings

The data on seigneurial holdings in the Inventaire Marcellier makes it possible to trace a considerable number of the families that acquired domains during the latter part of the sixteenth century. The *inventaire* is made up of thirty-five manuscript volumes located in the Archives départementales de l'Isère. Because of the difficulty of undertaking a systematic analysis of the evolution of all the holdings in the province, I have limited my analysis to the Valentinois-Diois region. I selected this region both because it is relatively typical of the distribution of property holdings in the province and because other sources are available for the Valentinois-Diois that allow the researcher to fill in missing information or to check entries in the *inventaire*.

Data on the ownership of 113 of the 193 seigniories listed in the *inventaire* for the Valentinois-Diois can be isolated for periods before and after the Wars of Religion. The *inventaire* quotes extensively from the most important documents concerning each holding. The ownership of almost all the seigniories can be determined for the years 1540–2, when an official *dénombrement* was carried out by the Chambre des comptes and all the owners of *cens*, toll stations, jurisdictions, or parts of a seigniory were listed. For the following periods and for the years after the Wars of Religion such information is less abundant. The *inventaire* does generally list documents that affected the ownership of the holdings: acts of homage, sales of seigniories, or procedures of transfer to and from the Crown domain (*aliénation* and *réunion*). In some cases I have had to resort to other sources of information to complete the data on individual domains. Record series such as the one compiled by André Lacroix on archival holdings in the Montélimar or Nyons regions, or his invaluable *Inventaire sommaire des archives départementales de la Drôme* have been useful in filling the gaps. The same is true of Brun-Durand's *Dictionnaire topographique du Département de la Drôme*, which lists the families that had possessed each domain.

The following list contains the results of this effort to reconstitute ownership. The list is complicated by the fact that most of the documents consulted list only family names. It is therefore impossible to follow the individual evolution of each holding, since the nuclear families that owned them cannot be identified apart from extended family groups. In the list I have hyphenated families that were joined by marriage, such as Clermont-Montoison for Aiguebonne in 1556 or La Tour-Montauban for Auriple in 1683. In other cases where there is multiple ownership, the different families have been listed individually. This is the case for Bonneval and for Montclar in 1540. These cases of multiple ownership pose a problem for the researcher following the evolution of ownership, since the different subsequent sources of information do not always indicate exactly who sold his holdings to the new owner. For each of the seigniories listed the reference given is to the volume and initial page of the Inventaire Marcellier where the holding is treated, and in cases where other sources were used, the reference to the source is noted according to the reference codes following. This reference is followed in parentheses by volume and page where the data was found.

CODE TO REFERENCES

A J. Brun-Durand, *Dictionnaire topographique du Département de la Drôme*, Paris 1891
B André Lacroix, *Inventaire sommaire des archives départementales de la Drôme*, 8 vols., Valence 1872–1910
C André Lacroix, *L'Arrondissement de Montélimar*, 8 vols., Valence 1868–93, repr. Paris 1973
D André Lacroix, *L'Arrondissement de Nyons*, 2 vols., Valence 1888–1901

Name of seigniory	Inventaire Marcellier	Evolution of holding
Aiguebonne	I, 3–4	1520 d'Eurre, 1550 Reynier (A 2), 1565 Clermont-Montoison (A 2), 1588 Dufour de la Répara (A 2)
Aix	I, 5–20	1540 Montauban, 1578 La Tour Gouvernet, 1648 La Tour Gouvernet
Alançon	I, 27–33	1540 Bologne, 1643 Bologne
Aleyrac	I, 38–42	1543 Adhémar de Monteil, 1686 Adhémar de Monteil
Ancone	I, 58–76	1541 Pracontal, 1677 Pracontal
Aoust	I, 77–83	1539 Biship of Die, 1625 Solvaing de Cheylon (B VII 395)
Aubenas	I, 87–94	1541 Lers, 1612 Lers
Auriple	I, 97–113	1540 Clermont, 1548 Diane de Poitiers, 1683 La Tour-Montauban (B VIII 105–6)
Autichamp	I, 114–24	1543 Beaumont, 1603 Beaumont, 1621 Beaumont
Baix-aux-Montaignes	I, 125–60	1537 Bertrand, 1548 Cornilliane-Eurre, 1580 Arbalestier de Beaufort
Barbières	I, 161–73	1540 Beaumont, 1606 Claude Frère
Barcelone	I, 174–84	1540 Odoard and Eurre, 1583 Thomé, 1584 Glane de Cugy d'Eurre, 1613 Glane de Cugy d'Eurre, 1615 Lebéron
Barry	I, 188–205	1540 Sauvaing, 1596 La Tour Gouvernet
La Bâtie	I, 206–7	1540 Boulogne (A 23), 1550 Eurre (A 23), 1600 Alric (A 23)
Brete et la Batie de Brete	I, 208–11	1540 Laydette-Eurre, 1603 Eurre
Batie, Roland	I, 212–17	1540 Beaumont, 1589 Ponet, 1591 Blain
Batie de Vere	I, 218–28	1540 Bane, 1684 Bane

Name of seigniory	Inventaire Marcellier	Evolution of holding
Beaufort and Gigors	I, 230–66	1521 Adhémar-Clermont and Adhémar-Eurre, 1573 Clermont, Peloux and Eurre, 1602 Beaumont, 1657 Arbalestier
Baume-Corniliane	I, 272–8	1540 Corniliane, 1601 Abries-Corniliane
Beaumont	I, 281–5	1540 Poitiers, 1576, Chartelier, 1607 Bishop of Valence
Beauvrières	I, 286–8	1540 d'Agoult, 1603 Armand de Lus (A 30)
Beconne	I, 289–96	1540 Vesc, 1621 Vesc
Bonlieu	I, 297–300	1540 Adhémar, 1582 Brunier (A 42)
Bonneval	I, 301–4	1540 Rozard and Montauban, 1620 Montauban
Bellegarde	I, 305–16	1540 Artaud, 1601 Montauban
Chabrillan	II, 475–509	1540 Moreton-Eurre, 1631 Moreton-Eurre
Chabeuil	I, 327–474	1540 Eurre, 1558 des Monts, 1603 des Monts
Chamaret	II, 510–16	1540 Adhémar de Monteil, 1678 Adhémar de Monteil
Chamel	II, 517–18	1540 de Pierre, 1624 Reynier
Charens	II, 519	1540 Bishop of Die, 1576 Brotin (A 72)
Châteaudouble	II, 523–626	1540 Plonier, 1545 Benoît Théocrène (A 75–6), 1550 Diane de Poitiers (A 75–6), 1576 Jules Centurion, 1593 Du Puy Montbrun
Châteauneuf de Mazenc	II, 636–94	1540 Vesc, 1554 Montauban-d'Agoult, 1602 Florent de Renard, 1617 Blain
Châteauneuf de Rhône	II, 695–704	1540 Bishop of Viviers, 1600 Bishop of Viviers
Chatelarnaud	II, 705–19	1540 Salvaing, 1599 Montoison

Name of seigniory	Inventaire Marcellier	Evolution of holding
Charpey	II, 720–72	1540 Beaumont, 1612 Clermont and Lattier (B II 39)
Chalar	II, 776–82	1540 Salvaing, 1621 Salvaing
Clansayes	II, 783–7	1398 Adhémar, 1600 Adhémar (C II 286–8)
Comps	II, 798–804	1540 Vesc, 1602 Vesc
Condillac	II, 805–8	1540 Forez, 1592 Forez-Mirabel
Cormillon	II, 809	1541 Grolée-Mevouillou, 1615 La Tour Gouvernet (D I 65)
Coubonne	II, 810–14	1540 Clermont, 1682 Clermont
Dieulefit	II, 905–12	1540 Commanderie de Poët-Laval and Vesc, 1630's Poët-Laval and Vesc (B IV)
Divajeu	II, 913–18	1540 Mirabeau and Eurre, 1558
Espeluche	II, 980–6	1540 Vesc, 1609 Vesc
Espel	II, 987–1003	1539 Januaing, 1621 Piègres and Baume
Eurre	V, 2906	1540 Eurre and Beaumont, 1562 Glane de Cugy d'Eurre (B II 179), mid-seventeenth-century Eurre
Fiancey	III, 1076–8	1540 Silve, 1626 d'Orne (A 144)
Garde Adhémar	III, 1080–1994	1540 Adhémar de Guyers, 1557 Adhémar-Escalin, 1585 Adhémar-Escalin, 1620, Adhémar de Monteil
Gigors	III, 1099–1118	1540 Eurre, 1645 Arbalestier (A 160)
Grâne	III, 1119–42	1540 Du Puy, 1560 Diane de Poitiers (A 167), 1562 Benoît Théocrène (A 167), 1570 Gardes, 1590 Reynier

Name of seigniory	Inventaire Marcellier	Evolution of holding
Jansac	III, 1143–89	1540 Commanderie de Poët-Laval, 1564 Monteynard (A 182), 1601 Borel de Pontenas (A 182)
Lemps	III, 1158–87	1540 Clermont and Hostun, 1600 Artus Prunier
Loupie	III, 1189–97	1540 Tholon, 1576 Morges, 1601 Tholon
Laval de Tourne	III, 1204–7	1543 d'Agoult and Montauban, 1560 Montauban
Luc-en-Diois	III, 1214–24	1543 l'Hère and Montauban, 1560 Montauban, 1580 Arnaud
Manas	III, 1225–9	1540 Commanderie de Poët-Laval, 1600 Commanderie de Poët-Laval (c v)
Marches	III, 1441–8	1539 Salvaing, 1582 Broé, 1612 Lattier
Marsanne	III, 1449–88	1540 Adhémar de Monteil, 1582 Brunier, 1621 Adhémar-Brunier
Mirabel	III, 1232–5	1540 Demiras and Montmeyran, 1553 Inhabitants of the village, 1660 Arbalestier
Montboucher	III, 1242–57	1540 Darbonfils and Odoard, 1577 Ventador (A 225), 1595 Bezanger
Montclar	III, 1369–1440	1540 Reynaud, Montoison and Arbalestier, 1583 Gramont, 1606 Arbalestier
Montgros	III, 1260–5	1540 Picon (A 230), 1635 Simiane (A 230)
Montjoux	III, 1489–1502	1540 Vesc, 1607 Vesc, 1624 Rigot
Montmeyran	III, 1503–60	1540 Clermont-Montoison, 1548 Couches (A 232), 1574 Clermont-Tallard
Montoison	III, 1475–88	1540 Clermont, 1610 Clermont
Motte-Chalençon	III, 1582–8	1540 Eynard, 1590 Eurre and Chabrillan (A 238), 1627 Morte and Laval (A 238)
Odiffret	III, 1589–96	1540 Eynard, 1602 Silo
Orcinas	III, 1597–1603	1540 Cliou, 1601 Lattier, 1621 Lattier

Name of seigniory	Inventaire Marcellier	Evolution of holding
Ourches	III, 1618–22	1540 Eurre, 1621 Eurre
Pennes	III, 1625	1540 Vesc, 1603 Vesc
Piègros	III, 1626–52	1540 Salvaing, 1597 Dejony, 1645 Lens
Pierrelatte	IV, 1654–88	1543 Adhémar-Escalin, 1552 Royal Domain (C VII 36–7), 1598 Adhémar-Escalin (C VII 36–7)
Pisançon	IV, 1689–1710	1542 Beavieu and Vauperge, 1545 Créqui (A 273), 1570 Poitiers-St Valliers (A 273), 1595 La Croix Chevrières
Poët-Celard	IV, 1710–23	1540 DuPuy-Blain, 1585 Blain, 1621 Blain
Poët-Laval	IV, 1724–36	1540 Commanderie de Poët-Laval, 1605 Commanderie de Poët-Laval
Pont de Barret	IV, 1741–51	1540 St Ferréol, Gaubert, Eurre, Adhémar, 1680 St Ferréol (C VII 128–9)
Portes	IV, 1752–5	1540 Eurre and Bedot, 1564 Guyon and Lolle, 1598 Monery, 1603 Bompard
Pousin	IV, 1756–1812	1530 Dablon, 1559 Diane de Poitiers, 1577 Ventador and Gardon
Puygiron	IV, 1813–31	1540 Berenger, 1601 Berenger
Puy St Martin	IV, 1832–6	1540 Adhémar and Eurre, 1600 Eurre (A 293)
Quint-Pontaix	IV, 1837–1912	1539 Sauvaing, 1543 Guillaume de Poitiers, 1566 Royal Domain, 1594 La Tour Gouvernet
Rac	IV, 1913–22	1540 Odoard, 1624 Roque-Goutard
Ravel	IV, 1925–7	1540 Beranger, mid-sixteenth-century Perrined (A 296)
Roche Baudin	IV, 1927–33	1540 Clermont-Montoison

Name of seigniory	Inventaire Marcellier	Evolution of holding
Rochefort, Samson	IV, 1934–97	1540 DuPuy and Salvaing, 1573 Bocsozel, 1593 Lattier, 1620 Lattier and DuPuy, 1623 Claude Frère
Rocheguide	IV, 1997–2005	1540 Baume, 1667 Blocaud
Roche-sur-Grane	IV, 2006–11	1527 DuPuy, 1628 Beaumont
Roche St Secret	IV, 2012–25	1540 Faure de Bologne, 1545 Faure de Bologne, 1601 Faure de Bologne
Rochette	IV, 2026–30	1540 Beauvoir, 1606 Baume
Roussas	IV, 2032–41	1540 Beaumont, 1561 Chapuyer, 1601 Chapuis, 1621 Chapuis
St Dizier	IV, 2055–8	1540 Cliou, 1619 Valserre
St Ferréol	IV, 2058–9	1540 Pelissier, 1578 l'Hère de Glandage, 1619 Bertrand and Morges (A 339)
St Genis	IV, 2060–75	1540 Marsanne, 1585 Marsanne, 1620 Marsanne
St Gervais	IV, 2076–86	1540 Commanderie de Poët-Laval, 1573 Moreton de Chabrillan, 1595 Eurre
St Paul-3-Châteaux	IV, 2095–2102	1540 Bishop of St Paul, 1627 Bishop of St Paul
Salette	IV, 2120–22	1540 Guyon and Commanderie de Poët-Laval, 1621 Guyon
Saou	IV, 2123–83	1540 Eurre, 1593 Blain
Sauzet	V, 2284–8	1540 Moreton, 1573 Albert de Montluc, 1591 Blacons-Mirabel
Savasse	V, 2186–2209	1540 Montes and Marcel, 1600 Montes and Rostaing des Montes
Soyans	V, 2394–2412	1540 Clermont, 1548 Diane de Poitiers, 1592 Du Mas (A 380–81)
Stablet	V, 2415–23	1540 Guillelaret, 1621 De la Tour
Suze	V, 2424–36	1540 Baume, 1572 Baume, 1625 Baume

Name of seigniory	Inventaire Marcellier	Evolution of holding
Touche (La)	v, 2456–62	1540 Eurre, 1621 Eurre
Treschenu	v, 2464–5	1540 Claret, 1589 Claret
Truinas	v, 2465–78	1540 Galien, Commanderie de Poët-Laval, Pontoz, Eurre, 1558 Girard and Eurre, 1560 Eurre, 1584 Philibert, 1603 *avocat* Charancy from Die, 1612 Eurre
Upie	v, 2851–2904	1539 Rabot, 1593 Blacons-Mirabel
Vache (La)	v, 2479–2488	1540 Poitiers, 1594 Manuel de la Fay
Vachères	v, 2489–2493	1540 Grammont, 1621 Rostaing de Grammont
Valdrôme	v, 2790–2797	1540 d'Agoult and Pierre, 1603 d'Agoult (A 402)
Vassieux	v, 2798–2800	1540 Baume and Planchette, 1597 Lattier (A 407), 1602 Gironde, 1603 Muret, 1622 Engilbond (A 407)
Vaunaveys	v, 2801–2824	1540 Clermont, 1610 Clermont
Véronne	v, 2832–2842	1540 Eurre, 1695 Moreton de Chabrillan (A 413), 1680 Moreton d'Expilly
Vesc	v, 2843–2845	1540 Vesc and Clermont, 1578 l'Hère, 1616 Léberon

Ennoblements 1578–1625

This list of ennoblements has been drawn up on the basis of two sources of information. The first is the acts of ennoblement registered in the parlement of Grenoble. These acts give the name of the candidate for nobility, his seigneurial holdings, those who sponsored or recommended him for ennoblement, the reason for which he was to be granted a title, and, after 1602, the indemnity he was to pay for his possessions to become tax exempt. The acts of ennoblement are scattered through the Generalia of the parlement, and they can be located through an invaluable manuscript inventory, prepared by G. Letonnelier, in the Archives départementales de l'Isère. The second major source for identifying ennoblements is numerous official texts and rolls drawn up during the seventeenth century. I have added a separate series of ennoblements located through such texts by Christiane Masson-Faucher ('L'Anoblissement en Dauphiné au xviie siècle') and Guy Allard (*Nobiliaire du Dauphiné*, and 'Rôle des anoblis dans le Dauphiné depuis 1582 et la valeur de leurs biens,' BM Grenoble R80, t 9, f 776).

ACTS OF ENNOBLEMENT, 1578–1625

Name	Seigniories held	Date of ennoblement	Indemnity paid	Reason for ennoblement	Source AD Isère
d'Avity, Claude		1610	60 écus	official – maître d'ordonnance	B 2924, f 992
Aymon, Jean-Louis	Franquières	1603	116 écus	army – service against Savoy	B 2919, f 1
Baulne, Bon de la		1615	133 écus	official – service as judge	B 2919, f 1164
Bellefin, Jacques de		1578		army – service in king's army	B 2914, f 120
Beins, Jean de		1612	100 écus	army – service with Governor Ornano and Lesdiguières	B 2920, f 209
Bernard, Pierre		1609	600 écus	lt particulier in St Marcellin; negotiated to break up Catholic League	B 2919, f 209
Bonnet, Jacques		1606		services as docteur-en-droit and professor at the University of Valence	B 2928, f 1031
Bonnet, Jean		1606		lt particulier in the sénéchaussée of Valence-Diois at Crest; uncovered a conspiracy in 1585	B 2928, f 1031
Bremond, Noël		1607		army – service with Lesdiguières	B 2917, f 655
Brissac, Henri de		1608	400 écus	official – served in the Chambre des comptes; was conseilleur and secretary to the king	B 2918, f 371 and f 1287
Busselin, Arnault de	Jacquelliers	1603	40 écus	army	B 2916, f 82
Calignon, Louis	Laffrey	1602	456 écus	army – arquebusier; received letters of ennoblement from king in 1592	B 2916, f 71

ACTS OF ENNOBLEMENT, 1578–1625

Name	Seigniories held	Date of ennoblement	Indemnity paid	Reason for ennoblement	Source AD Isère
Calignon, Soffrey		1607	50 écus	official – member and president of the Parlement	B 2917, f 351
Catilhon, Isabeau and Boniot		1615		official – avocat général	B 2914, f 1195
Chervas, Pierre-André de		1605		army – captain	B 2918, f 35
Davin, Antoine		1606	30 écus	army doctor	B 2917, f 918
Dubonnet-Finé, Charles		1606	60 écus	directed negotiations between Maréchal d'Ornano and the government of Grenoble	B 2917, f 560
Ducros, Charles		1606		official – *avocat consistorial*	B 2918, f 1
Engilboud, Hercule		1608	60 écus	army – captain	B 2918, f 1233
Falcon-Saint, Jehan	Roysset	1603	75 écus	army – captain	B 2916, f 51
Fillon, Melchior de		1602		official – royal judge	B 2918, f 21
Faure, Arnaud du	Blains	1605	40 écus	army – wartime injury	B 2916, f 80
Froment, Claude		1602		official – University of Valence	B 2918, f 728
Four, Jehan	Repara	1618	38 écus	army – his nobility was re-established	B 2921, f 1
Gauteront, Anthoyne		1602	100 écus	army – service under Guise	B 2916, f 45
Gillibert, Claude		1612	140 écus	army – sergeant-major	B 2919, f 791

ACTS OF ENNOBLEMENT, 1578–1625

Name	Seigniories held	Date of ennoblement	Indemnity paid	Reason for ennoblement	Source AD Isère
Gilliers, Gaspard, Philibert, and Philippe		1605	100 écus	army – nobility re-established	B 2919, f 564
Garagol, Antoine		1605	150 écus	official – royal judge at Romans; resisted the rebels of 1579	B 2917, f 115
Gratet, Pierre	Gragnien	1594		army – service with royalists and Lesdiguières	B 2915, f 11
Jomaron, Gaspard		1603	200 écus	army service	B 2918, f 666
Lange, Louis de	Montmiral	1613	30 écus	army service	B 2919, f 496
LeBlanc, Pierre	Nyons	1609	200 écus	official – parlement of Grenoble	B 2918, f 628
LeBlanc, Jean	Percy	1602	300 écus	army – captain	B 2921, f 279
Lionne, Sébastien de		1602	300 écus	army – service in royal forces	B 2916, f 28
Manen de Montault, Jean		1612		army	B 2919, f 1254
Meysonnier, Isaac		1606	40 écus	army – twenty years' service	B 2916, f 815
Michalon, Jacques		1602		army	B 2916, f 27
Morard, François		1586		official – secretary to Maugiron	B 2914, f 132
Motte, Pierre de la	Busselin	1603		army	B 2916, f 81
Morte, Jean de la	La Motte Chalençon, Laval	1607	200 écus 245 écus	negotiator with Duke of Savoy	B 2917, f 591
Natarel, Estienne		1595		army	B 2916, f 27

ACTS OF ENNOBLEMENT, 1578–1625

Name	Seigniories held	Date of ennoblement	Indemnity paid	Reason for ennoblement	Source AD Isère
Pellisson, Louis, François, and Geoffroy		1611		services to the town of Vienne and officials in the Chambre des comptes	B 2924, f 309
Peloux, Imbert	Sibveltaire	1602	100 écus	projects for Henry III	B 2916, f 38
Perrotin, François		1612		official – maréchal to the queen	B 2918, f 1356
Perrotin, Mathieu	Bertonnière	1608	30 écus	army	B 2918, f 1014
Philibert, François	Montalquier	1602		army – counsellor to Lesdiguières	B 2917, f 315
Pina, Balthazar de	Ocuarieu	1602	80 écus 30 écus in 1630	letters of ennoblement issued in 1595	B 2922, f 46
Poisle, Jehan de		1581		negotiations with the Romans rebels in 1579–80	B 2914, f 122
Prat, Etienne du		1605	40 écus	army	B 2917, f 144
Perroy, Paul		1609	400 écus	official – treasurer of war and of the Estates	B 2919, f 284
Rigot de Bourdeaux, Esprit de		1606	305 écus	army	B 2917, f 539
Vignon, Antoine and Jacques	Mas Plantières	1619	80 écus (Jacques)	army	B 2920, f 403
Vignon, André de	Tarnezieu	1616	60 écus	army	B 2921, f 796

ACTS OF ENNOBLEMENT, 1578–1625

Name	Seigniories held	Date of ennoblement	Indemnity paid	Reason for ennoblement	Source AD Isère
Villeneuve, Louis		1603	15 écus	doctor in Grenoble during plague epidemic	B 2916, f 62
Villard, Jean		1608	1,500 écus	army	B 2919, f 111

Name	Seigniories held	Date of ennoblement	Indemnity paid	Reason for ennoblement	Source
Armand	Lus	1606	50 écus	official – in Conseil du roi	Masson-Faucher and Allard, 'Rôle'
Basset, Félix		1586		avocat in the parlement	Allard, Nobiliaire and 'Rôle'
Bertrand		1618		official – treasurer	Masson-Faucher
Boissat, Pierre		1602	200 écus		Masson-Faucher
Calignon, Pierre		1612			Masson-Faucher
Cuisinel, Louis and Marc		1585			Masson-Faucher
Gallifet, Alexandre de		1609			Masson-Faucher
Garcin, Jean de Sisteron		1603	60 écus		Allard, Nobiliaire
Lancellin, Nicolas	Ambonil and La Rolière	1601		army	Allard, Nobiliaire and 'Rôle'
LeFebvre, Henri, Nicolas and Jacques		1599			Masson-Faucher

Name	Seigniories held	Date of ennoblement	Indemnity paid	Reason for ennoblement	Source AD Isère
Leusse, Antoine and Laurent		1615	70 écus	re-established in nobility through position as canon of St-Maurice-sur-Vienne	Masson-Faucher
Marchier, Ennemond		1605	20 écus	official – *avocat* in the parlement	Allard, *Nobiliaire*
Michel, Sixte de	Beauregard	1602			Masson-Faucher
Micha, François de	Montchamp	1606			Masson-Faucher
Rame, Gaspard		1602	30 écus		Masson-Faucher
Revol, Claude, François, Antoine, et Guillaume		1602	150 écus		Masson-Faucher
Suffixe de Joachim	La Croix		40 écus		Masson-Faucher
Vocance, Antoine		1588			Allard, *Nobiliaire*

Notes

INTRODUCTION

1 Here I am using absolutism in its broadest sense, that is, to mean a
process aimed at increasing the power and responsibilities of the central
government or the Crown at the expense of local and provincial levels
of government. I see the process as identical to the concept of *state
building*, a term preferred by numerous socio-economic historians.
2 Mariéjol, *Henri IV et Louis XIII*, chaps. 2, 3
3 Ibid., 389–406
4 Ibid., 406
5 Mousnier, 'Le Conseil du roi de la mort d'Henri IV au gouvernement
personnel de Louis XIV,' in *La Plume, la Faucille et le Marteau*, 141–78;
Valois, introduction to *Inventaire des arrêts du Conseil d'état, règne d'Henri IV*;
Doucet, *Les Institutions de la France au XVIᵉ siècle, I*, 131–53; Pagès, 'Le
Conseil du roi sous Louis XIII,' 293–324, and 'Le Conseil du roi et la
vénalité des offices,' 245–82
6 Michaud, *La Grande Chancellerie et les écritures royales au seizième siècle, 1515–
1589*; Doucet, *Institutions, I*, 102–11; Sutherland, *The French Secretaries
of State in the Age of Catherine de Médicis*
7 Doucet, *Institutions, I*, 422–36; Esmonin, 'Des intendants du Dauphiné des
origines à la Révolution,' in *Etudes sur la France des XVIIᵉ–XVIIIᵉ siècles*,
71–113; Mousnier, 'Etat et Commissaire. Recherches sur la création des
intendants des provinces,' in *La Plume, la Faucille et le Marteau*, 179–99
8 Zeller, 'L'Administration monarchique avant les intendants. Parlements et
gouverneurs,' 180–215; Pagès, 'Autour du "grand orage." Richelieu et
Marillac. Deux politiques,' 63–97; J.R. Major, 'Bellièvre, Sully and the
Assembly of Notables of 1596,' 1–34. As a result of his work on provincial

and local institutions, Major differs with the view that Richelieu was an
all-out advocate of absolutism; see Major, *Representative Government in
Early Modern France*, 581–606.

9 Major, 'Henry IV and Guyenne,' 375–7
10 Ranum, *Richelieu and the Councillors of Louis XIII*
11 Bonney, *Political Change in France under Richelieu and Mazarin, 1624–1661*
12 Mousnier, *La Vénalité des offices sous Henri IV et Louis XIII*
13 Mousnier, *Les XVI*ᵉ *et XVII*ᵉ *siècles*, 176–81
14 Mousnier, *Vénalité des offices*, 666. Since his work on the sale of offices,
Mousnier has become interested in social categories and social mobility.
Refusing the concept of *classes*, Mousnier has developed the argument
that the rank of individuals in a social hierarchy should be determined by
a value system that can be extracted from official documents, documents
from the royal court, marriage registers, notarial minutes, court judgments, and the like. From an examination of such documents, he has
proposed nine social strata into which individuals should be divided. The
criticism of his classification revolves around the imposition of categories
'from above' and the use of wealth of individuals to determine his
hierarchies. See Mousnier, *L'Echantillon de 1634, 1635, 1636* and *Les
Hiérarchies sociales de 1450 à nos jours*. For a critique of these views
see Arriaza, 'Mousnier and Barber,' 39–57; Rotelli, 'La Structure sociale
dans l'itinéraire historiographique de Roland Mousnier,' 145–82; and
Goubert, 'L'Ancienne Société d'ordres,' 35–40.
15 Mousnier, *Vénalité des offices*, 666
16 Porchnev, *Les Soulèvements populaires en France de 1623 à 1648*
17 Ibid., 538–61
18 See Salmon, 'Venality of Office and Popular Sedition in Seventeenth-
Century France,' 21–43; and Mandrou, 'Les Soulèvements populaires et
la société française du XVIIᵉ siècle,' 756–65. A 1957 conference organized
by *Past and Present* brought together some thirty historians to discuss
the theme of seventeenth-century revolutions: see *Past and Present* 13
(1958). The debate resulted in an article by H.R. Trevor-Roper, 'The
General Crisis of the Seventeenth Century,' in *Past and Present* 16 (1959):
31–64, and in a collective response by several historians, including
Mousnier, in 'Trevor Roper's General Crisis,' *Past and Present* 18 (1960):
8–51.
19 Bercé, *Histoire des croquants*, II, 537–603
20 Pillorget, *Les Mouvements insurrectionnels de Provence entre 1596 et 1715*,
450–68

21 Lublinskaya, *French Absolutism*, 321–6
22 Ibid., 103–45, 320–33. For further comment on the role of the commercial bourgeoisie in its alliance with absolutism, see William Beik, *Absolutism and Society in Seventeenth Century France: State Power and Provincial Aristocracy in Languedoc*. I wish to thank Professor Beik for giving me access to the manuscript of his introduction.
23 Chaunu, 'L'Etat,' in *L'Etat et la Ville*, 16
24 Ibid., 17
25 See the important monographs applying these criteria: Le Roy Ladurie, *Les Paysans de Languedoc*; Goubert, *Beauvais et Beauvaisis de 1600 à 1730*; Deyon, *Amiens, capitale provinciale;* Gascon, *Grand Commerce et vie urbaine au xvie siècle. Lyon et ses marchands*; and Jacquart, *La Crise rurale en Ile-de-France, 1550–1670*.
26 Richet, *La France moderne, l'esprit des institutions*, 37–60
27 Goubert, *L'Ancien Régime*, II, espec. chaps. 5, 10
28 Of course, *élections* were created in Guyenne in 1621, but the provincial Estates continued. In Languedoc *élections* were imposed in 1622 but withdrawn after pressure from the lieutenant-general. See Major, 'Henry IV and Guyenne,' 382–3.
29 Chomel, 'Le Dauphiné sous l'ancien régime,' 310
30 Dupont-Ferrier, *Les Officiers des bailliages et sénéchaussées et les institutions monarchiques locales en France à la fin du moyen age*, 671–748

CHAPTER 1: PRELUDE TO THE *TAILLE* AFFAIR

1 Dussert, 'Les Etats du Dauphiné aux xive et xve siècles,' 282–3; Chomel, 'De la principauté à la province (1349–1456),' in Bligny, ed., *Histoire du Dauphiné*, 161–89; J. Chevalier, *Mémoires pour servir à l'histoire des comtés de Valentinois et de Diois*, I, 404–5; Guiffrey, *Histoire de la réunion de Dauphiné à la France*, 72–82
2 The act of *transport*, dated 30 Mar. 1349, is printed in French translation in Blet, Esmonin, and Letonnelier, eds., *Le Dauphiné, Recueil de textes historiques*, 55–71; its integral Latin version is printed in Guiffrey, *Histoire de la réunion de Dauphiné à la France*, pièce justificative XXVII, 223–47. The *statut*, dated 14 Mar. 1349, is printed in Valbonnais, *Histoire de Dauphiné et des princes qui ont porté le nom de Dauphin*, II, 582, doc. CCLXVIII.
3 The *bailliages* of Viennois and of the Montagnes and the *sénéchaussée* of Valentinois
4 On the position of *trésorier général* of Dauphiné and of the Chambre des

comptes, see Dupont-Ferrier, *Les Officiers des bailliages et sénéchaussées*;
J. Chevalier, *Mémoires pour servir*, II, 173–4; Chomel, 'De la principauté à
la province,' in Bligny, ed., *Histoire du Dauphiné*, 177.

5 Dussert, 'Les Etats du Dauphiné de la Guerre de Cent Ans aux Guerres
de Religion,' 219

6 Ibid., 219–20

7 Ibid., 223–4

8 J. Chevalier, *Mémoires pour servir*, II, 173–4

9 Lacroix, *L'Arrondissement de Montélimar, géographie, histoire et statistique*, V,
357. On the general question of strengthening municipal privileges, see
B. Chevalier, 'The Policy of Louis XI toward the *Bonnes Villes*: The
Case of Tours,' 276; and Major, *Representative Government in Early Modern
France*, 172–4.

10 Lacroix, *L'Arrondissement de Montélimar*, V, 358–60

11 Dussert, 'Les Etats ... de la Guerre de Cent Ans aux Guerres de Religion,'
220–1

12 J. Chevalier, *Mémoires pour servir*, II, 36

13 Van Doren, 'Wars, Taxes and Social Protest,' 143; see also Van Doren,
'War Taxation, Institutional Change and Social Conflict in Provincial
France – The Royal *Taille* in Dauphiné, 1494–1559,' 75–9

14 Guy Pape, cited in Lacroix, 'Claude Brosse et les Tailles,' 31: 187. Van
Doren has demonstrated that the list of inhabitants eligible for exemptions
was actually much longer than even Guy Pape implied; it included
winners of marksmanship contests, those who discovered or betrayed
plots to capture towns during the civil wars, and manufacturers, printers,
and artists who were offered exemptions to entice them to settle in
towns. See Van Doren, 'Wars, Taxes and Social Protest,' 201–89.

15 Lacroix, 'Claude Brosse,' 31: 189. See also Van Doren's treatment of
these exemptions in 'Wars, Taxes and Social Protest,' 201–14.

16 Dussert, 'Les Etats ... de la Guerre de Cent Ans aux Guerres de Religion,'
271–6. Dauphiné did not apply a pure *taille personnelle* system. The
province's system represented a mixed approach: most villages had no
cadastre, and their assessments seem to have been based upon the previous
annual *taille* rolls, but many villages and virtually all towns had *cadastres*.
Further complicating the system was the fact that lands could be transferred from noble to roturier categories between *cadastres*, and generally
the villages did not include noble holdings in their registers. E. Esmonin
goes so far as to claim that we should really be speaking of a *taille
mixte*, since the *taille personnelle* was rarely applied without numerous

exceptions; see *Etudes sur la France des XVIIe et XVIIIe siècles*, 168; and Major, *Representative Government in Early Modern France*, 76–80.

17 Van Doren, 'Wars, Taxes and Social Protest,' 142–4; see also Van Doren, 'War Taxation, Institutional Change,' 70–96.

18 Van Doren, 'War Taxation, Institutional Change,' 59

19 Dussert, 'Les Etats ... des Guerres de Cent Ans aux Guerres de Religion,' 284

20 Ibid., 281.

21 Ibid., 285

22 Ibid., 285; Van Doren Papers, Deliberations of 1542 Estates, BMG, R7568, ff 12–13

23 Van Doren, 'War Taxation, Institutional Change,' 59

24 The prices went from 35 francs per hectolitre in 1541 to 37 in 1542, 70 in 1543, 89.7 in 1544, and 89.7 in 1545 before dropping back to 29.7 in 1546. See Robert Latouche, 'Le Prix du blé à Grenoble du XVe au XVIIIe siècle,' 347.

25 At its 1538 meeting the provincial Estates ruled that the traditional system of exempting privileged groups from regular *taille* levies should be maintained. They refused to approve the preparation of *cadastres* for communities that did not already have them, and they upheld the exemptions for the *avocats consistoriaux* in defiance of the communities that were trying to tax them as *roturiers*; see Van Doren Papers, Conclusion of the Estates at Grenoble, concerning an attempt by some communities to tax rural holdings of nobles and clerics, 19 Mar. 1538, AC Vienne, CC 39; also referred to by Dussert, 'Les Etats ... des Guerres de Cent Ans aux Guerres de Religion,' 286. The attack upon the *avocats consistoriaux* in Dauphiné corresponded to a general sixteenth-century debate over the place of the *parlementaires*, the officials and nobles of the robe within the French social structure: were they with the third estate or with the nobles? Denis Richet has underscored the controversy, showing that there were even plans to create a separate 'fourth estate' in which the *parlementaires* would be placed; see 'Autour des origines idéologiques lointaines de la Révolution française,' 3–6.

26 Sclafert, *Le Haut-Dauphiné au moyen age*; Faucher, *Plaines et bassins du Rhône moyen*

27 This movement towards rural acquisitions by urban residents began at the end of the fifteenth century and intensified during the late sixteenth and seventeenth centuries. It was common to most regions of France; see Le Roy Ladurie, 'Sur Montpellier et sa campagne aux XVIe et XVIIe

siècles,' 223–30; Estèbe, 'La Bourgeoisie marchande et la terre à Toulouse au XVIᵉ siècle, 1519–1560,' 457–64; Jacquart, *La Crise rurale en Ile-de-France*, 101–34, 232–53, 331–57, 716–52.

28 Van Doren Papers, Deliberations of Estates, Grenoble, 8–13 Aug. 1547, AD Isère, J5 24/2, no. 1, ff 1 and 20

29 The original 1540 *dénombrements* and 1541 *hommages* for Montbonnot have been destroyed, but sections of the acts that they contained were summarized in the seventeenth-century Inventaire Marcellier, a manuscript inventory to the holdings of the Chambre des comptes; see AD Isère, Inventaire Marcellier, Graisivaudan, 4ᵉ vol., 'Montbonnot,' ff 2154–93.

30 Ibid., Deliberations of the Estates, 1547, ff 1, 11

31 Dussert, 'Les Etats ... des Guerres de Cent Ans aux Guerres de Religion,' 288. Dussert's opinion on the possibility that the villages and towns could have reached an agreement is corroborated by the fact that at the 1547 Estates they formed a common front to contest the purchase of property by clerics; Van Doren Papers, Deliberations of the Estates, 1547.

32 Van Doren Papers, Deliberations of the Estates, 15–16 July 1548, AC Romans, AA2, f 20

33 Ibid., f 29

34 Van Doren Papers, 'Arrêt du Conseil privé,' Lyon, 30 Sept. 1548, AD Isère, J524/1, f 6, and AD Isère, IC4 30, ff 9–10

35 Dussert, 'Les Etats ... des Guerres de Cent Ans aux Guerres de Religion,' 290. Van Doren Papers, letter from Authe Rives, *procureur* for the village of Cremieu, to consuls of Cremieu, 6 July 1549, AD Isère, 4E 245/58 (Cremieu CC); Extrait des conclusions d'une réunion des commis du pays, 12 July 1549, AC Romans, CC 478, no. 24; Pour l'examen de l'arrêt du Conseil privé pour la revision des feux,' 1549, AC Romans, CC 478, no. 108.

36 Van Doren Papers, Deliberations of the 1550 Estates, 9–13 Jan. 1550 (missing early sessions), AD Isère, J524/2, no. 2, ff 23–4

37 Ibid., Deliberations of the 1551 Estates, Feb. 16–21 1551, AD Isère, J524/2, no. 3, f 45

38 Dussert, 'Les Estats ... des Guerres de Cent Ans aux Guerres de Religion,' 292–3

39 Ibid., 293

40 Ibid., 64

41 Van Doren Papers, Deliberations of the Estates, 4–11 Mar. 1552, AC Romans, AA2, f 3

42 Ibid., In order to piece together the negotiations and agreements con-

cerning the *taille* question at the 1552 Estates, it is necessary to take note
of the variations in the different résumés of proceedings; see Deliberations of the Estates, AC Romans, AA2; and AC Cremieu, BB, ff 20–46.

43 Van Doren Papers, Deliberations of the Estates, 4–11 Mar. 1552, AC
Romans, AA2, ff 29–30

44 Ibid., Deliberations of the Estates, Mar. 1553, AC Vienne, AA 5–11, f 22

45 Dussert, 'Les Etats ... des Guerres de Cent Ans aux Guerres de Religion,'
297

46 Ibid., 300. Van Doren Papers, Extrait des registres du Conseil privé du
roy, 4 Aug. 1553, AC Valence, AA 10, ff 70–2

47 Van Doren Papers, Governor to *commis du pays*, 25 June 1553, AD Drôme,
E 3616, no. 65, ff 1–2; and Résumé of the meeting of *commis du pays*, 6
June 1553, AD Drôme, E 3616, no. 65

48 Transaction entre les trois ordres, 16 February 1554, in Dussert, 'Les
Etats ... de la Guerre de Cent ans aux Guerres de Religion,' 340–6. See
also Van Doren, 'Wars, Taxes and Social Protest,' 225–30.

49 Rambaud, *Plaidoyé pour le tiers estat du Dauphiné*, f 23, and *Second Plaidoyé
pour le tiers estate du Dauphiné*, f 58. See Dussert, 'Les Etats ... de la
Guerre de Cent Ans aux Guerres de Religion,' 302–3.

50 Ibid., 340–1. The legal memorandum on third-estate recourses for
contesting the 1554 vote, prepared by Pasquier et al. in 1596, noted that
a large number of the proxy votes had not been dated and should
have been considered invalid; see memo by Chopin, Pasquier, DuLaurens,
Chauvelin, Thoard, and Buisson, Paris, 26 May 1596, AD Drôme, C
1024/23.

51 Van Doren Papers, Deliberations of the Estates, 8–12 Apr. 1548, AC
Romans, AA2 f 1

52 Ibid., Deliberations of the Estates, 16–21 Feb. 1551, AD Isère, J524/2, no.
3, f 37

53 Dussert, 'Les Etats ... des Guerres de Cent Ans aux Guerres de Religion,'
xiv. The authorized proportion of representation was 36 representatives
of the clergy, 270 of the nobility, and 115 of the third estate.

54 Ibid., 303

55 Ibid., 304

56 Chorier, *Histoire générale de Dauphiné*, II, 538

57 Van Doren Papers, Offres que le tiers estat demandes estre accordez par
les deux premiers estats, Feb. 1554 (1555 ns), AC Vienne, AA 5–8

58 Ibid., ff 8–15

59 Van Doren Papers, Jean Vincent and De Combes to Council of Vienne,
23 July 1555, AC Vienne, CC 45

60 Ibid., De Combes to Council of Valence, 25 July 1555, AC Valence, AA 10, ff 253–6

61 Ibid., Council of Valence to *commis des états*, 26 May 1555, AC Valence, AA 10, ff 241–2; and Duc de Clermont to Council of Vienne, 11 Nov. 1555, AC Vienne, AA 5–13

62 Arrêt du Roi-Dauphin Henri II sur le différend des trois ordres du Dauphiné au sujet des tailles, Fontainebleau, June 1556, in Dussert, 'Les Etats ... des Guerres de Cent Ans aux Guerres de Religion,' 346

63 Van Doren, 'War Taxation, Institutional Change,' 92

64 In 1560 at the Estates-General of Orléans the third estate of Dauphiné appealed to the king, who issued an edict in 1562 that added further restrictions concerning ennoblement by the purchase of a noble fief. He distinguished among kinds of fiefs: those that did not include the right to dispense justice or that were worth less than 300 *livres* could not ennoble their owners. The importance of this problem seems to indicate that land purchases by non-nobles and subsequent ennoblement were becoming more frequent. See Lacroix, 'Claude Brosse et les Tailles,' 31:388. At the 1560 Estates the third estate seems to have discussed demands for a global transformation of the *taille* from *taille personnelle* to *taille réelle* everywhere in the kingdom, but these discussions never progressed far enough for such a request to be entered in the third-estate cahier. See Picot, *Histoire des Etats généraux*, II, 237–8.

CHAPTER 2: THE CRISIS OF 1579

1 The chronology of the wars has been treated by Long, *La Réforme et les Guerres de Religion en Dauphiné de 1560 à l'Edit de Nantes (1598)*, and Charronnet, *Les Guerres de Religion et la société protestante dans les Hautes-Alpes (1560–1579)*. Of a more analytical nature is the chapter by L. Scott Van Doren on the composition and recruitment processes of the two armies; see Van Doren, 'Wars, Taxes and Social Protest,' 98–140.

2 Lacroix, 'Claude Brosse et les Tailles,' 31: 388–96; Romans, *Documents sur la réforme et les Guerres de Religion en Dauphiné*, and 'Catherine de Médicis en Dauphiné'; Dussert, 'Catherine de Médicis et les Etats de Dauphiné'; Cavard, *La Réforme et les Guerres de Religion à Vienne*; Chomel, 'Guerres de Religion et "Remuements des peuples": la fin des libertés provinciales,' in Bligny, ed., *Histoire du Dauphiné*; La Roy Ladurie, *Carnival in Romans*; and Van Doren, 'Wars, Taxes and Social Protest,' 'War Taxation, Institutional Change,' 'Civil War Taxation and the Foundations of Fiscal Absolutism,' 35–53, and 'Revolt and Reaction in Romans, 1579–1580,' 71–100

3 These official *taille* levies are calculated from the *lançons* listed by Van Doren in 'War Taxation, Institutional Change,' app. 57–60, and 'Civil War Taxation,' app. 42–9.

4 Le Roy Ladurie, *Carnival*, 40. The Le Roy Ladurie graph was plotted by dividing the amount of the annual *taille* levy for each *feu* (based upon the Van Doren tables) by the average annual price of wheat in Grenoble (obtained from the Registres des gros fruits of the Chambre des comptes, AD Isère, B4385, B4388, B4380). In Graph 1 I have taken the liberty of extending this method of calculation up to 1600.

5 Clamageran, *Histoire de l'impôt en France*, II, ii, 155–332; Van Doren, 'War Taxation, Institutional Change,' and 'Civil War Taxation,'; Wolfe, *The Fiscal System of Renaissance France*; Chamberland, 'Les Recettes de l'Epargne en 1581 et une erreur de Forbonnais,' 105–6, and 'Le Budget de 1597,' 16–19. I wish to thank Christopher Stocker for suggesting these references to me.

6 J.B. Collins has provided further proof of this discrepancy in a *pays d'élection*; he illustrated the differences between revenues listed in the royal Epargne and revenues actually collected in Champagne in the early seventeenth century. See Collins, 'Sur l'histoire fiscale du XVIIᵉ siècle,' 325–42. Collins and Roger Chartier further debate the question in the same issue of the *Annales*, 34(1979): 242–347.

7 Chamberland, 'Les Recettes de l'Epargne en 1581,' 103–7

8 Van Doren, 'Civil War Taxation,' 22

9 AC Vienne, Third-Estate Cahiers: Vaunaveys, CC 42; Condorcet and Châteauneuf-de-Mazenc, CC 43. These cahiers were a part of the third-estate effort to prove the injustices of the *taille personnelle* system.

10 Van Doren Papers, Remonstrances, doléances et requêtes que font les états et quelques villes, 1573, with reply 15 Jan. 1574, AD Drôme, C 1073, no. 6. Requête présentée au roy, 24 Nov. 1576 and 16 Mar. 1577, AD Drôme, C 1023. Doléances du tiers état, Apr. 1579, in Dussert, 'Catherine de Médicis et les Etats du Dauphiné,' 166–75

11 Van Doren Papers, Supplie au Duc de Mayenne des villages du pays contre les villes, Dec. 1581, AD Isère, 4E 245/1 (Cremieu AA)

12 Tilley, *The Vendée* 177–87; Chartier and Nagle, 'Les Cahiers de doléances de 1614,' 1484–94; Robin, *La Société française en 1789: Semur-en-Aixois* 255–71

13 In 1598 the *avocats* of the third-estate cause ordered all towns and villages to send them dossiers similar to those prepared unilaterally by a number of villages in the 1570s and in 1596. The dossiers were to list the consuls and syndics who had held office, the taxes levied to pay *tailles*

and military impositions, the *roturier* holdings that had been acquired by nobles or exempted inhabitants, and the loans that the community had negotiated. The *avocats* asked that information on all these points extend back to 1518, but no cahier went any further back than 1570. See instructions in *Avertissement pour le tiers estat de Dauphiné pour plus amples instructions du procès dudict tiers estat contre les deux premiers ordres dudict païs* (Lyon 1598), BM Grenoble, E29175.

14 Piémond, *Mémoires de Eustache Piémond*

15 Ibid., 376–7. AC Vienne, CC 44, St-Antoine cahier, 22 Sept. 1596. The cahier for 1598 is printed in the *Mémoires*, 369–92.

16 Wolfe, *Fiscal System of Renaissance France*, 195–202

17 Piémond, *Mémoires*, 214–34

18 The method of imposing *tailles* upon the villages during the wars can be reconstituted from the *Mémoires* of Piémond and from the controversy over the creation of three *receveurs*. For the latter, see Van Doren Papers, Requête présentée au roi par le procureur des trois états de Dauphiné pour la suppression de l'edit de trois receveurs audit pais, 24 Nov. 1574; Autre requête aux mêmes fins que la précédente, 14 Feb. 1577; and Edit de suppression de l'edit des trois receveurs, 4 Mar. 1577, AD Isère, IC 3/39. This reconstitution also owes much to discussions with L. Scott Van Doren.

19 Résumé of the provincial Estates meeting, 4 July 1578, in Fauché-Prunelle, 'Le Livre du roy,' 557–61. A similar agreement with the Huguenots was negotiated in 1589; see Trêve de 26 mars 1589, in Goulart, *Mémoires de la Ligue*, III, 289–90. I wish to thank L.S. Van Doren for sending me these references.

20 Van Doren Papers, Requête présentée au roi par le procureur des trois états de Dauphiné pour la suppression de l'edit des trois receveurs audit pais, 24 Nov. 1574; Autre requête aux mêmes fins que la précédente, 14 Feb. 1577; and Edit de la suppression de l'edit des trois receveurs, 4 Mar. 1577, AD Isère, IC 3/39

21 Ibid., Deliberations of the Estates, 2–4 May 1569, AD Isère, 4E 245/61, f 3

22 Deliberations of the Estates: 1575, AD Isère, 4E 241/1; 1576, AD Isère, 4E 245/62; 1586, AD Drôme, C 1024/2; 1587, AD Drôme, C 1024/10

23 Piémond, *Mémoires*, 219, 220, 226–7. In 1587 Piémond noted that the Baron de la Roche imposed a *taille* of six *écus* per feu 'demande qui lui avait esté refusée par le dernier Estat, mais que la force a contraint le peuple de payer' (202).

24 Van Doren, 'Wars, Taxes and Social Protest,' 146–7

25 A levy had been imposed in 1567 without the permission of the Estates, but at that time the commissioners, who had been ordered by the king to impose the tax, had consulted both the parlement and the *commis*; see Van Doren, 'Civil War Taxation,' 38–9.

26 Ibid., 39

27 Ibid.

28 Ibid.

29 Gay, *Mémoires des Frères Gay*, 29

30 Rapport par Morard sur l'exécution de l'arrêt prescrivant le demantèlement des places fort du Valentinois-Diois, 11 Jan. 1582, in J. Chevalier, *Mémoires pour servir à l'histoire des comtes*, I, 532–6

31 Van Doren, 'Civil War Taxation,' 40

32 Barbiche, 'Les Commissaires députés pour le "régalement" des tailles en 1598–99,' 68–78

33 Le Roy Ladurie, *Carnival*, 41–2

34 Le Roy Ladurie, *Carnival*, 61

35 Consuls of Blois to consuls of Nyons to convoke the *élus* from the region of the Baronnies, 23 Apr. 1571, AC Nyons, CC29

36 Consuls of Grenoble to Mgr de Gordes, 1 Mar. 1572, AM Grenoble, BB 24, in Prudhomme, *Inventaire sommaire des archives communales, ville de Grenoble*, I, 42

37 Du Blanc to consuls of Châteauneuf-de-Mazenc, 26 Oct. 1575, AC Châteauneuf-de-Mazenc, EE 2, in Lacroix, *Inventaire sommaire des archives départementales de la Drôme*, IV, 145

38 Cahiers of Seyssuel and Classe, 1572, AC Vienne, CC 42

39 28 July 1571, AC Châteauneuf-de-Mazenc, BB 1, cited in Van Doren, 'Wars, Taxes and Social Protest,' 241

40 7 Oct. 1573, AM Grenoble, BB 25, in Prudhomme, *Inventaire sommaire*, V, 43

41 Aug. 1574, AM Grenoble, BB 26, in Prudhomme, *Inventaire*, V, 43

42 Van Doren Papers, Deliberations of the Estates, Grenoble, 2–4 May 1569, AD Drôme, III E 57, ff 3–5

43 Ibid., f 2

44 Ibid., f 6

45 Dussert, 'Catherine de Médicis et les Etats,' 132. The ten officially recognized cities were Grenoble, Valence, Romans, Vienne, Gap, Crest, Montélimar, Briançon, Die, and Embrun.

46 Van Doren Papers, Remonstrances, doléances et requêtes que font les estats et quelques villes, 1573, with reply of 15 Jan. 1574, AD Drôme, C

1073, no. 6. Requête présentée au roy, 24 Nov. 1576 and 16 Mar. 1577, AD Drôme, C 1023. Doléances du tiers estat, Apr. 1579, in Dussert, 'Catherine de Médicis et les Etats,' 166–75

47 See mandates given on 8 Mar. 1552 and 4 Feb. 1554 in AM Grenoble, BB 15, in Prudhomme, *Inventaire sommaire des archives communales, ville de Grenoble*, I, 25, 29.

48 Van Doren Papers, Article 17, Cahier des Remonstrances, 1573, with reply 15 Jan. 1574, AD Drôme, C 1023/6

49 Ibid., Deliberations of the Estates, Grenoble, 1–3 Mar. 1574, AD Isère, IC 3

50 Ibid., copy of the thirty-two articles presented to the king, in Loutchitzky, *Documents inédits pour servir à l'histoire de la Réforme et de la Ligue*, 2–19

51 It should be noted that in 1556 the clergy had been made subject to *tailles extraordinaires* for their rural holdings and the nobles were to be taxed for *taillable* holdings that were not located in *taille réelle* areas.

52 Van Doren Papers, Antoine Giffard, résumé des principaux articles de son cahier, 20 Oct. 1576, AD Isère, 4E 245/62, f 1. The *baillis* of the Viennois had assembled a preliminary meeting for 11 Oct. at Vienne to discuss the grievances to be presented; then on 14 Oct. the clergy, nobles, and third-estate representatives for the Viennois had drafted their cahiers. See Cavard, *La Réforme et les Guerres de Religion à Vienne*, 200.

53 Announcement by Annet de Maugiron de Leyssins of the convocation of the Estates at Blois and of an assembly to prepare for the Estates at St Marcellin on 10 Oct., St Marcellin, 27 Sept. 1576, AC Tain, AA 2

54 Agreement concluded 28 Oct. 1576, Dussert, 'Catherine de Médicis et les Etats,' 133–4

55 Cavard, *La Réforme et Les Guerres de Religion à Vienne*, 201

56 Van Doren Papers, Cahier des plaintes et doléances du tiers estat de Dauphiné, Blois, 24 Nov. 1576 and Mar. 1577, AD Drôme, C 1023

57 In the absence of minutes of the 1578 Estates meeting, one has to depend on the summary in Fauché-Prunelle, 'Procès-verbal des Etats de 4 juillet 1578,' 557–61.

58 Van Doren Papers, description of procedures in Supplie au Duc de Mayenne des villages du pays contre les villes, Dec. 1581, AD Isère, 4E 245/1 (Cremieu AA)

59 In 1550, because of the king's intervention, the Estates had accorded a *commis* to the villages for a one-year trial period, but in 1551 the post was not renewed.

60 Dussert, 'Catherine de Médicis et les Etats,' 127–8

61 Le Roy Ladurie, *Carnival*, 79–80

62 Piémond, *Mémoires*, 64
63 Van Doren Papers, Assemblée des six villes et seize villages, 10 Mar.
   1579, AD Drôme, c 1023/9
64 This is evident from a cahier submitted from the town of Cremieu; see
   Plaintes et doléances du tiers estat de Cremieu, 1579, in Délachenal,
   Une petite ville de Dauphiné, Histoire de Cremieu, 481–2.
65 For further information on the 1579 Estates, see Dussert, 'Catherine de
   Médicis et les Etats,' 128; Cavard, *La Réforme et les Guerres de Religion
   à Vienne*, 216–19; and Brun-Durand, ed., in Piémond, *Mémoires*, 72–3, n
   1.
66 Dussert, 'Catherine de Médicis et les Etats,' reproduces the Doléances du
   tiers estat, Apr. 1579, 166–75.
67 The information on discussions at the Estates is available from summaries
   in Le Livre du roy in AC Briancon; see Dussert, ibid., 141, who bases
   his information on Fauché-Prunelle, 'Le Livre du roy,' 562–3.
68 Gutton, *Villages du Lyonnais sous la monarchie (xvr–xvir siècles)*, 99–100,
   and *La Sociabilité villageoise sous l'ancien régime*, 123–54; St-Jacob, *Documents
   relatifs à la communauté villageoise en Bourgogne du milieu du xvir siècle à
   la Révolution*
69 These *communautés d'habitants* were composed of delegates from the
   twenty-two *vigneries* or *bailliages*, and in each of these districts one town
   held a predominant position. During the sixteenth century the *procureur
   du pays* generally used the consuls of those towns to communicate with
   the villages. In the reorganization of the Estates following the Wars
   of Religion, it was left to the principal towns to convene the assembly of
   the *vignerie* to select delegates to the Estates. If at least three villages
   did not reply to the convocation, the town consuls could designate the
   delegates. See Busquet, *Histoire des institutions de la Provence de 1482
   à 1790*, 260–2.
70 Guérin, 'Un soulèvement populaire à Romans à la fin du xvie siècle,' 58
71 Ibid., 44–6
72 On the visit of Catherine to Dauphiné, see Dussert, 'Catherine de Médicis
   et les Etats du Dauphiné,' 143–4.
73 Catherine to the king, Agen, 19 Mar. 1579, in Romans, *Documents*, doc.
   181, 311–12
74 On the bishop of Valence, see Catherine to the king, 18 July 1579,
   Romans, *Documents*, doc. 188, 330–2. Following Catherine's visit the
   bishop cracked down on the rebels, and official satisfaction with his
   measures is evident in Fustier to the king, 5 Apr. 1580, Romans, *Documents*, doc. 230, 404–7. On Romans, see Judge Guérin, 'Un soulèvement

populaire à Romans à la fin du XVIᵉ siècle,' 60. The effects of Catherine's remarks in Romans have been treated in Le Roy Ladurie, *Carnival*, 150–2.

75 Dussert, 'Catherine de Médicis et les Etats du Dauphiné,' 151–2. It is true that some members of the third estate were not pleased that Catherine had been sent as judge; there was even a movement to appeal over her head directly to the king, a movement of which Catherine was well aware. See Catherine to the king, Grenoble, 5 Aug. 1579, Romans, Documents, doc. 195, 342.

76 Chomel, 'Guerres de Religion et "Remuements des peuples": la fin des libertés provinciales,' in Bligny, ed., *Histoire du Dauphiné*, 228–9

77 Consuls of Sauzet to consuls of Donzière, 20 Oct. 1578; see Van Doren, 'Revolt and Reaction,' 76.

78 Le Roy Ladurie, *Carnival*, 87; and Lacroix, *L'Arrondissement de Montélimar*, VI, 174

79 Guérin, 'Un soulèvement populaire,' 40; and Le Roy Ladurie, *Carnival*, 97

80 Cavard, *La Réforme*, 215–16

81 Baron de Coston, *Histoire de Montélimar et des principales familles qui ont habité cette ville*, II, 394

82 Le Roy Ladurie, *Carnival*, 117–25

83 Van Doren, 'Revolt and Reaction,' 75

84 These goals were never listed clearly in any one document; they can be pieced together from letters: Lyonne, treasurer of the Estates to d'Hautefort, president of the parlement, Grenoble, 3 Mar. 1579, Romans, *Documents*, doc. 178, 304–7; Catherine to the king, Agen, 19 Mar. 1579, ibid., doc. 181, 311–12; Guérin, 'Un soulèvement populaire,' 42; Le Roy Ladurie, *Carnival*, 84.

85 Le Roy Ladurie, *Carnival*, 82–3

86 Van Doren, 'Revolt and Reaction,' 85–7

87 Le Roy Ladurie, *Carnival*, 21–2

88 Van Doren, 'Revolt and Reaction,' 86–7

89 Guérin, 'Un soulèvement populaire,' 45

90 Consuls of Vienne to Lieutenant-Governor Maugiron, 17 Mar. 1579, Romans, *Documents*, doc. 180, 309–10

91 Cavard, *La Réforme*, 220

92 Le Roy Ladurie, *Carnival*, 132–7

93 Guérin, 'Un soulèvement populaire,' 60–2. See also Le Roy Ladurie, who corrects numerous aspects of the Guérin text concerning the repression carried out by the judge and his 'gens de bien,' *Carnival*, 198–276.

94 Consuls and *commis* of the third estate of Dauphiné present at Grenoble to consuls of Romans, 12 May 1579, Romans, *Documents*, doc. 185, 332
95 Catherine to the king, Grenoble, 5 Aug. 1579, Romans, *Documents*, doc. 195, 341–4
96 Van Doren, 'Revolt and Reaction'
97 Le Roy Ladurie, *Carnival*, 175–227
98 Van Doren Papers, 'Demande des consuls de St-Auban faite aux consuls, mandements et habitants de St-Euphémie, 17 Jan. 1579, AD Drôme, E 2944/35
99 Cavard, *La Réforme*, 260–2
100 Van Doren Papers, Supplie de Piégros au Duc de Mayenne, 28 Aug. 1581, AD Drôme, E 4027/29
101 Ibid., Supplie au Duc de Mayenne des villages du pays contre les villes, Dec. 1581, AD Isère, 4 E 245/1 (Cremieu AA)
102 Ibid., Ordre de Mayenne de nommer négociateurs, 13 Dec. 1581, AD Isère, 4 E 245/1 (Cremieu AA)
103 Ibid., Décision des villes et liste des négociateurs, 14 Dec. 1581, AD Isère, 4 E 245/1 (Cremieu AA)
104 Ibid., Rôle des tailles de 1582, Grenoble, July 1582, AM Grenoble, CC 11, f 2
105 Ibid., Abrégé des délibérations des Etats, 12 Jan. 1583, AD Isère, 4 E 245/1 (Cremieu AA), f 2
106 Ibid., Articles des accords et conventions de l'Assemblée de Romans, 24 Oct. 1583, 2 copies; AD Drôme, E 3744/30, and AD Isère, J 524/1, no 1
107 Richet, 'Autour des origines idéologiques lointaines de la Révolution française: élites et despotisme,' 1–23; Mandrou, *Introduction à la France moderne*, 141–63; and Goubert, *L'Ancien Régime*, I, *La Société*, 199–203, 217–35

CHAPTER 3: FROM RURAL TO URBAN CONTESTATION

1 AC Vienne, Third-Estate Cahiers, St-Paul-Trois-Châteaux and Gigors, CC 42; Châteauneuf-de-Mazenc and Livron, CC 43
2 These rates can be calculated from the debts listed in the third-estate cahiers, AC Vienne, cahiers of Rac, 1599, Vaunaveys, 1599, CC 43, and Gigors, 1599, CC 42.
3 Piémond, *Mémoires*. This graph is drawn up from the data on weather conditions noted annually by Piémond for each month of the growing season. On the larger question of the relation between weather and economic conjuncture, see Le Roy Ladurie, *Les Paysans de Languedoc*, I,

chaps. 1, 2; 'Le Climat des xɪᵉ et xvɪᵉ siècles: séries comparées,' *Annales* 20 (1965): 903, 921. Also see the theses that concentrate upon the role of population growth and food consumption in the sixteenth-century crisis: Abel, *Crises agraires en Europe, xɪɪɪᵉ–xxᵉsiècle*, 159–205; and Slicker Van Bath, *The Agrarian History of Western Europe*, 195–206.

4 Deliberations, Romans consulate, 25 Feb. 1587, 22 Oct. 1590, AM Romans, BB 17, cited in Lacroix, *Inventaire sommaire des archives départementales*, vi, 331–2. J. Chevalier, *Essai historique sur l'Eglise et la ville de Die*, iii, 236–7. For Grenoble, see Morel, 'Le Vagabondage et la Mendicité au xvɪᵉ siècle,' 104–22; and Bonarel, 'La Population de Grenoble – Etude socio-démographique,' chap. 2. Hickey, 'Changing Expressions of Charity in Early Modern France,' 12–22

4 Le Roy Ladurie, *Carnival*, 2–3. A similar influx of peasants from Dauphiné was noted by Richard Gascon, who described population increases in the city of Lyon between 1529 and 1563; see 'Immigration et croissance au xvɪᵉ siècle: l'exemple de Lyon,' 988–1001.

5 Paris Registers, Church of St-Sauveur, Crest, 1587, AC Crest, GG 1

7 Piémond, *Mémoires*, 183

8 Ibid., 228

9 Ibid., 262

10 Jacquart, 'Immobilisme et catastrophes, 1560–1660,' in Duby and Wallon, *Histoire de la France rurale*, ii, 282–300, and 'Réflexions sur la communauté d'habitants,' 1–25. On the rural communities of Ile-de-France, see Jacquart, *La Crise rurale en Ile-de-France, 1550–1670*, 555–81. The villages of Burgundy have been treated by St-Jacob in 'Mutations économiques et sociales dans les campagnes bourguignonnes à la fin du xvɪᵉ siècle,' 34–49. For south-western France, see Bercé, *Histoire des croquants*, i, 186–205.

11 U. Chevalier, 'Annales de la ville de Romans pendant les Guerres de Religion de 1549 à 1599,' 170–5

12 See Graph 2.

13 Consuls to Maugiron, for permission to assemble cities and towns, 8 Sept. 1590, AC Vienne, AA 7/1, and Cahier présenté aux nobles par les villages de la province, Voiron, 1590, AC Vienne, AA7/2. The context of this meeting is provided in Chorier, *Histoire de Dauphiné*, 741–2.

14 Cahier présenté aux nobles par les villages de la province, Voiron, 1590, AA 7/2, reproduces the St-Marcellin demands, pp 8–22.

15 Cahier soumis par les députés des villes et villages à Monsieur St-André, Voiron, 1590, AC Vienne, AA 7/3

16 Réponse de la noblesse du Dauphiné au cahier des députés des villes et villages, Voiron, 21 Nov. 1590, AC Vienne, AA 7/4

17 Deliberations of the Estates, Grenoble, 18–28 May 1591, AC Vienne, AA 7/ 5, p 21

18 Lacroix, 'Claude Brosse et les Tailles,' 54–5, argues that *avocats* Rambaud, Vincent, Delagrange, Expilly, Audeyer, and Chevrières became involved in the case in 1591; this incorrect information was based on a remark by Chorier, *Estat politique de la province de Dauphiné*, III, 670.

19 Deliberations of the Estates, Grenoble, 18–28 May 1591, AC Vienne, AA 7/ 6, pp 43–4

20 Ibid., 47

21 Ibid.

22 Ibid., 44. The third estate cited this 1591 agreement in its later arguments before the king's council; see Pièces produites devant Jacques Talon, conseilleur du roi, 1633, AC Vienne, CC 39.

23 Chorier, *Estat politique*, III, 670

24 Van Doren Papers, Deliberations of the Estates, Grenoble, 25 Jan. 12 Feb. 1592, AM Grenoble, R 7568, f 153

25 Piémond, *Mémoires*, mentions of Estates meetings, Grenoble; 2 July 1594 (sic), 329; St-Marcellin, 22 Nov. 1594, 335, and Grenoble, 15 Jan. 1595, 339. Piémond seems to have erred in dating the 2 July 1594 meeting; see Deliberations of the Estates, Grenoble, 5 Aug. 1594, BMG, R 7568, ff 171–216.

26 Van Doren, 'Civil War Taxation,' Table 2, pp 50–2

27 Deliberations, Valence consulate, 17 June 1592–8, Nov. 1595, AC Valence, BB12

28 The last-minute attempts of the nobles to convince the third estate to withdraw its appeal to the king are described in Cavard, *La Réforme*, 393–4.

29 Piémond, *Mémoires*, 353

30 Ibid., 356; Piémond reproduced Marchier's speech, pp 354–66.

31 Dufos, *Défense de la noblesse de Dauphiné*, 24–5; and Piémond, *Mémoires*, 366–7. For third-estate reactions, see Delagrange, 'Réplique du tiers estat du Dauphiné à la défense de la noblesse du même pays,' in *Réponses et salutations des pièces produites par les gens du tiers estat*.

32 Piémond, *Mémoires*, 366

33 Ibid., 367–8. Van Doren Papers, Arrêt du Conseil d'estat pour le paiement des tailles (Lyon 1595), Harvard Law School

34 Dussert, 'Les Etats ... de la Guerre de Cent Ans,' 154–5, 301 n 3.

35 Deliberations, Grenoble consulate, 10 Oct. 1592, AM Grenoble, BB 44; summarized in Prudhomme, *Inventaire sommaire des archives communales, ville de Grenoble*, I, 90

36 Dussert, 'Les Etats ... de la Guerre de Cent Ans,' 250 n 3
37 Van Doren Papers, Villes closes de ce pays du Dauphiné, nd (c 16), AC Vienne, cc 44. L. Scott Van Doren is currently preparing a study of the walled towns of Dauphiné.
38 Lists of participants are not available for most of the meetings of the assembly, but the representation from the walled towns was particularly evident at the 1602 assembly at Crest, where over half of the eighty delegates were from outside the ten cities and the majority were from walled towns. See summary of the Assembly, Crest, 14 July 1602, AD Drôme, c 1024/13. Even at the more selective meeting at St-Marcellin in 1597, five of the seventeen delegates were from walled towns and among them was Claude Delagrange, one of the principal defenders of the third-estate cause; summary of the assembly, St-Marcellin, 11 Oct. 1597, AD Drôme, c 1024/9.
39 Cavard, La Réforme, 280–1
40 Ibid., 255
41 Summary of the Estates meeting, Grenoble, 18–28 May 1591, AC Vienne, AA 7/6, 53
42 Summary of the Estates meeting, Grenoble, 5 May 1599, AC Vienne, AA 7/16, p 12; Deliberations, Romans Consulate, 17 Dec. 1601, AC Romans, BB 21; and summary of the Assemblée des consuls et syndics des villes et villages, Crest, 15 July 1602, AD Drôme, c 1024, f 1
43 Lacroix, 'Claude Brosse et les Tailles,' 32: 144
44 Arrêt concernant la suspension des sentences données contre M Achilles du Faure, Paris, 13 July 1604, AN, E 6ᵇ, ff 58–9
45 Notaire Pierre Blanc, Valence, 1587, rent of a house with shop to Jean Sepoule, AD Drôme, 2E 319, f 24; and 1589 disengagement of Faure as tutor for heirs of Claude Guilheton, ibid., 2E 2319, f 130. Notaire Jean Mounier, Valence, 1608, request for payment due from Françoise de Rey, widow of noble Pierre de Gillibert, for whom Faure had procured numerous documents necessitating trips to Grenoble, Romans, and other cities, AD Drôme, 2E 2020, f 9
46 Deliberations, Valence consulate, 26 Mar. 1593, 26 Oct. 1594, AC Valence, BB 12
47 Valeur des pinatelles suivant le règlement de la cour Grenoble, 13 Mar. 1593, BM Grenoble, 3084
48 Lettres patentes de S.M. concernant les dettes contractées au temps de l'affaiblissement des monnaies, 5 Dec. 1606, BM Grenoble, o 3084
49 Taille royale, Valence, 1588, AC Valence, CC 13, f 23
50 Taille royale, Valence, 1606, AC Valence, CC 13, f 4

51 Taille royale, Valence, 1615, AC Valence, CC 13, f 23
52 Paris register, Church of St-Jean, Valence, 28 Aug. 1599, Alex Sepolla, femme de Sieur Faure, AC Valence, GG 1. See also taille royale, Valence, 1588, AC Valence, CC 13, f 2.
53 Cavard, *La Réforme*, 359, 376
54 Summary of the Estates meeting, St-Marcellin, 5 Dec. 1595, AC Vienne, AA 7/9, p 24
55 Ibid., 27–8; the text of Charbotel's reply is printed in Cavard, *La Réforme*, 393–4.
56 Cavard, La Réforme, 400
57 Summary of Assemblée des députés des villes et autres lieux, St-Marcellin, 11 Oct. 1597, AD Drôme, C 1024/9; summary of the Assemblée des consuls et syndics des villes et villages, Crest, 15 July 1602, AD Drôme, C 1024, f 1
58 Lacroix, 'Claude Brosse et les Tailles,' 32: 144
59 Parisot, 'Essai sur les procureurs au parlement de Bourgogne,' 64–5. Pierre de l'Etoile commented on the death of *procureur* Dardes, 'It was said that he was an honest man. I would like to believe it, but since he was a *procureur*, I am sceptical'; *Journal de Henri III, de Henri IV et de Louis XIII*, XLIX, 199.
60 Balsan, *Valence au grand siècle*, 106–13
61 Taille royale, Grenoble, 1591, AM Grenoble, CC 15
62 Ibid., 1610, AM Grenoble, CC 25
63 Parish Register, parishes of St-Hughes and St-Jean, Grenoble, 1 Mar. 1598, AM Grenoble, GG 11
64 Taille royale, Grenoble, 1613, AM Grenoble, CC 28; and 1614, AM Grenoble, CC 29
65 Financial receipts, 4 Oct. 1597, AM Grenoble, CC 721, in Prudhomme, *Inventaire sommaire des archives communales, ville de Grenoble*, II, 70
66 Financial account of Claude Roux, treasurer, 1599–1600, Valence, AD Drôme, CC 38
67 Lacroix, 'Claude Brosse et les Tailles,' 32: 155; summary of the Estates meeting, Grenoble, 1594, BM Grenoble, R7568; and summary of the Estates meeting, St-Marcellin, 1595, AM Vienne, AA 9/7
68 Rochas, 'Antoine Rambaud,' in *Biographie du Dauphiné*, I, 336–7; and Lacroix, 'Claude Brosse et les Tailles,' 32: 155. Députés de la noblesse to Bellièvre, Grenoble, 8 May 1606, BN mss fr 15.899, f 555
69 Lacroix, 'Claude Brosse et les Tailles, 32: 155
70 Brun-Durand, 'Antoine Rambaud,' in *Dictionnaire biographique et biblio-iconographique de la Drôme*, II, 292–4

71 Rambaud et M de Villeneuve, médecin du roi, Paris, 1 Mar. 1598, in
   Rambaud, *Plaidoyé pour le tiers estat du Dauphiné*, 121, BM Grenoble, 02988
72 Ibid.
73 Rochas, 'Antoine Rambaud,' 337; and Brun-Durand, 'Antoine Rambaud,'
   293
74 Rambaud, *Plaidoyé pour le tiers estat du Dauphiné*, 68
75 Expilly, 'Plaidoyé trente-et-un ou Très-humbles remonstrances au roi ...
   sur le procès intenté par le tiers estat contre la noblesse dudit pays,'
   in *Plaidoyez de M. Claude Expilly*, 383, AD Drôme, Ancienne Bibliothèque
   3213; and Audeyer, *Très-humbles remonstrances en forme d'avertissement au roi
   par les officiers de la cour du parlement de Dauphiné sur le procès intenté par
   le tiers estat*, 57–61, BM Grenoble, Bd 416
76 Rambaud, *Second plaidoyé pour le tiers estat du Dauphiné* ff 75–6; Rambaud
   to Alian, Paris, 1 Mar. 1598, in *Plaidoyé pour le tiers estat*, app., 122–5;
   and Rambaud to Vincent, Paris, 1 Mar. 1598, 'Lettre servant d'apologie
   ou défense pour le premier plaidoyé du tiers estat du Dauphiné,' in
   Plaidoyé pour le tiers estat, app., separate pagination, 1–18
77 Laurens, *Le procès des tailles, (1537–1639), Claude Brosse – Antoine Rambaud*,
   30
78 Lacroix, 'Claude Brosse et les Tailles,' 32: 155, 158
79 Le Roy Ladurie, *Carnival*, chap. 14
80 This frequent assumption is evident in most treatments of the *taille*
   question, which tend to speak of the exploited 'third estate' or the 'people.' See Lacroix, 'Claude Brosse et les Tailles,' 31: 189–90, 289–90;
   Dussert, 'Les Etats de Dauphiné de la Guerre de Cent Ans,' 274–6. Even
   Le Roy Ladurie, in *The Carnival*, 5–13, analyses urban social structures
   in terms of the property controlled by the elite, without mentioning the
   taxes paid on that property. The extension of this argument is the
   Marxist interpretation of Porchnev, *Les Soulèvements populaires en France
   de 1623–1648*, 263–78.
81 The parlement in 1558 was composed of 2 presidents, 20 councillors, 8
   clerks, and 4 *huissiers*, but by 1599 there were 7 presidents, 33 councillors,
   and 2 *avocats-généraux* in addition to the clerks and *huissiers* for whom I
   do not have figures. For 1558 see Chomel, 'Pouvoir royal et croissance
   urbaine,' *Histoire de Grenoble*, 103. The statistics for 1599 are calculated
   from Vindry, *Les Parlementaires français au XVIᵉ siècle*, 1, 59–99.
82 This dominance of the social elite by the legal profession is characteristic
   of towns that possessed a parliament; in Toulouse, where the members
   of the parlement and the royal and municipal officials constituted only 15
   per cent of the population, 150 magistrates, as compared to 78 nobles

and 40 officials, paid more than 120 *livres* in the city assessments. The same context is evident in Aix-en-Provence: see Dolan-Leclerc, 'Renaissance: le premier siècle du régime français,' 113–16; and for Rouen, see Dewald, *The Formation of a Provincial Nobility*.

83 Taille royale et négociable, Grenoble, 1591, AM Grenoble, CC 15

84 Taille royale, Valence, 1588 AC Valence, CC 13.

85 Taille royale, Romans, 1578, AC Romans, CC 92. After 1578 *taille* rolls in Romans were constituted by districts, as in Grenoble. Unfortunately they do not list a sufficient number of occupations to be analysed in the manner of the Grenoble roll.

86 Le Roy Ladurie, *Carnival*, chap. 14

87 On the basis of data concerning the economic mobility of the third-estate elite I have previously argued that their advancement was not hindered by their *taille* status. When one examines the even more rapid advancement of those who benefited from ennoblements, however, it appears that the *taille* status was more important than I previously thought. I will be expanding upon this point in the next two chapters. See Hickey, 'Une Remise en question: procès des tailles et blocage social,' 25–49.

88 Similar confrontations between merchants and officials or legal groups occurred in Paris; see Brodes, *L'Administration provinciale et municipale en France au XVIIe siècle*, 213; see also Salmon, who concentrated upon Paris during the period of the Catholic League, *Society in Crisis: France in the Sixteenth Century*, 247–8.

89 Cavard, *La Réforme*, 8–10. It is true that in their selections the merchants did maintain a certain balance among the social groups represented on the consulate, and towards the end of the sixteenth century the major controversy was the extent to which the representation of the legal professions should be increased.

90 Règlement de 1447. See introduction to *Fastes consulaires et municipaux de la ville de Grenoble depuis l'année 1244* (Grenoble nd), 4; see also Chorier, *Estat politique*, III, 636–9.

91 Deliberations, Grenoble consulate, 1591–7; see elections between 15 and 31 Dec. of each year, AM Grenoble, BB 43–BB 59.

92 Balsan, *Valence au Grand Siècle*, 28

93 Deliberations, Valence consulate, 1595–1601; see elections on 26 Apr. of each year, AC Valence, BB 13. See also election regulations for 1601, BB 13, ff 336–7.

94 Deliberations, St-Marcellin consulate, 1588–1603; see elections held on 24 June each year, AC St-Marcellin, BB 1. Tailles royales, St-Marcellin, 1592 and 1599, AC St-Marcellin, FF 15. Lacroix, *St-Marcellin, Excursions*

dans la vallée de l'Isère, 72. Bonnin emphasizes that fiscal requirements for participation at meetings of the community of inhabitants were tightened up in the course of the seventeenth century; see Bonnin, 'La Terre et les paysans en Dauphiné au XVIIᵉ siècle,' I 326–7.

95 Hickey, 'Une Remise en question,' 41–4, 46–9; Masson-Fauchier, 'L'Anoblissement en Dauphiné au XVIIᵉ siècle (1598–1668)'

96 These accusations were repeated frequently in the memoirs and tracts written by the third-estate delegates in the 1590s; see Rambaud, *Plaidoyé pour le tiers estat*, 90–2, and *Second plaidoyé*, ff 12, 76. See also Vincent, *Discours en forme de plaidoyé pour le tiers estat de Dauphiné*, ff 37–8, BM Grenoble, o 2987.

97 Taille royale et négociable, Grenoble, 1591, AM Grenoble, CC 15/395. Nobles were listed frequently in the rolls without being assessed. Another older source of noble residence patterns can be seen in the Comptes de la santé drawn up in 1567 after the plague epidemic; see AM Grenoble, CC 1132.

98 Ibid.

99 Taille royale, Romans, 1595, CC 95; and Le Roy Ladurie, *Carnival*, 229–35

100 Taille royale, Valence, 1588, CC 13

101 Pillorget, *Mouvements insurrectionnels en Provence*, 157–61

102 Deliberations, Grenoble consulate, 5, 12, 17, and 30 Jan. 1592, AM Grenoble, BB 44, ff 7, 16, 23, 29

103 Chorier, *Histoire de Dauphiné*, II 751

104 Procès de Claude Frère, 17 Jan. – 7 Mar. 1592, AC Valence, FF 22

105 Deliberations, Valence consulate, 30 Oct. 1592, AC Valence, BB 12

106 Consuls of Montélimar to consuls of Nyons, 1 Nov. 1594, AC Nyons, CC 31, in Lacroix, *L'Arrondissement de Montélimar*, VI, 197–8

107 Deliberations, St-Marcellin, 24 June 1596, AC St-Marcellin, BB 1, ff 180–4

108 Ibid., 3 July 1596, AC St-Marcellin, BB 1, f 185

109 Ibid., 7 July 1596, AC St-Marcellin, BB 1, f 185

110 On disturbances elsewhere, see Bercé, *Histoire des croquants*, I, 257–93; and Pillorget, *Mouvements insurrectionnels en Provence entre 1596 et 1715*, 224, 250, 274

CHAPTER 4: THE LAWYERS

1 Mandrou, *Magistrats et sorciers en France au XVIIᵉ siècle*, 121–37; Kelley, *Foundations of Modern Historical Scholarship, Law and History in the French*

Renaissance, 271–300; Huppert, *The Idea of Perfect History*, 72–87; Weill, *Les Théories sur le pouvoir royal en France pendant les Guerres de Religion*, 99–121; Church, *Constitutional Thought in Sixteenth-Century France*

2 Nadal, *Histoire de l'Université de Valence*, 37–44

3 Devert, 'Recherches sur la vie et l'oeuvre de Jean de Montluc, 1502–1579,' I, 24–31; II, 1, 300–11

4 Nadal, *Histoire de l'Université de Valence*, 45–51, 59–73; 'Montluc,' in Brun-Durand, *Dictionnaire biographique ... de la Drôme*, II, 166–9; Berriat-St-Prix, *Histoire du droit romain suivi de l'histoire de Cujas*, 591–7

5 Mesnard, 'La place de Cujas dans la querelle de l'humanisme juridique,' 531–2

6 Berriat-St-Prix, *Histoire du droit romain*, 565–74; Registre des diplômes accordés par l'Université de Valence, 1562–75, AD Drôme, D 17

7 Mesnard, 'La place de Cujas,' 531–2

8 Summary of the Estates meeting, St-Marcellin, 5–19 Dec. 1595, AC Vienne, AA 7/9, pp 27–9

9 Cavard, *La Réforme*, 394

10 The questions asked were noted in the introduction to each reply; see replies of Simon Marion, Antoine Arnauld, Bouthillier, and Robert, Paris, 9 May 1596, AD Drôme, C 1024/22; and René Chopin, Etienne Pasquier, DuLaurens, Chauvelin, Thoard, and Buisson, Paris, 26 May 1596, AD Drôme, C 1024/23. DuLaurens remained one of the principal legal councillors for the third estate up to the 1602 judgment.

11 Chopin, Pasquier, et al., ibid.

12 Ibid., 4

13 Ibid., 5

14 Ibid., 7

15 Delagrange, *La Juste Plainte et remonstrance faite au roi et à nosseigneurs de son Conseil d'estat par le pauvre peuple de Dauphiné*, BM Grenoble, O 2961; Rambaud, *Plaidoyé pour le tiers estat*, BM Grenoble, O 2988; Vincent, *Discours en forme de plaidoyé pour le tiers estat de Dauphiné*, BM Grenoble, O 2987

16 Dufos, *Défense de la noblesse de Dauphiné*, BM Grenoble, Bd 555

17 Cavard, *La Réforme*, 400

18 Ibid.

19 Summary of Assembly of Deputies from towns and other localities, St-Marcellin, 11–15 Oct. 1597, AD Drôme, C 1024/9, 11

20 Ibid., 4

21 Ibid., 6

22 Ibid., 6

23 Delagrange, *Stylus curiae majoris Viennesii et Valentinesii* (Lyon 1581); and Lacroix, 'Claude Brosse et les Tailles,' 32: 157

24 The arguments developed in his *Juste Plainte* are supported by examples that suggest that Delagrange had consulted numerous notables, town magistrates, and historical and juridical texts. The successive tracts and pleas of Rambaud and Vincent expanded upon these arguments concerning exemptions from the *taille*, the military service of the nobles, and the exaggerated number of exemptions.

25 Piémond notes that he headed the commission named by D'Ornano in 1592 to oversee the financial management of St-Antoine Abbey: *Mémoires*, 307

26 Lacroix, 'Claude Brosse et les Tailles,' 32: 158

27 Rôle des tailles, St-Marcellin, 1591, AC St-Marcellin, FF 15

28 Delagrange expressed these fears to the St-Marcellin assembly; see Summary of Assembly of Deputies from towns and other localities, St-Marcellin, 11–15 Oct. 1597, AD Drôme, C 1024/9, p 4

29 Rôle des tailles, St-Marcellin, 1592, AC St-Marcellin, FF 15

30 Rôle de tailles, St-Marcellin, 1593, ibid.

31 Brun-Durand, 'Jean Vincent,' in *Dictionnaire biographique ... de la Drôme*, II, 407

32 Ibid., 407–8

33 Chomel, 'Guerres de Religion et "Remuements des peuples," ' in Bligny, ed., *Histoire du Dauphiné*, 245

34 Deliberations, Valence Consulate, 17 Jan. and 6 Mar. 1592, AC Valence, BB 12, f 32

35 *Avertissement pour le tiers estat de Dauphiné pour plus ample instruction du procès* (Lyon 1598), BM Grenoble, E 29175

36 Trebillod, 'Etude de registre de l'assemblée de la noblesse en Dauphiné entre 1602 et 1622,' 8

37 Ibid., 3; and Piémond, *Mémoires*, 349

38 Registre des assemblées de la noblesse, 28 May 1602–13 July 1622, AD Isère, IJ 175

39 Ibid.

40 It is specifically mentioned that the council existed in 1597; see *Secondes Escritures pour l'estat des nobles du Dauphiné*, 49, BM Grenoble, t 1411.

41 Delagrange, 'Response du tiers estat et commun peuple aux escritures du second estat,' in *Juste Plainte*, p 1

42 Piémond, *Mémoires*, 348–9

43 Rivoire de la Batie, *Armorial de Dauphiné*, 15–16

44 Parish registers of St-Hugues and St-Jean Church, 10 July 1578, AM
   Grenoble, GG 2

45 Aquin, *Le Plaidé des docteurs et avocats consistoriaux du parlement de Dauphiné*,
   BM Grenoble, T 1414

46 Deliberations, Council of the Nobility, Grenoble, 18 Aug. 1602, Registre
   des assemblées de la noblesse, AD Isère, IJ 175, f xlix

47 Piémond, *Mémoires*, 366–7

48 Basset, president of the provincial Estates, to consuls of Vienne, 7 May
   1599, on the positions of the third estates; ibid., 8 May 1599, on the
   positions of the privileged orders; ibid., 8 May 1599, containing resolutions passed in the Estates noting the impossibility of reaching an agreement, AC Vienne, AA 7/17

49 Antoine Rambaud to Alian, avocat consistorial, Paris, 1 Mar. 1598,
   Rambaud, *Plaidoyé pour le tiers estat*, app., 124. Antoine Rambaud to Vincent, Paris, 1 Mar. 1598, 'Lettre servant d'apologie ou défense du premier plaidoyé du tiers estat de Dauphiné,' in *Plaidoyé pour le tiers estat*,
   app., 15

50 Catilhon, La Vie de Messire Expilly, chevalier, conseiller du roi en son
   conseil d'estat et président au parlement de Grenoble, 15; Rivoire de la
   Batie, *Armorial*, 210

51 Allard, 'Rôle des anoblis dans le Dauphiné depuis 1582 et la valeur de
   leurs biens,' BM Grenoble, R 80, t 9, f 776. I have found neither letters of
   ennoblement nor any other document that could further corroborate
   this point.

52 The numerous biographies of Expilly's activities all refer back to Boniel
   de Catilhon for details; see Olivier, 'Expilly,' 65–94; and Martin, *Histoire et
   vie de Claude Expilly*.

53 Expilly, *Plaidoyez de M. Claude Expilly*, plaidoyé 31, pp 359–403. Edmond
   Maignien notes that this plaidoyé, mistakenly dated 1601 in the edition
   above, had been dated 1600 in its first edition; see Maignien, *Petite revue
   des bibliophiles dauphinois*, IV (1913–15): 64–71. This Maignien reference
   was found in the Van Doren Papers.

54 Boniel de Catilhon, *La Vie de M. Expilly*, 52

55 Baptism of Claude, son of noble François de la Porte and of Marguerite
   Audeyer, 14 Aug. 1605, parish register of St-Hugues and St-Jean Church,
   AM Grenoble, GG 17; legal case between noble Jean Audeyer, seigneur
   of Montbel, and the consuls of Grenoble, 1644, AM Grenoble, FF 105

56 Deliberations, Grenoble consulate, 21 Dec. 1625, AM Grenoble, BB 92

57 'Jean de la Croix,' in Brun-Durand, *Dictionnaire Biographique ... de la Drôme*,
   II, 43–4

58 Trebillod, 'Etude du régistre de l'assemblée de la noblesse,' 6
59 Allard, *Nobiliaire du Dauphiné*, BM Grenoble, V 4153
60 Rabot, *La Maison des Rabot*
61 See Registers, 1590–1610, in St-Alphonse Olive Papers, AD Isère, 32 J, 4–12
62 Chomel, 'Pouvoir royal et croissance urbaine,' in *Histoire de Grenoble*, 106–7
63 Chorier, *Etat politique*, III, 670
64 Delagrange, *La Juste Plainte et remonstrance*, ii–iv
65 Ibid., v–ix
66 Ibid., xii–xvi
67 Ibid., xvi–xvii
68 Ibid., xxiii, xxxvi. This point is supported by Van Doren, who showed that the *ban* and *arrière ban* were poorly adapted to the military needs of the province during the Wars of Religion; see 'War, Taxes and Social Protest,' 103–7.
69 Ibid., xxvii–xxix
70 Vincent, *Discours en forme de plaidoyé pour le tiers estat de Dauphiné*, ff 20–4
71 Rambaud, *Plaidoyé pour le tiers estat de Dauphiné*, 41–2
72 Ibid., 65–9, 72–7, 86–98
73 Vincent, *Discours*, f 27
74 Ibid., f 34
75 Ibid., ff 38–9
76 Anonymous, *La Vérité des justes défenses de la noblesse du Dauphiné aux insultes, demandes, plaintes et doléances du tiers ordre*, BM Grenoble T 1412; and Expilly, *Plaidoyez*, plaidoyé 31
77 Expilly, *Plaidoyez*, 361; and *La Vérité*, 8–9
78 Expilly, *Plaidoyez*, 387–8
79 Ibid., 361
80 Ibid., 373; and *La Vérité*, 10
81 Expilly, *Plaidoyez*, 386–91; and *La Vérité*, 45–7. Of course, neither side was accurate in its examination of the question concerning *tailles* as *réelle* or *personnelle*. The *feux* assessments combined considerations of the number of tax-paying heads of family with ponderation of the quantity and the quality of the landholdings in the community.
82 Expilly, *Plaidoyez*, 389
83 Ibid., 376
84 *La Vérité*, 12
85 Ibid., 4–5; and Expilly, *Plaidoyez*, 399
86 Expilly, *Plaidoyez*, 399. The nobles were not all that mistaken in their

evaluation of the third-estate elite; see Hickey, 'Une Remise en question,' 31–45

87 Expilly, *Plaidoyez*, 383–4; and *La Vérité*, 68–71
88 Expilly, *Plaidoyez*, 383
89 *La Vérité*, 5–6, 74
90 Ibid., 76–7
91 Anonymous, *Secondes escritures pour l'estat des nobles du Dauphiné contenant contradits contre la production et réponses aux invectives injurieuses du tiers état*, 56, BM Grenoble, T 1414
92 Delagrange, 'Réponses et salutations des pièces produites par les gens du tiers estat ... aux secondes escritures ainsi intitulées et prétendus contre-dits baillés par l'estat des nobles,' in *Réponses et salutations des pièces produites par les gens du tiers estat*, 53–4, BM Grenoble, R 4389
93 *Secondes escritures*, 23
94 This division in the ranks of the second estate explains the production of several independent pamphlets defending specifically the privileges and the exemptions of the nobles of the robe. See Audeyer, *Très-humbles remonstrances en forme d'avertissement au roy par les officiers de la cours de parlement de Dauphiné*, BM Grenoble, Bd 416; de la Croix, *Apurement des défenses du parlement de Grenoble*, BM Grenoble, R 4080; Aquin, *Le plaidé des docteurs et avocats consistoriaux* BM Grenoble, U 4399.
95 Boissat, *Remerciement au roy par les anoblis du Dauphiné*, 5, BM Grenoble, O 2614
96 Rambaud, *Second plaidoyé pour le tiers estat du Dauphiné*, 75–7, BM Grenoble, O 2989
97 Ibid., 80–1
98 Delagrange, *Réponses et salutations des pièces produites*, 98, 186
99 Ibid., 2–3
100 Delagrange, 'La response du tiers estat et commun peuple aux escritures du second estat,' in *Juste plainte*, xxvii
101 *Secondes écritures*, 84
102 Lesdiguières to Chancellor Bellièvre, Grenoble, 19 Sept. 1599, BN, mss fr 15.899, f 541
103 Arrêt du Conseil d'état, 21 Dec. 1632, portant que les sieurs des deux premiers ordres et officiers seroient signifiés pour venir défendre si bien leur semble à la dite requête, AM Vienne, CC 45. The involvement of Lesdiguières is also reflected in the fact that his secretary, Florent de Reinart, was sent to the royal court during the *taille* appeal and was accused of spreading rumours unfavourable to the third estate; see Cavard, *La Réforme*, 403–4.

104 Arrêt et règlement donné par le roi en son conseil entre les trois ordres de Dauphiné sur les tailles et impositions, 15 Apr. 1602, in Giroud, ed., *Recueil des édits, déclarations, lettres patentes et ordonnances du roi ... concernant en général et en particulier la province de Dauphiné*, 167–72

105 Delagrange, *Réponses et salutations des pièces produites*, 397

106 Lacroix, 'Claude Brosse et les Tailles,' 32: 159–60; Laurens, *Le Procès des tailles*, 41–2

107 Deliberations, Assembly of towns and villages, Crest, 15 July 1602, AD Drôme, C 1024/13

108 Rambaud, *Plaidoyé pour le tiers estat*, 93; Vincent, *Discours en forme de plaidoyé*, ff 34–5; Delagrange, *Réponses et salutations*, 2

109 Third estate cahiers, AC Vienne, CC 42, CC 43

110 Bonnin, 'La Terre et les Paysans en Dauphiné au XVIIᵉ siècle (1580–1730),' II, 460–8

111 Jacquart, *La Crise rurale en Ile-de-France*, 104–8

112 Ibid., 248–53

113 Le Roy Ladurie, 'Sur Montpellier et sa campagne aux XVIᵉ et XVIIᵉ siècles,' 223–30

114 Hickey, 'The Socio-Economic Context of the French Wars of Religion. A Case Study: The Valentinois-Diois,' 165

115 Delagrange, *Réponses et salutations*, 95–6; Rambaud, *Second plaidoyé*, ff 12–16; Vincent, *Discours*, ff 27–8

116 Expilly, *Plaidoyez*, plaidoyé 31, 376; *Secondes escritures*, 35

117 Goubert, *L'Ancien Régime*, I, *La Société* 170–7; Wood, *The Nobility of the Election of Bayeux, 1463–1666*, 29–42. In Dauphiné these acts are scattered through the registers of generalia of the parlement of Grenoble, AD Isère, B 2914–B 2919, B 2921–B 2922. There is a manuscript inventory for these *anoblissements*, prepared by G. Letonnelier. My list of ennoblements also takes account of the titles for which Christiane Masson-Fauchier found official documents, although the actual letters of ennoblement could not be located; see 'L'Anoblissement en Dauphiné au XVIIᵉ siècle (1598–1668).'

118 Expilly, *Plaidoyez*, 376

119 Wood, *The Nobility of the Election of Bayeux*, chap. 2

120 The question of how representative the leaders of the contestation movement were reflects the thesis of Boris Porchnev that the class identification of an individual makes it difficult for him to assume the leadership and the grievances of another class. Certainly the difficulties of this fusion were evident in the *taille* dispute. In one of his pamphlets

Rambaud noted that the towns were worse off than the villages (*Second plaidoyé*, f 35), a declaration that was patently false. The same division was evident within the nobility, where the old nobles seem to have been tempted to abandon the defence of the *anoblis*. In Dauphiné, however, the problem never became critical and both in 1579 and in the 1590s the leaders of the contestation were criticized rarely by their constituents. See Porchnev, *Les soulèvements populaires*, 578–81.

CHAPTER 5: TOWARDS ROYAL INTERVENTION

1 Buisseret, 'A Stage in the Development of the French Intendants,' 27–38; Barbiche, 'Les Commissaires députés pour le "régalement" des tailles en 1598–99,' 61; Major, 'Henri IV and Guyenne,' 363–83; Antoine, 'Le Régalement des tailles de 1623–1625,' 27–63; Bonney, *Political Change in France under Richelieu and Mazarin*, 29–39; Doucet, *Les Institutions de la France au XVIᵉ siècle*, I, 431–6; Mousnier, 'Etat et Commissaire, recherche sur la création des intendants des provinces, 1634–1648,' in *La Plume, la Faucille et le Marteau*, 179–99.
2 Doucet, *Les Institutions*, 433
3 Esmonin, 'Les Intendants du Dauphiné des origines à la Révolution,' in *Etudes sur la France des XVIIᵉ et XVIIIᵉ siècles*, 72–3
4 Lacroix, 'Claude Brosse et les Tailles,' 32: 241–2. A 1628 pamphlet defending Brosse against charges of embezzlement notes that he was elected in 1599; see A Monsieurs les Deputez des bailliages, Chastellains, consuls et notables, 1628, 11, BM Grenoble, O 3072.
5 Ibid., 239–40
6 Ibid., 239
7 See explanations of the functioning of this system in Factum pour Messire Louis de Clermont, seigneur de Rochebaudin ... contre les consuls, 1682, AD Drôme, E 491. The consuls argued that the system had originated during the sixteenth century.
8 Van Doren Papers, Arrêt et règlement par le roi en son conseil entre les trois ordres de Dauphiné, 15 Apr. 1602, in Giroud, *Recueil*, I, 172
9 Cahier présenté au roi par ceux du tiers estat de Dauphiné pour avoir interprétation de l'arrêt donnaae par sa majesté le 15 avril 1602; and Articles respondus à Fontainebleau, 28 avril 1603, BM Grenoble, O 3006
10 Van Doren Papers, summary of the principal resolutions of the provincial Estates, Grenoble, July 1603, AD Isère, 4 E 245/1 (Cremieu AA), f 3
11 Van Doren Papers, deliberations and conclusions of the provincial

Estates, Valence, Nov.–Dec. 1604, with continuation of the session in Feb. 1605 and modification of the conclusions, 2 May 1605, AD Isère, IC 4/20, ff 11–12

12 Van Doren Papers, Acte de sommation et protestation, 29 Oct. 1603, AD Drôme (Romans), E 3749/41

13 Deliberations, Council of the Nobility, 10 Jan. 1604, in Registre des assemblées de la noblesse, AD Isère, IJ 175, f 164

14 Arrêt donné par le roi en son Conseil d'estat au profit des communautés villageoises du Dauphiné,' 4, BM Grenoble, O 3015

15 Van Doren Papers, deliberations and conclusions of the provincial Estates, Valence, Nov.–Dec. 1604, with modifications of the conclusions, 2 May 1605, AD Isère, IC 4/20, ff 11–13

16 Report on the 1605 Estates to the Council of the Nobility, 8 Mar. 1605, f 189; and Requête du commis des villages présentée aux Etats, 7 Feb. 1605, in Registre des délibérations de la noblesse, 1605–1658, document partly restored by Archives Nationales, AD Isère, uncatalogued register

17 The presence of Brosse at the hearings of the Conseil d'estat is attested to in Basset, president of the Estates, to Sillery, chancellier and garde des sceaux, Grenoble, Sept. 1605; AMAE, Mémoires et Documents, France 1546 (Dauphiné), f 49.

18 M Aleron for the commissioners sent by the king to revise the *feux* to Bellièvre, chancellier, Grenoble, 21 Aug. 1605, BN, mss fr 15.899, f 569

19 Arrêt donné par le roi en son Conseil d'estat au profit des communautés villageoises de Dauphiné, 14 Sept. 1605, BM Grenoble, X 3015, pp 3–5; and second *arrêt* under the same title, directed at stopping legal actions, 3 Mar. 1607, BM Grenoble, X 3015, pp 5–7

20 Brosse to the consuls of Loriol announcing an assembly of the villages of the region at Loriol, 30 Dec. 1605, AD Drôme, E 5363 (Loriol, CC 37), in Lacroix, *Inventaire*, IV, 144

21 Letters patent, 23 Aug. 1606, BN mss fr 4014, f 130 in Esmonin, *Etudes*, 72

22 Arrêt donné par le roi en son Conseil d'estat au profit desdites communautés villageoises, 5 Aug. 1606; and Instructions que le roi entend être suivies et gardées par les commissaires, 5 Aug. 1606, in Arrêt donné par le roi en son Conseil d'estat au profit des communautés, Grenoble, 1619, 8–23, BM *Grenoble*, O 3015

23 Ibid.

24 Esmonin, *Etudes*, 73

25 Claude Expilly to Sillery, conseilleur au Conseil privé et garde des sceaux,

Grenoble, 14 Oct. 1605, AMAE, Mémoires et Documents, France, 1546, f 51

26 See listings of verifications of village debts under virtually each community in sections on legal proceedings (procédures), série FF of communal archives lists in Lacroix, *Inventaire*, IV–VIII.

27 Expilly, 'Remonstrance faite en 1624 lorsque les Etats ... rendre compte aux commissaires députés du roi,' in *Plaidoyez*, 464–74

28 Fillon, *procureur du roi* in the parlement, to Monsieur, Grenoble, 29 May 1610, AMAE, Mémoires et Documents, France, 1546, f 80; Fillon to Monsieur, Grenoble, 1 Dec. 1612, ibid., f 82; Fillon to Monsieur, Grenoble, 10 Feb. 1614, ibid., f 83; Aubery, le Provost, and Ferran, inspectors and deputies for the auditing of village accounts, to Chancellier Bellièvre, Grenoble, 31 Apr. 1620, ibid., f 84

29 Fillon to Monsieur, Grenoble, 29 May 1610, ibid.

30 Aubery, le Provost, Ferran to Chancellier Bellièvre, 31 Apr. 1620, ibid., f 84

31 Cahier presented by Claude Brosse in 1620 along with replies from the king, in Registre des assemblées de la noblesse, AD Isère, IJ 175, ff 533–541. See also Lacroix, 'Claude Brosse et les Tailles,' 32: 366–7.

32 Arrêt et règlement donnés par le roi en son conseil, 15 Apr. 1602, in Giroud, *Recueil*, 171

33 Van Doren Papers, summary of the principal resolutions taken in the meeting of the Estates, Grenoble, July 1603, AD Isère, 4 E 245/1, ff 1–3 (Cremieu AA)

34 Deliberations, Council of the Nobility, Grenoble, 27 Sept. 1603, in Registre des assemblées de la noblesse, AD Isère, IJ 175, ff 140–1

35 Deliberations, Council of the Nobility, Grenoble, 10 June 1604, ibid., f 164

36 Van Doren Papers, deliberations and conclusions of the provincial Estates, Valence, Nov. and Dec. 1604, recalled in Feb. 1605 with modifications in their conclusions in 2 May 1605, AD Isère, IC 4/20, f 8

37 Requête du commis des villages présentée aux Etats, Valence, 7 Feb. 1605, AD Isère, Registre des délibérations de la noblesse, 1605–58, AD Isère, uncatalogued register, f 4

38 Deliberations, Council of the Nobility, Grenoble, 8 Mar. 1605, in Registre des assemblées de la noblesse, AD Isère, IJ 175, ff 184–5

39 Deliberations, Assembly of the Nobility, Grenoble, 27 June–1 July 1606, ibid., f 203

40 Deliberations, Council of the Nobility, Grenoble, 7 July and 22 Aug. 1606, ibid., ff 230 and 223

41 Summary of the deliberations of the provincial Estates, Romans, 10–16 June 1607, in Lacroix and Bellet, *Inventaire des archives communales antérieur à 1790: Tain* 3–4; and deliberations, General Assembly of the Nobility, Romans, 10–16 June, Registre des assemblées de la noblesse, AD Isère, IJ 175, ff 236–47

42 Deliberations, General Assembly of the Nobility, Grenoble, 3 Apr. 1609, ibid., f 293

43 Sieur de Villars reported to the Council of the Nobility on the 'positive' results of the delegation's meeting with the king, 10 July 1609 ibid., ff 305–6, but the conditions that Henry IV attached to dropping the wine tax were only explained before the General Assembly of the Nobility, Grenoble, 22 Dec. 1609, ibid., ff 311–12.

44 Deliberations, Council of the Nobility, Grenoble, 19–21 Nov. 1609, ibid., ff 297–301

45 Deliberations, Assembly of the Nobles and Clergy, Grenoble, 28 Dec. 1609, ibid., f 311

46 Ibid., 29 and 30 Dec., ff 312–16

47 Ibid., 31 Dec., ff 317–18

48 Ibid., 7 Jan. 1610, ff 320–1

49 Deliberations, General Assembly of the Nobility and Clergy, Valence, 5 Feb. 1611, ibid., ff 345–50

50 Deliberations, General Assembly of the Nobility, Valence, 11 Feb. 1611, ibid., ff 353–60

51 All the revenues from the salt farm were to be turned over to the third estate, with the exception of 6,000 *écus* for the upkeep of roads and 4,700 *écus* for the doctors of the University of Valence.

52 Deliberations, General Assembly of the Nobility, Valence, 15 and 22–4 Feb. 1611, Registre des assemblées de la noblesse, AD Isère, IJ 175, ff 361–75

53 Deliberations, General Assembly of the Nobility and Clergy, Grenoble, 7 Jan.–8 Feb. 1616, ibid., ff 417–22

54 Deliberations, General Assembly of the Nobility and Clergy, Grenoble, 30 Jan.–18 Feb. 1621, ibid., ff 542–52

55 Ibid., Grenoble, 10 Feb.–10 March 1622, ff 562–78

56 Lacroix, 'Claude Brosse et les Tailles,' espec. 32: 239–48, 363–71, and 33: 75–80, 234–7, 307–23; Laurens, *Le Procès des tailles (1537–1639). Claude Brosse – Antoine Rambaud*, 50–68; Le Roy Ladurie, *Carnival*, 335–7

57 Chorier, *La Vie d'Artus Prunier*, 170

58 Arrêt évoquant au Conseil ... tous les procès que pourront avoir pendant deux ans Claude Brosse, 5 Aug. 1606, AN, E 11ᵇ, f 29 vo

59 Arrêt prolongeant pendant deux ans l'évocation générale du procès de Claude Brosse, 14 Aug. 1608, AN, E 18ª, f 226 vo

60 Arrêt règlement d'un acompte de 20,000 livres sur les 30,000 ... à Claude Brosse, 23 Aug. 1608, AN, E 18ª, f 262

61 Brosse to the consuls of Loriol, 30 Dec. 1605, AC Livron, in Lacroix, *Inventaire*, VI, 178; Brosse to consuls of Châteauneuf-de-Mazenc, 30 Dec. 1605, AC Châteauneuf-de-Mazenc, CC 37, in ibid., IV, 444; Brosse to councils of Condillac, 23 Dec. 1605, AC Condillac, CC 21, in ibid., IV, 358–9

62 Deliberations of the village syndics, Châteauneuf d'Isère, 15 June 1617, AC Châteauneuf d'Isère, BB 9, in Lacroix, *Inventaire*, V, 397

63 Deliberations of the *commis du pays*, Grenoble, 28 Mar.–5 Apr. 1618, AC Vienne, AA 7/47, f 16

64 Arrêt du Conseil d'estat obtenu par C. Brosse ..., le 3 Sept. 1631 portant cassation de celui du parlement de Grenoble donné contre lui le 21 Jan. 1631, BM Grenoble, O 9992. Despite the questionable nature of most of these monetary grants and the refusal of officials to sanction them, it is clear from the *taille* levy receipts in the archives of La Garde Adhémar that most of the sums claimed by Brosse were, in fact, paid by the rural communities. La Garde Adhémar, Account Books, 1615–1626, AC La Garde Adhémar, CC 10/7, CC 11/19, and mandates, CC 29

65 Lacroix, 'Claude Brosse et les Tailles,' 32: 367

66 Registre du Conseil d'état, 30 Aug. 1623, AM Vienne, AA 7/38, 1–7

67 Ibid., 2

68 Deliberations, Romans Consulate, 14 Aug. 1624, AC Romans, BB 26, in Lacroix, *Inventaire*, VI, 342

69 Consuls of Montélimar to consuls of La Garde Adhémar, 20 July 1624, AC La Garde Adhémar, CC 54, in Lacroix, ibid., V, 64

70 Consuls of Charpey and Etoile to consuls of Livron, proposing a local assembly to protest the concessions made by Brosse, 1628, AC Livron, CC 111, in Lacroix, ibid., VI, 187. Consuls of Montélimar to consuls of Allex, asking for a similar meeting, 4 July 1628, AC Allex, CC 102, in Lacroix, ibid., VII, 353

71 That the privileged orders were behind the legal suits can be seen from a series of pamphlets written to defend Brosse. They underlined all that he had done for the villages and accused the nobles of generating the rumours and accusations against him. See A Monsieurs les deputez des bailliages, chastellains, consuls et notables des communautés villageoises de Dauphiné, Aug. 1628, BM Grenoble, O 3072; A Monsieurs les chastellains, consuls et notables des communautés, des villes et villages du

Dauphiné, 1 Mar. 1629; and Lettre du Sieur d'Ambhonneur, 1 May 1628, in which Brosse is defended against those who accuse him of embezzlement. He is said to be as poor as when he became syndic twenty-five years earlier. It is even argued that he sold off his own holdings to continue the *taille* struggle; see 28–9, BM Grenoble, O 3071.

72 Deliberations, Assemblée du pays, 9–23 Mar. 1628, AC Vienne, AA 7/48, 22

73 See *arrêt* from the *procureur du roi* ordering imprisonment, 7 Jan. 1631, in Lacroix, 'Claude Brosse et les Tailles,' 32: 370–1; and *arrêt* of the court of the king's councillors concerning trial and fine, 21 Jan. 1631, ibid., 33: 75–8.

74 Arrêt du Conseil du roi pour la saisie des papiers de Brosse, 30 Jan. 1631, in Lacroix, ibid., 79; and *arrêt* of the King's council annulling judgment of the Grenoble court, 6 Mar. 1631, ibid., 80

75 The support of the Crown for Brosse is further demonstrated by the fact that his son Jean-François was named *président* of the *élection* of Vienne in 1637 even as his father continued to work for the confirmation of the *taille réelle* status: Lacroix, 'Claude Brosse et les Tailles,' 32: 318.

76 Mariéjol, *Henri IV et Louis XIII*, 389–93

77 Bitton, *The French Nobility in Crisis, 1540–1640*, 18–23

78 Porchnev, *Les Soulèvements populaires*, 122–4

79 Deyon, 'A propos les rapports entre la noblesse française et la monarchie absolue pendant la première moitié du XVIIIᵉ siècle,' 345

80 The advocates of the crisis theory for France follow in the historiographical footsteps of Pierre de Vaissière, *Gentilhomme campagnard de l'ancienne France*, 215–260; Henri Druout, *Mayenne et la Bourgogne: Etude sur la Ligue (1587–1596)*, I, 32–53; and Lucien Romier, *Le Royaume de Catherine de Médicis*, I, p III, chaps. 2, 4.

81 Weary, 'Royal Policy and Patronage in Renaissance France: The Monarchy and the House of La Trémoille'

82 Major, 'Noble Income, Inflation and the Wars of Religion in France,' 21–48

83 Wood, *The Nobility of the Election of Bayeux, 1463–1666. Continuity through Change.* In a very telling critique of Wood's book Denise Angers has argued that his analyses are too exclusively based upon the nobiliar *recherches* and that he is not sufficiently critical of the source; see her review in *Histoire sociale* 14 (Nov 1981): 531–3.

84 Wood, *Nobility of the Election of Bayeux*, 55, 64, 67

85 Ibid., 47–53

86 Ibid., 143–7

87 Registre des assemblées de la noblesse, AD Isère, IJ 175, 28 May 1602–13 July1626. See also the so-called Registre des délibérations de la noblesse, 1605–1658, AD Isère, uncatalogued, which contains few deliberations but a number of petitions, memoirs, and official acts.

88 See chap. 4, n 117.

89 Inventaire, Marcellier, compiled by François Marcellier, a seventeenth-century manuscript listing of the holdings of the Chambre des comptes, 35 vols., AD Isère, archivist's office

90 General Assembly of the Nobility, Côte St-André, 3 June 1602, in Registre des assemblées de la noblesse, AD Isère, IJ 175, ff 9–11

91 Council of the Nobility, Grenoble, 23 Oct. 1602, ibid., ff xxv–xxvi, second version of request in ff LXVII–LXVIII. This was the same Marchier who, as lawyer for the third estate, had attacked the exemptions of the privileged orders before the king in 1595.

92 General Assembly of the Nobility, Grenoble, 11 July 1603, ibid., ff LXXX–LXXXI

93 Ennemond Marchier, in Allard, *Nobiliaire de Dauphiné*, BM Grenoble, V 4153; and Council of the Nobility, Grenoble, 3 Aug. 1607, ibid., f 248

94 Council of the Nobility, Grenoble, 2 Sept. 1609, ibid., f CCXCVI

95 Act of ennoblement, Charles Dubonnet-Fine, 1606, AD Isère, B 2917, f 560

96 Council of the Nobility, Grenoble, 13 Mar. 1615, in Registre des assemblées de la noblesse, AD Isère, IJ 175, ff 411–12

97 Act of ennoblement, Imbert Pelloux, 1602, AD Isère, B 2916, f 38

98 General Assembly of the Nobility, Valence, 15 Feb. 1611, Registre des assemblées de la noblesse, AD Isère, IJ 175, f 363

99 Trebillod, 'Etude du registre de la noblesse,' 7

100 Expilly, *Plaidoyez*, plaidoyé 31, 376

101 Allard, *Dictionnaire historique, chronologique, géographique, généalogique ... du Dauphiné*, 1, 70–6

102 Perroy, 'Social Mobility among the French Noblesse in the Later Middle Ages,' 31; and Wood, *Nobility of the Election of Bayeux*, 43–53

103 It is true, as James Wood noted, that noble lines are a poor test of the real evolution of the nobility, in the sense that at the same time that one line might be composed of one or two nuclear families, another might contain eight or ten families. Over the course of a century the families included in one line might triple or quadruple, while another line might regress. Unfortunately, in the absence of more numerous *ban* rolls or inquiries into noble titles in Dauphiné, it is impossible to reconstitute the progression or regression of nuclear noble families in the province.

104 Romier, *Le Royaume de Catherine de Médicis*, I, 181–8; Druout, *Mayenne et la Bourgogne*, I, 32–53; Raveau, *Agriculture et les classes paysannes: la transformation de la propriété dans le haut Poitou au XVIe siècle*, chap. 2

105 Inventaire Marcellier, AD Isère. On the historical value of the document, see Letonnelier, 'Notice historique sur les archives de la Chambre des comptes du Dauphiné,' in *Répertoire des registres du fonds de la Chambre des comptes du Dauphiné*, i–xiv

106 Lacroix, *Inventaire*, II–VIII; Brun-Durand, *Dictionnaire topographique du département de la Drôme*; Lacroix, *L'Arrondissement de Montélimar*, and *L'Arrondissement de Nyons*

107 Wood, *Nobility of the Election of Bayeux*, 142–9

108 Long, *La Réforme et les Guerres de Religion en Dauphiné 1560–1598*, 240–1; Cavard, *La Réforme*, 392–404

109 Gérard Giordanengo has demonstrated that there were few acquisitions of noble holdings by non-nobles from the thirteenth to the middle of the fourteenth century and that from the mid-fourteenth to the sixteenth century only three cases can be verified either in the Inventaire Marcellier or in the legal decisions of Guy Pape. See Giordanengo, 'Les Roturiers possesseurs de fiefs nobles en Dauphiné aux XIVe et XVe siècles,' 322–4.

110 Inventaire Marcellier, Valentinois, IV f 2032

111 Ibid., IV, f 2114

112 Ibid., V, f 2798

113 For explanations of the origins of these acts, see above, chap. 4, 000.

114 Masson-Fauchier, 'L'Anoblissement en Dauphiné au XVIIe siècle (1598–1668)'

115 See Appendix 1; see also Allard, 'Rôle des anoblis dans le Dauphiné depuis 1582 et la valeur de leurs biens,' BM Grenoble, R 80, t 9, f 776.

116 Act of ennoblement of Louis de Villeneuve, 1603, AD Isère, B 2916, f 62; act of ennoblement of Jean de Villard, 1608, AD Isère B 2919, f 111; see also Allard, 'Rôle des anoblis,' BM Grenoble, R 80, t 9, f 776.

117 Wood, *Nobility of the Election of Bayeux*, 69–98

118 Act of ennoblement of Jacques de Bellefin, 1578, AD Isère, B 2914, f 120

119 Act of ennoblement of Jean de Bein, 1612, AD Isère, B 2920, f 209

120 It is true that the use of military criteria for ennoblement in Dauphiné may be more indicative of a certain traditionalist rhetoric than of the reality of the situation; nevertheless, the perpetuation of this rhetoric testifies to the unchanging ideological position of the second estate in Dauphiné when compared to its development in other regions of the

country. See Schalk, 'The Appearance and Reality of Nobility in France during the Wars of Religion,' 19–31; Delumeau, 'Fondements idéologiques de la hiérarchie sociale: le discours sur le courage,' 273–87.

121 Delagrange, *Réponses et salutations des pièces produites par les gens du tiers estat*, 286, 397
122 Esmonin, *Etudes sur la France des XVIIe et XVIIIe siècles*, 43–4
123 Barbiche, 'Commissaires députés pour le "régalement" des tailles,' 61
124 Antoine, 'Le Régalement des tailles de 1623–25,' 27–63

CHAPTER 6: THE FISCAL AND SOCIAL FOUNDATIONS FOR CROWN INTERVENTION

1 Bonney, *Political Change in France*, 30; d'Aguesseau to d'Herbault, 1626, AMAE, Mémoires et Documents, France, 1546, ff 136–56
2 Favier, 'Les Assemblées du Dauphiné après la suspension des Etats en 1628,' 59
3 Lacroix, 'Claude Brosse et les Tailles,' 32: 367–71, 33: 75–80, 234–7, 307–23
4 For purposes of consistency I have continued the method of calculation applied to *taille* levies from 1540 to 1610 in Graph 1. Expressing the levies in *quartals* of wheat has the advantage of compensating for inflation and providing a more realistic evaluation of the effect of *tailles*.
5 See above, chap. 5, 143–5.
6 Edict pour la création des procureurs, Dec 1620, and 1623, AD Isère, B 2346, f 1, and list of those purchasing positions, AD Isère, B 2346, f 6
7 Nomination de Michel Antoine, 1623, ibid., B 2345, f 157
8 Baudet, president of the Grenoble parlement, Rapport extrait du registre du parlement, 9 Jan. 1626, AC Mirabel, BB 2, in Lacroix, *Inventaire*, III, 387
9 Consuls of Mirabel to maréchal of Créqui, 24 Oct. 1626, AC Mirabel, BB 2, in Lacroix, *Inventaire*, III, 387
10 Van Doren Papers, Supplie de Claude Brosse et ordonnance conforme du duc de Créqui, 23 July 1628, AD Drôme, E 3887
11 Graph 7, of the levies and loans collected at La Garde Adhémar, has been drawn up from the account books of the community, 1615–26, AC La Garde Adhémar, CC 10/7–CC 11/19, and from the official mandates presented, CC 29. This data was corrected with a new series of *taille lançons* that L.S. Van Doren is currently preparing for the period after 1610.

12 Baudet, Rapport, 9 Jan. 1626, and Van Doren Papers, summary of the conclusions of the Assembly of the Ten Cities, AD Drôme, c 1025, 31

13 Deliberations, Consulate of Romans, 4 Mar. 1627, AC Romans, BB 27, in Lacroix, *Inventaire*, VI, 343

14 Deliberations, Consulate of Nyons, 8 Mar. 1626, AC Nyons, BB 23, in Lacroix, ibid., III, 432

15 Van Doren Papers, Deliberations and conclusions of the General Assembly of Grenoble, 20 Oct.–2 Nov. 1627, AD Drôme, 3025/7, 1–2

16 Arnaud, *Histoire des protestants du Dauphiné aux XVI, XVII et XVIII siècles*, II, 17–20, 27–32

17 D'Aguesseau to d'Herbault, conseilleur au roi en son Conseil d'état, Grenoble, 14 Sept. 1626, AMAE, Mémoires et Documents, France, 1546, f 136

18 Six of these letters were signed by d'Aguesseau and two by Lesdiguières; see ibid., ff 136–56.

19 Lesdiguières to d'Herbault, Valence, 26 Aug. 1626, ibid., f 152

20 D'Aguesseau to d'Herbault, Grenoble, 14 Sept. 1626, ibid., ff 154–6

21 Van Doren Papers, Deliberations and conclusions of the General Assembly of Grenoble, 20 Oct.–2 Nov. 1627, AD Drôme, E 3025/7, ff 1–4. It is never mentioned clearly that the delegates to the assemblée générale protested against the imposition of *élections*; however, when they cited their opposition to the establishment of new official positions and to the 'nouveautés' that threatened the liberties and privileges of the province, they meant the proposals for *élections*.

22 Major, 'Henry IV and Guyenne,' 383, and *Representative Government in Early Modern France*, 519–68

23 Bercé, *Histoire des croquants*, I, 88–9

24 Barbiche, 'Les Commissaires députés pour le "régalement" des tailles de 1623–1625,' 27–63

25 D'Argenson to Richelieu, Grenoble, 17 Apr. 1631, AMAE, Mémoires et Documents, France, 1546, f 227

26 Claude Frère to Richelieu, 18 Apr. 1631, ibid., f 228. Frère's connections with the cardinal can be seen in his correspondence with Richelieu. Besides a letter on 19 Sept. 1628, in which he indicated that he had done all he could to register the 1628 edict at a time when the anger of the privileged orders had subsided, Frère sent Richelieu unsigned notes in 1631 reporting on Huguenot activities in the region. See Frère to Richelieu, 19 Sept. 1628, ibid., f 180; unsigned (in Frère's handwriting) to Richelieu, 1631, ibid., f 233; Claude Frère to Richelieu, 24 June 1631, ibid., f 234.

27 Arrêt du Conseil d'état portant que les sieurs des deux premiers ordres ... venir défendre si bien leur semble à la dite requête,' 21 Dec. 1632, AC Vienne, CC 45

28 See the 1633 cahiers scattered among those for 1596 and 1598 in AC Vienne, CC 42, CC 44, CC 46.

29 For the third estate, F. de Guérin, *Très-humbles remonstrances au roy par les gens du tiers estat*, BM Grenoble, O 3082. For the privileged orders, Anonymous, *Très-humbles remonstrances faites au roy par les députés de la noblesse*, BM Grenoble, O 9940; *Très-humbles remonstrances au roy par les officiers du parlement de Grenoble*, BM Grenoble, O 3087; *Remonstrances des présidents, trésoriers-généraux de France, avocat et procureur de S.M. au Bureau des Finances*, BM Grenoble, O 8091; *Avertissement pour la noblesse de Dauphiné*, BM Grenoble, O 7944

30 Inventaire des pièces qu'ont remis par devant Monseigneur de Talon,' 14 July 1633, AC Vienne, CC 42

31 Arrêt portant règlement entre les trois ordres de la province de Dauphiné sur la réalité des tailles, 31 May 1634, in Giroud, *Recueil*, I, 178–9, 180–2

32 Mémoires concernant le fait du cadastre de Dauphiné, 1643–44 (in fact it concentrates upon the procedures that accompanied the adoption of the 1634 edict), BN mss fr 18723, ff 211–16

33 Talon to Richelieu, Romans, 16 June 1635, AMAE, Mémoires et Documents, France 1546, f 269

34 Talon from Seguier, Romans, 16 June 1635, in Lublinskaya, ed., *Documents pour servir à l'histoire de France au XVII* siècle*, doc. 319, pp 341–3

35 Dauphiné Estates, Règlements pour les tailles avec les notes faites par Talon, Grenoble, June 1635, ibid., doc. 321, pp 344–9

36 Talon, Relation des affaires de Dauphiné, Romans, June 1635, doc. 322, p 351. Talon's accusation of the council was also repeated in a cahier by Claude Brosse; see Lacroix, 'Claude Brosse et les Tailles,' 33: 304–10.

37 Mémoires concernant le fait du cadastre, 1643–4, BN mss fr 18723, f 212

38 See above, nn 26, 27.

39 Memoires concernant le fait du cadastre, 1643–4, BN mss fr 18723, f 212

40 Arrêt portant règlement entre les trois ordres de la province sur la réalité des tailles, 31 May 1634, in Giroud, *Recueil*, I, 179–80

41 Requête des estats [in fact, nobles and officials] de Dauphiné contre le Conseiller d'estat Talon, 1635, BN, Coll. Dupuy, 869, ff 83–4

42 Porchnev, *Les Soulèvements populaires*, 123

43 Arrêt du conseil donné en exécution et interprétation de règlement fait par S.M., 31 May 1634, 9 Jan. 1636, in Giroud, *Recueil*, I, 186–9; Arrêt et règlement sur les différends des trois ordres, 6 Apr. 1639, ibid., 191–4.

I have not consulted the 1637 edict, but its existence is mentioned in the preamble of the 6 Apr. 1639 document, 191.

44 M de Vallambert, pour la noblesse, to Richelieu, Grenoble, 30 Nov. 1636, AMAE, Mémoires et Documents, 1546, f 298

45 Monsieurs de la noblesse to Richelieu, Grenoble, 31 May 1637, AMAE, Mémoires et Documents, 1546, f 300

46 Bonney, *Political Change in France under Richelieu and Mazarin*, 355

47 Monsieurs de la noblesse to Richelieu, Grenoble, 20 Nov. 1628, in Romans, 'Catherine de Médicis en Dauphiné,' 153–60, 293–305

48 Van Doren Papers, Règlement fait pour le fait des tailles, 24 Oct. 1639, in *Plaidoyez de Maistre Jean Basset* (Grenoble 1648), seconde partie, livre III, titre II, chap. 1, 204–6, Harvard Law School Library

49 Talon estimated that freezing the existing noble-to-*roturier* ratio of land distribution in the province actually increased the value of noble land by a third, since it was perpetually tax free and an attractive investment: Talon to Seguier, Romans, 16 June 1635, in Lublinskaya, *Documents*, doc. 320, p 342.

50 Talon to Seguier, Romans, 16 June 1635, in Lublinskaya, *Documents*, doc. 320, p 343

51 This charge against Brosse was contained in a 1634 pamphlet by the Sieur du Four la Repara, an *anobli* who had received his title in 1618. Brosse denied the accusation in Lettre du Sieur Brosse, 10 Nov. 1634, BM Grenoble, 1382, pp 1–9. An even more conclusive refutation of the charge is the accusation repeated in the Romans consulate that Brosse was secretly negotiating with the first two orders on a *taille* compromise: see Deliberations, Consulate de Romans, 4 Sept. 1637, AC Romans, BB 29, in Lacroix, *Inventaire*, VI, 348. There was even a dispute between Brosse and the consuls of the major cities over taxation of the *francs fiefs*. At that time the consuls contested the right of Brosse even to participate in the Assembly of the Ten Cities: see Van Doren Papers, Réponse faite par Monsieurs les Consuls, 17 Mar. 1639, AC Valence, EE 2.

52 Van Doren Papers, Règlement fait pour le fait des tailles, 24 Oct. 1639, in *Plaidoyez de Maistre Jean Basset* (Grenoble 1648), seconde partie, livre III, titre II, chap. 1, pp 204–6, Harvard Law School Library

53 M de la Chambre des comptes to Richelieu, Grenoble, 6 Nov. 1639, AMAE, Mémoires et Documents, 1546, f 352; Gens de la cour de parlement to Richelieu, 5 Nov. 1639, ibid., f 353

54 In 1658–60 the second estate forced the king to abandon a new *feux* evaluation: AD Isère, B 2778–B 2779. Another indication of its opposition is the participation of the nobility in the popular risings that continued

to affect Dauphiné in the 1640s: see Porchnev, *Les Soulèvement populaires*, 113–17.

55 Mousnier, *La Vénalité des offices*, 455–529

56 Porchnev, *Les Soulèvements populaires*, 561–74

57 Lublinskaya, *French Absolutism*, chap. 5, 220–71

58 See Bercé, *Histoire des croquants*, I, 88–9.

59 Van Doren Papers, Délibérations et conclusions prises en l'assemblée générale de tous les commis du pays, consuls des villes et commis de villes et députés des villes et bailliages de la province de Dauphiné, Grenoble, 20 Oct.–2 Nov. 1627, AD Drôme, E 3025/7

60 Conclusions de l'assemblée des dix villes et députés des bailliages, Grenoble, 9–23 Mar. 1628, AC Vienne, AA 7/48, p 3

61 Ibid., 11

62 Brosse, Mémoire des règlements obtenus par Sieur Brosse, in A Monsieurs Deputez des bailliages, chastelains, consuls et notables des comunautés villageoises de Dauphiné, Vienne, 20 Aug. 1628, BM Grenoble, 3072, pp 21–3

63 Arrêt du Conseil du roi, Lyon, 26 June 1630, in Favier, 'Les Assemblées du Dauphiné,' 67–9

64 See above, chap. 5, 147–8.

65 Requête des Etats de Dauphiné [sic: nobles] contre le Conseilleur d'estat Talon, 1635, BN, Coll. Dupuy, 869, ff 83–4; M Vallambert pour la noblesse to Richelieu, Grenoble, 20 Nov. 1636, AMAE, Mémoires et Documents, 1546, f 298

66 Arrêt du Conseil d'estat du roy portant deboutement des récusations proposées contre Monseigneur de Talon, 21 Feb. 1637, BM Grenoble, X 1388, pp 1–4

67 Deliberations, Consulate of Romans, 4 Sept. 1637, BB 29, in Lacroix, *Inventaire*, VI, 348

68 Hickey, 'Politics and Commerce in Renaissance France: The Evolution of Trade along the Routes of Dauphiné,' 150–1; and Van Doren Papers, Règlement fait pour le fait des tailles, 24 Oct. 1639, in *Plaidoyez de Maistre Jean Basset*, III, 204–6, Harvard Law School Library

EPILOGUE

1 On the different cabals organized by the *parlementaires* against the new Crown institutions, see the article by Jacques Solé that summarizes various aspects of the correspondence of Chancellor Séguier: 'Le Dauphiné dans la correspondance du Chancellier Séguier,' 391–3.

2 See Parlement de Grenoble to Séguier, Valence, 25 Aug. 1644, in
Lublinskaya, *Documents*, doc. 333, p 359; Lozières to Séguier, Valence, 12
Jan. 1645, ibid., doc. 335, pp 362–3; Parlement to Séguier, Grenoble,
15 Mar. 1645, ibid., doc. 338, pp. 364–5; Dufaure to Séguier, Grenoble,
15 Mar. 1645, ibid., doc. 338, pp 364–5; Dufaure to Séguier, Grenoble,
15 Mar. 1645, ibid., doc. 339, pp 365–6; Parlement to Séguier, Grenoble,
17 Oct. 1645, ibid., doc. 348, p 373; Parlement to Séguier, Grenoble,
23 June 1646, ibid., doc. 353, p 376; Louis XIV to Séguier, Paris, 7 Aug.
1648, in Mousnier, ed., *Lettres et Mémoires adressés au Chancelier Séguier
(1633–1649)*, II, doc. 341, pp 861–862; Louis XIV to Séguier, Paris, 7 Aug.
1648, ibid., doc. 342, pp. 862–3; Séguier to Le Tellier, Paris, 30 May
1649, ibid., doc. 368, pp 930–2; Le Tellier to Séguier, Campiègne, 8 May
1649, ibid., doc. 33, pp 1008–9.

3 Bonnin and Solé, 'Les deux derniers siècles de la monarchie absolue,'
chap. II of Bligny, ed., *Histoire de Dauphiné*, 290–4, 309–12. See also Egret,
*Le Parlement de Dauphiné et les affaires publiques dans la deuxième moitié du
XVIII siècle.*

4 Favier, 'Les Assemblées du Dauphiné,' 64

5 Deliberations, Grenoble Consulate, 3 Dec. 1641, 14 Jan. 1642, AM
Grenoble, BB 107, in Prudhomme, *Inventaire, Grenoble*, I; Van Doren
Papers, Créqui, duke of Lesdiguières, requête du procureur syndic des
trois ordres, Grenoble, 8 June 1655, in Maignien, *Catalogue des livres
et manuscrits du fonds dauphinois de la Bibliothèque Municipale de Grenoble*,
II, 6, doc. 8469, BM Grenoble, X 3553; Van Doren Papers, Delibéra-
tions, Assemblée du pays, 8–12 Aug. 1655, BM Grenoble, R 7565,
ff 333–80

6 Arrêt pour la vérification et paiement des dettes du pays, 27 June 1646,
BM Grenoble, X 1319; Arrêt du Conseil d'estat concernant la forme de
procéder que tiendra les officiers des villes et communautés ... tant pour
la liquidation que paiement de leurs dettes, 16 Jan. 1644, BM Grenoble,
X 1320; Révocation de toute commission extraordinaire ... avec décharge
à ses sujets des restes des tailles avant l'année 1647 et remise d'un demi
quartier de celles pour les années 1648 et 1649, 13 July 1648, BM
Grenoble, P 9627

7 Favier, 'Les Assemblées du Dauphiné,' 66

8 Arrêt du Conseil d'estat du roi portant défense à messieurs de l'ordre de
la noblesse de faire aucune assemblée générale, ni particulière, 1636
[between 29 Nov. and 31 Dec.], Maignien, *Fonds dauphinois*, II, 5–6, doc.
8466; *arrêt* repeated on 28 Aug. 1637, BM Grenoble, X 1389

9 Registre des délibérations de la noblesse (1605–1658), AD Isère, uncatalogued register
10 Major, *Representative Government in Early Modern France*, 653–5
11 Edicts were issued ordering the verification and reduction of rural debts
  in 1641, (BM Grenoble, x 1629); 1642 (BM Grenoble, x 3134); 1646
  (BM Grenoble, x 1319); and 1655 (BM Grenoble, o 3103). Special edicts
  were issued, restating which groups were to be taxed, in 1640 (Giroud,
  Recueil, I, 202); 1641 (AD Drôme, c 6414); 1642 (BM Grenoble, x 1390);
  1646 (BM Grenoble, x 1391); and 1648 (BM Grenoble, x 1342).
12 Délibérations, assemblée du pays, 8–21 Aug. 1655, BM Grenoble, R 7568,
  ff 333–80
13 Fauché-Prunelle, *Essai sur les anciennes institutions autonomes ou populaires
  des Alpes Cottiennes-briançonnaises*, II, 73
14 Favier, 'Les Assemblées du Dauphiné,' 60; Registre des assemblées tenues
  pour les affaires du bailliage de Gap pendant le consulat du Sr. François
  Marchand, 1644, AM Gap, ff 102
15 Favier, 'Les Assemblées du Dauphiné,' 60
16 Bonnin, 'Les Milieux dominants en Dauphiné au XVIIᵉ siècle,' 47–66
17 Lettres patentes du roy portant commission pour procéder à la révision
  générale des feux, 28 Oct. 1658, BM Grenoble, o 9951, 4
18 Registres de la révision des feux, 1658–60, AD Isère, B 2778, B 2779
19 See Bonnin, 'Les Deux Derniers Siècles de la monarchie absolue (1634–
  1790): Les hommes et leur vie matérielle,' chap. 10, and Bonnin and
  Solé, 'Les Deux Derniers Siècles de la monarchie absolue (1634–1790):
  La politique, le religieux, les mentalités,' chap. 11, in Bligny, ed., *Histoire
  du Dauphiné*, 273–4, 290–4. Crown suspicions of the *parlementaires* are
  evident in the secret notes that Colbert ordered drawn up by his intendant
  in 1663 on the strong points and weaknesses of the different officials
  of the parlement: see Depping, *La Correspondance administrative sous le règne
  de Louis XIV* II, 78–87.
20 Colbert to d'Herbigny, 23 Nov. 1679, in Clément, ed., *Lettres, instructions
  et mémoires de Colbert*, IV, 136
21 'L'Organisation du parlement en 1698,' in Blet, Esmonin, and Letonnelier, eds., *Le Dauphiné, recueil de textes historiques*, 172–5
22 Bonnin, 'La Terre et les Paysans en Dauphiné,' 413–19
23 Colbert to d'Herbigny, Versailles, 7 Nov. 1680, in Clément, *Lettres ... de
  Colbert*, II, 145–6
24 Colbert to d'Herbigny, Versailles, 27 Dec. 1680, ibid., 145
25 Bonnin, 'La Terre et les Paysans en Dauphiné,' 462–3

26 Lacroix, 'Claude Brosse et les Tailles,' 33: 310–22
27 Third-Estate Cahiers, Châteauneuf-de-Mazenc, AC Vienne, CC 43, and *courcier* or *livre des mutations*, 1604–1769, AC Châteauneuf-de-Mazenc, CC 2, in Lacroix, *Inventaire*, IV, 136
28 Third-Estate Cahiers, Mollars, AC Vienne, CC 43, and 1666 *cadastre*, AC mollars, CC 5, in Lacroix, *Inventaire*, III, 341
29 Gaudissard and Pascal, 'L'Appropriation citadine dans les campagnes de l'Isère au XVIIᵉ siècle,' 70–84
30 Ibid., 208–11
31 Delille, 'La Propriété foncière à Vourey aux XVIᵉ et XVIIᵉ siècles'
32 Goubert, *L'Ancien Régime*, II, *Les Pouvoirs*, 148–51; Chaunu, 'L'Etat,' in *Histoire économique et sociale de la France*, I, pt 1, 184–91; Immanuel Wallerstein, *The Modern World System*, 28–9, 133–9; Lublinskaya, *French Absolutism*, 312–22; Yves-Marie Bercé, *Histoire des croquants*, I, 88–118
33 Van Doren, 'Civil War Taxation and the Foundation of Fiscal Absolutism,' 35–53
34 Mariéjol, *Histoire de France depuis les orignes jusqu'à la Révolution*, chaps. 2, 3; Pagés, 'Le Conseil du roi sous Louis XIII,' 293–324; Zeller, 'L'Administration monarchique avant les intendants,' 180–215; Major, *Representative Government in Early Modern France*, 375–9
35 Major, *Representative Government in Early Modern France*, 375–9, 487–531
36 Porchnev, *Les Soulèvements populaires*, 538–582; Mousnier, *Les XVIᵉ et XVIIᵉ siècles*, 176–82; Lublinskaya, *French Absolutism*, 330–2
37 Declaration of *procureur* François Roux, Van Doren Papers, Deliberations of the Estates, Grenoble, 4 Mar. 1552, AC Romans, AA 2, f 3

Bibliography

PRINCIPAL MANUSCRIPT SOURCES

Grenoble

AD Isère: Archives départementales de l'Isère. The principal institutional holdings for the old province of Dauphiné are contained in series B, the archives of the parlement. The series also contains scattered records from the Chambre des comptes. Through this series debates over the *feux* revisions or appointments to offices can be traced. The series was catalogued in a series of published inventories by Auguste Prudhomme and J.J.A. Pilot de Thorey. Series B also contains the Generalia of the parlement, in which acts of ennoblement are located. For these acts there is a manuscript inventory compiled by G. Letonnelier. In addition, the departmental archives contain the Registre des assemblées de la noblesse, 1602–22 (2 J 130), the holdings of a certain number of communal archives, such as those of St Marcellin, which are contained in series 4E, and the seventeenth-century manuscript Inventaire Marcellier (35 vols.), which lists the holdings, subsequently dispersed, of the Chambre des comptes.

BM Grenoble: Bibliothèque municipale de Grenoble. The Fonds dauphinois of this library contains virtually all the tracts and printed legal pleas published on the *taille* question during the period from 1595 to 1639. It also contains an outstanding collection of royal edicts and *arrêts* applicable to Dauphiné during the early seventeenth century. In addition to such collections of printed works, the library contains the personal papers of Guy Allard, a seventeenth-century provincial historian, and the papers of Abbé Dussert. The collection was catalogued by Edmond Maignien in five published volumes, *Catalogue des livres et manuscrits du fonds dauphinois de la Bibliothèque de Grenoble*.

AM Grenoble: Archives municipales de Grenoble. The municipal council deliberations, series BB, are useful in completing gaps in the Estates records. The *cadastres*, series CC, yield considerable information on the standing of the different socio-professional groups. Auguste Prudhomme produced a very complete finding aid to these holdings.

Valence
AD Drôme: Archives départementales de la Drôme. The principal resource of these holdings is the well-inventoried communal archives, in which numerous mentions of Estates meetings, local assemblies, and village grievances can be found, principally in series BB and CC. Some of the local holdings, such as AC Buis, Etoile, and Mollans, have been centralized at Valence, but most have remained in the villages. The Archives départementales also contains some holdings of the deliberations of provincial Estates and third-estate assemblies (C 1024–5) and a large collection of notarial registers (series 2E). The finding aid to these archives was compiled by André Lacroix.
AC Valence: Archives communales de Valence. Held by the Bibliothèque municipale, these archives are useful for the deliberations of the town consulate, series BB, and for their *cadastres*, series CC. André Lacroix compiled the finding aid.

Vienne
AC Vienne: Archives communales de Vienne. A large number of village cahiers, tracts, and legal position papers concerning the *taille* dispute are contained in CC 39 and CC 42–7 (these are available in microfilm at the AD Isère). Other documents summarizing deliberations of the provincial Estates, the *assemblées du pays*, and several royal decrees are in AA 7.

Romans
AC Romans: Archives communales de Romans. Lodged in the Bibliothèque municipale and listed in the Lacroix finding aid on the Drôme, series BB contains deliberations of the consulate and series CC contains the *cadastres*.

La Garde Adhémar
AC La Garde Adhémar: Archives communales de La Garde Adhémar. One of the best series of fiscal records for villages of the Drôme is contained in series CC.

Van Doren Papers

L. Scott Van Doren has succeeded in reconstituting a large number of transcriptions and microfilms of Estates meetings for the sixteenth and early seventeenth centuries. These documents have been scattered about in communal and *départemental* holdings. The papers also include numerous important documents on the *taille* question. They are in the possession of Professor L. Scott Van Doren of Boston College.

Paris

AMAE: Archives du Ministère des Affaires etrangères. Catalogued as Mémoires et Documents, France 1546 (Dauphiné), a series of letters, petitions, and reports from Dauphiné to the chancellery, covering the period from 1605 to the 1660s.

BN: Bibliothèque nationale. Several important letters in mss fr concern the *feux* revisions in 1605 and Lesdiguière's opposition to reversing the *taille personnelle* in 1599–1600. In the same series is the Mémoire concernant le fait du cadastre de Dauphiné, written in 1643–4.

AN: Archives nationales. The principal relevant documents are the decrees issued by the conseil d'état concerning the individuals active in the *taille* affair. They are contained in series E and were inventoried by Noël Valois.

PRINTED SOURCES

Anonymous. *Avertissement pour le tiers estat de Dauphiné pour plus amples instructions du procès dudict tiers estat contre les deux premiers ordres dudict païs.* Lyon 1598 [BM Grenoble]

– *La Vérité des justes défenses de la noblesse du Dauphiné aux insultes, demandes, plaintes et doléances du tiers ordre.* Grenoble 1599 [BM Grenoble]

– *Secondes escritures pour l'estat des nobles du Dauphiné contenant contradits contre la production et réponses aux invectives injurieuses du tiers estat.* Grenoble 1602 [BM Grenoble]

– *Très-humbles remonstrances faites au roy par les députés de la noblesse.* Paris 1633 [BM Grenoble]

– *Très-humbles remonstrances au roy par les officiers du parlement du Grenoble.* Paris 1633 [BM Grenoble]

– *Avertissement pour la noblesse de Dauphiné.* Paris 1634 [BM Grenoble]

– *Remonstrances des présidents, trésoriers-généraux de France, avocat et procureur de S.M. au Bureau de Finances ...* Paris 1634 [BM Grenoble]

Aquin, Jean. *Le Plaidé des docteurs et avocats consistoriaux du parlement de Dauphiné.* Grenoble 1599 [BM Grenoble]

Audeyer, Jean-Claude. *Avertissement pour le tiers estat de Dauphiné pour plus ample instructions du procès.* Lyon 1598 [BM Grenoble]

– *Très-humbles remonstrances en forme d'avertissement au roy par les officiers de la cour de parlement de Dauphiné sur le procès intenté par le tiers estat.* 1601 [BM Grenoble]

Blet, H., E. Esmonin, and G. Letonnelier. *Le Dauphiné, Recueil de textes historiques.* Grenoble 1938

Boissat, P., seigneur de Litieu. *Remerciement au roy par les anoblis du Dauphiné.* Vienne 1602 [BM Grenoble]

Catilhon, Boniel de. *La Vie de Messire Expilly, chevalier, conseilleur du roi en son Conseil d'estat et président au parlement du Grenoble.* Grenoble 1660

Clément, Pierre, ed. *Lettres, instructions et mémoires de Colbert.* 8 vols. Paris 1861–82

de la Croix, Jean. *Apurement des défenses du parlement de Grenoble.* Paris 1602 [BM Grenoble]

Delagrange, Claude. *Stylus curiae majoris Viennesii et Valentinessi.* Lyon 1581 [BM Grenoble]

– *La Juste Plainte et remonstrance faite au roi et à nosseigneurs de son Conseil d'estat par le pauvre peuple de Dauphiné.* Lyon 1597 [BM Grenoble]

– *Réponses et salutations des pièces produites par les gens du tiers estat du Dauphiné.* Paris 1599 [BM Grenoble]

Depping, G.B., ed. *La Correspondance administrative sous le règne de Louis XIV.* Vol. IV. Paris 1855

Dufos, Julien. *Défense de la noblesse de Dauphiné contre les demandes du tiers estat de la même province contenues en deux requêtes du 23 juillet 1595 et 14 mai 1597.* Paris 1601 [BM Grenoble]

de l'Etoile, Pierre. *Journal de Henri III, de Henri IV et de Louis XII.* Vols. XLV–XLIX of *Mémoires pour servir à l'histoire de la France.* Paris 1926

Expilly, Claude. *Playdoyez de M. Claude Expilly.* Lyon 1636 [AD Drôme]

Giroud, Alexandre, ed. *Recueil des édits, déclarations, lettres patentes et ordonnances du roi ... concernant en général et en particulier la province de Dauphiné.* 26 vols. Grenoble 1690

Goulart, Simon. *Mémoires de la Ligue.* 20 vols. Amsterdam 1758

Guérin, Antoine (presumed author). 'Un soulèvement populaire à Romans à la fin du XVIe siècle.' In *Un soulèvement populaire (Romans, 1580)*, ed. P. Venault, P. Blon, and J. Farges. Paris 1979

Guérin, François de. *Très-humbles remonstrances au roy par les gens du tiers estat.* Paris 1634 [BM Grenoble]

Lublinskaya, Alexandra, ed. *Documents pour servir à l'histoire de France au xvi*
siècle*. Moscow and Leningrad 1966

Mousnier, Roland, ed. *Lettres et mémoires adressés au Chancelier Séguier (1633–
1649)*. 2 vols. Paris 1964

Musy, Georges. *Très-humbles remonstrances au roy*. Paris 1634

Rabot, Jean de. *La Maison des Rabot*. ed. Jules Chevalier. Valence 1886

Rambaud, Antoine. 'Lettre servant d'apologie ou défense du premier plaidoyé
du tiers estat du Dauphiné.' Paris 1598. In *Plaidoyé pour le tiers estat*, app.

– *Plaidoyé pour le tiers estat du Dauphiné*. Lyon 1598 [BM Grenoble]

– *Second plaidoyé pour le tiers estat du Dauphiné*. Paris 1598 [BM Grenoble]

Romans, Joseph. *Documents sur la réforme et les Guerres de Religion en Dauphiné*.
Grenoble 1890. Repr. in *Bulletin de la société de statistique de l'Isère*, 3ᶜ série,
15 (1890)

Vincent, Jean. *Discours en forme de plaidoyé pour le tiers estat de Dauphiné*. Paris
1598 [BM Grenoble]

SECONDARY WORKS

Abel, W. *Crise agraires en Europe, xiiᵉ–xxᵉ siècles*. paris 1973

Allard, Guy. *Nobiliaire du Dauphiné*. Grenoble 1671

– *Dictionnaire historique, chronologique, géographique, généalogique ... du Dauphiné*.
Ed. H. Gabriel. 2 vols. Grenoble 1864. Repr. Geneva 1970

Anonymous. *Fastes consulaires et municipaux de la ville de Grenoble depuis l'année
1244*. Grenoble nd

Antoine, Michel. 'Le Régalement des tailles de 1623–1625.' *Revue historique*
265 (1981): 27–63

Arnaud, Eugène. *Histoire des protestants du Dauphiné aux xviᵉ, xviiᵉ et xviiiᵉ
siècles*. 3 vols. Paris 1875–6

Arriaza, A. 'Mousnier and Barber: The Theoretical Underpinning of the
"Society of Orders" in Early Modern Europe.' *Past and Present* 89 (1980):
39–57

Balsan, Alain. *Valence au grand siècle*. Valence 1973

Barbiche, Bernard. 'Les Commissaires députés pour le "régalement" des tailles
en 1598–99.' *Bibliothèque de l'Ecole des chartes* 118 (1960): 68–78

Beik, William. *Absolutism and Society in Seventeenth-Century France: State Power
and Provincial Aristocracy in Languedoc*. Cambridge 1985

Bercé, Yves-Marie. *Histoire des croquants. Etude des soulèvements populaires au xviiᵉ
siècle dans le sud-ouest de la France*. 2 vols. Geneva 1974

Berriat-St-Prix, Jacques. *Histoire du droit romain suivi de l'histoire de Cujas*. Paris 1821

Bitton, Davis. *The French Nobility in Crisis, 1540–1640*. Stanford, Calif., 1969

Bligny, B., ed. *Histoire du Dauphiné*. Toulouse 1973

Bonarel, Monique. 'La Population de Grenoble – Etude socio-démographique.' Thèse de doctorat, UER Histoire, Université de Grenoble 1975

Bonney, Richard. *Political Change in France under Richelieu and Mazarin, 1624–1661*. Oxford 1978

Bonnin, Bernard. 'La Terre et les paysans en Dauphiné au XVIIe siècle.' 4 vols. Thèse de doctorat, UER Histoire, Université de Lyon 1980

– 'Les Milieux dominants en Dauphiné au XVIIe siècle.' In *Lyon et l'Europe. Mélanges d'histoire offerts à Richard Gascon*. Lyon 1980

Bordes, A. *L'Administration provinciale et municipale en France au XVIIe siècle*. Paris 1972

Brun-Durand, Joseph. *Dictionnaire topographique du Département de la Drôme*. Paris 1891

– *Dictionnaire biographique et biblio-iconographique de la Drôme*. 2 vols. Grenoble 1901

Buisseret, David. 'A Stage in the Development of the French *Intendants*: The Reign of Henri IV.' *Historical Journal* 9 (1966): 27–38

Busquet, R. *Histoire des institutions de la Provence de 1482 à 1790*. Marseilles 1920

Cavard, Pierre. *La Réforme et les Guerres de Religion à Vienne*. Vienne 1950

Chamberland, Albert. 'La Répartition de la taille en 1597.' *Revue Henri IV* 1 (1905); rev. edn (1912): 82–5

– 'Le Budget de 1597.' *Revue Henri IV* 1 (1905); rev. edn (1907–8): 15–20

– 'Les Recettes de l'Epargne en 1581 et une erreur de Forbonnais.' *Revue Henri IV* 3 (1909): 103–7

Chartier, R., and J. Nagle. 'Les Cahiers de doléances de 1614.' *Annales: ESC* 28, no. 6 (1973): 1484–94

Charronnet, Charles. *Les Guerres de Religion et la société protestante dans les Hautes-Alpes (1560–1579)*. Gap 1861

Chaunu, Pierre. *L'Etat et la Ville*. Vol. I., pt 1, of *Histoire économique et sociale de la France*, ed. Fernand Braudel and Ernest Labrousse. 4 vols. Paris 1977

Chevalier, B. 'The Policy of Louis XI toward the *Bonnes Villes*: The Case of Tours.' In *The Recovery of France in the Fifteenth Century*, ed. P.S. Lewis. New York 1971

Chevalier, Jules. *Mémoires pour servir à l'histoire des comptés de Valentinois et de Diois*. 2 vols. Paris 1897

– *Essai historique sur l'Eglise et la ville de Die*. 4 vols. Valence 1909

Chevalier, U. 'Annales de la ville de Romans pendant les Guerres de Religion de 1549 à 1599.' *Bulletin de la Société départementale d'archéologie et de statistique de la Drôme* 10 (1876): 170–5

Chomel, Vital. 'Le Dauphiné sous l'ancien régime.' *Cahiers d'histoire* 8 (1963): 303–36

– *Histoire de Grenoble.* Toulouse 1976

Chorier, Nicolas. *Histoire générale de Dauphiné.* 2 vols. Grenoble 1661. Repr. Grenoble 1971

– *Estat politique de la province de Dauphiné.* 4 vols. Grenoble 1671

– *La Vie d'Artus Prunier.* Ed. Alfred Vellot. Paris 1880

Church, William F. *Constitutional Thought in Sixteenth-Century France.* Cambridge, Mass., 1941

Clamageran, J.-J. *Histoire de l'impôt en France.* 3 vols. Paris 1868

Collins, J.B. 'Sur l'histoire fiscale du xviie: les impôts directs en Champagne entre 1595 et 1635.' *Annales: ESC* 34 (1979): 325–42

Coston, Baron de. *Histoire de Montélimar et des principales familles qui ont habité cette ville.* 4 vols. Montélimar 1878–91

Délachenal, R. *Une petite ville de Dauphiné, Histoire de Cremieu.* Grenoble 1889

Delille, Gérard. 'La Propriété foncière à Vourey au xvie et xviie siècles.' Mémoire de maîtrise, UER Histoire, Université de Grenoble 1968

Delumeau, Jean. 'Fondements idéologiques de la hiérarchie sociale: le discours sur le courage.' In *Théorie et pratique politique à la Renaissance.* xviie Colloque International de Tours. Paris 1977

Devert, Michel. 'Recherches sur la vie et l'oeuvre de Jean de MontLuc, 1502–1579.' 2 vols. Thèse de doctorat, Université de Bordeaux III 1978

Dewald, Jonathan. *The Formation of a Provincial Nobility.* Princeton 1980

Deyon, Pierre. 'A propos le rapports entre la noblesse française et la monarchie absolue pendant la première moitié du xviie siècle.' *Revue historique* 230 (1964): 341–56

– *Amiens, capitale provinciale, étude de la société urbaine au xviie siècle.* Paris 1967

Dolan-Leclerc, Claire. 'Renaissance: le premier siècle du régime français.' In *Histoire d'Aix-en-Provence.* Aix 1977

Doucet, Roger. *Les Institutions de la France au xvie siècle.* 2 vols. Paris 1948

Druout, Henri. *Mayenne et la Bourgogne: étude sur la Ligue (1587–1597).* 2 vols. Paris 1937

Duby, G., and A. Wallon, eds. *Histoire de la France rurale.* Vol. II. Paris 1975

Dupont-Ferrier, G. *Les Officiers des bailliages et sénéchaussées et les institutions monarchiques locales en France à la fin du Moyen Age.* Paris 1902. Repr. Geneva 1974

Dussert, Auguste. 'Les Etats du Dauphiné aux xive et xve siècles.' *Bulletin de l'Académie delphinale*, 5e série, 8 (1914)
– 'Les Etats du Dauphiné de la Guerre de Cent Ans aux Guerres de Religion (1457–1559).' *Bulletin de l'Académie delphinale*, 5e série, 8, 2e partie (1922)
– 'Le Baron des Adrets et les Etats du Dauphiné. Essai d'organisation protestante durant la première guerre de religion.' *Bulletin de l'Académie delphinale*, 5e série, 20 (1929): 93–136
– 'Catherine de Médicis et les Etats de Dauphiné.' *Bulletin de l'Académie delphinale*, 6e série, 2 (1931): 123–89
Egret, Jean. *Le Parlement de Dauphiné et les affaires publiques dans la deuxième moitié du XVIIIe siècle*. 2 vols. Grenoble 1942
Esmonin, Edmund. *Etudes sur la France des XVIIe et XVIIe siècles*. Paris 1964
Estèbe, Janine. 'La Bourgeoisie marchande et la terre à Toulouse au xvie siècle, 1519–1560.' *Annales du Midi* 76 (1964): 457–67
Fauché-Prunelle, A. 'Le Livre du roy.' *Bulletin de l'Académie delphinale*, 1ère série, 1 (1846)
– 'Procès-verbal des Etats de 4 juillet 1578.' *Bulletin de l'Académie delphinale*, 1ère série, 1 (1846): 557–61
– *Essai sur les anciennes institutions autonomes ou populaires des Alpes cottiennes-briançonnaises*. 2 vols. Grenoble and Paris 1856–7
Faucher, Daniel. *Plaines et bassins du Rhône moyen*. Valence 1967
Favier, René. 'Les Assemblées du Dauphiné après la suspension des Etats en 1628.' *Cahiers d'histoire* 24 (1979): 59–70
Gascon, Richard. 'Immigration et croissance au xvie siècle: l'exemple de Lyon.' *Annales: ESC* 25 (1970): 988–1001
– *Grand commerce et vie urbaine au XVIe siècle. Lyon et ses marchands*. 2 vols. Paris 1971
Gaudissard, Daniel, and Jean-Paul Pascal. 'L'Appropriation citaden dans les campagnes de l'Isère au xviie siècle.' Mémoire de maîtrise, UER Histoire, Université de Grenoble 1977
Gay, Thomas and Gaspard. *Mémoires des Frères Gay pour servir à l'histoire des Guerres de Religion en Dauphiné*. Ed. Jules Chevalier. Montbéliard 1888
Giordanengo, Gérard. 'Les Roturiers possesseurs de fiefs nobles en Dauphiné au xive et xve siècles.' *Cahiers d'histoire* 15 (1970): 322–34
Goubert, Pierre. *Beauvais et Beauvaisis de 1600 à 1730*. 2 vols. Paris 1960
– 'L'Ancienne Société d'ordres: verbiage ou réalité.' In *Colloque Franco-Suisse d'histoire économique*. Genève 1969
– *L'Ancien Régime*. 2 vols. Paris 1969, 1973
Guiffrey, J.J. *Histoire de la réunion de Dauphiné à la France*. Paris 1868

Gutton, Jean-Pierre. *Villages du Lyonnais sous la monarchie (XVIe–XVIIe siècles).* Centre d'histoire économique et sociale de la région Lyonnaise. Lyon 1968
– *La Sociabilité villageoise sous l'ancien régime.* Paris 1980
Hickey, Daniel. 'Politics and Commerce in Renaissance France: The Evolution of Trade along the Routes of Dauphiné.' *Canadian Journal of History* 6, no. 2 (1971): 133–51
– 'The Socio-Economic Context of the French Wars of Religion. A Case Study: The Valentinois-Diois.' PH D diss., McGill 1973
– 'Changing Expressions of Charity in Early Modern France.' *Renaissance and Reformation* ns 2 (1978): 12–22
– 'Une remise en question: procès des tailles et blocage social.' *Cahiers d'histoire* 23 (1978): 25–49
Huppert, G. *The Idea of Perfect History.* Urbana, Ill, 1970
Jacquart, Jean. *La Crise rurale en Ile-de-France, 1550–1670.* Paris 1974
– 'Réflections sur la communauté d'habitants.' *Bulletin du Centre d'histoire économique et sociale de la région lyonnaise* no. 3 (1976): 1–25
Kelly, Donald R. *Foundations of Modern Historical Scholarship, Law and History in the French Renaissance.* New York 1970
Lacroix, André. *L'Arrondissement de Montélimar, géographie, histoire et statistique.* 8 vols. Valence 1868–93. Repr. Paris 1973
– *Inventaire sommaire des archives départementales de la Drôme.* 8 vols. Valence 1872–1910
– *St-Marcellin, excursions dans la vallée de l'Isère.* Grenoble 1875
– *L'Arrondissement de Nyons.* 2 vols. Valence 1888–1901
– 'Claude Brosse et les Tailles.' *Bulletin de la Société départementale d'archéologie et de statistique de la Drôme* 2e série, 31 (1897): 181–90, 289–99, 389–96; 32 (1898): 54–68, 142–60, 233–48, 363–71; 33 (1899): 75–80, 234–7, 307–23
Lacroix, André, and Charles Bellet. *Inventaire des archives communales antérieur à 1790: Tain.* Valence 1909
Latouche, Robert. 'Le Prix du blé à Grenoble du XVe au XVIIIe siècle.' *Revue d'histoire économique et sociale* (1932): 337–51
Laurens, Charles. *Le Procès des tailles (1537–1639), Claude Brosse, Antoine Rambaud.* Grenoble 1867
Le Roy Ladurie, Emmanuel. 'Sur Montpellier et sa campagne aux XVIe et XVIIe siècles.' *Annales: ESC* 12 (1957): 223–30
– 'Le Climat des XIe et XVIe siècles: séries comparées.' *Annales: ESC* 20 (1965): 903–21
– *Les Paysans de Languedoc.* 2 vols. Paris 1966
– *Carnival in Romans.* Trans. Mary Feeney. New York 1979

Letonnelier, G. *Répertoire des registres du fonds de la Chambre des comptes du Dauphiné.* Grenoble 1947

Long, J.D. *La Réforme et les Guerres de Religion en Dauphiné de 1560 à l'Edit de Nantes (1598).* Paris 1856. Repr. Geneva 1970

Loutchitzky, Jean. *Documents inédits pour servir à l'histoire de la Réforme et de la Ligue.* Kiev 1875

Lublinskaya, Alexandra D. *French Absolutism: The Crucial Phase, 1620–1629.* Cambridge 1968

Maignien, Edmund. *Catalogue des livres et manuscrits du fonds dauphinois de la Bibliothèque municipale de Grenoble.* 5 vols. Grenoble 1906–24

Major, J.R. 'Henry IV and Guyenne: A Study Concerning the Origins of Royal Absolutism.' *French Historical Studies* 4, no. 4 (1966): 363–83

– 'Bellièvre, Sully and the Assembly of Notables of 1596.' *Transactions of the American Philosophical Society* ns 64, pt 2 (1974): 1–34

– *Representative Government in Early Modern France.* New Haven, Conn., 1980

– 'Noble Income, Inflation and the Wars of Religion in France.' *American Historical Review* 86, no. 1 (1981): 21–48

Mandrou, Robert. 'Les Soulèvements populaires dans la société française du XVIIᵉ siècle.' *Annales: ESC* 14 (1959): 756–65

– *Introduction à la France moderne.* Paris 1961

– *Magistrats et sorciers en France au XVIIᵉ siècle.* Paris 1980

Mariéjol, J.H. *Henri IV et Louis XIII.* Vol. VI, pt 2, of *Histoire de France depuis les origines jusqu'à la Révolution,* ed. Ernest Lavisse. 9 vols. Paris 1900–11. Repr. New York 1969

Martin, J.-C. *Histoire et vie de Claude Expilly.* Grenoble 1803

Masson-Fauchier, Christiane. 'L'Anoblissement en Dauphiné au XVIIᵉ siècle (1598–1668).' Mémoire de maîtrise, UER Histoire, Université de Grenoble II 1971

Mesnard, Pierre. 'La Place du Cujas dans la querelle de l'humanisme juridique.' *Revue historique de droit français et étranger* 4ᵉ série, 28ᵉ année (1950): 526–337

Michaud, H. *La Grande Chancellerie et les écritures royales au seizième siècle, 1515–1589.* Paris 1967

Morel, M.J. 'Le Vagabondage et la mendicité au XVIᵉ siècle.' *Bulletin de la société dauphinoise d'ethnologie et d'anthropologie* 7 (1901): 104–22

Mousnier, Roland. *Les XVIᵉ et XVIIᵉ siècles.* Vol. IV, *Histoire générale des civilisations.* Paris 1965

– *Les Hierarchies sociales de 1450 à nos jours.* Paris 1969

– *La Plume, la Faucille et le Marteau.* Paris 1970

- *La Vénalité des offices sous Henri IV et Louis XIII.* Rouen 1945. Rev. edn, Paris 1971
- *L'Echantillon de 1634, 1635, 1636.* Vol. 1 of *La Stratification sociale à Paris aux XVIIᵉ et XVIIIᵉ siècles.* Paris 1976

Mousnier, Roland, J.H. Elliot, et al. 'Trevor-Roper's General Crisis.' *Past and Present* 17 (1960): 8–42

Nadal, Abbé J.C. *Histoire de l'Université de Valence et les autres établissements d'instruction de cette ville.* Valence 1861

Olivier, J. 'Expilly.' *Revue de Dauphiné* 6 (1839): 65–94

Pagès, Georges. 'Autour du "grand orage," Richelieu et Marillac. Deux politiques.' *Revue historique* 79(1937): 63–97
- 'Le Conseil du roi sous Louis XIII.' *Revue d'histoire moderne* 6 (1937): 293–324
- 'Le Conseil du roi et la vénalité des offices pendant les premières années du ministère de Richelieu.' *Revue historique* 82 (1938): 245–82

Parisot, P. 'Essai sur les procureurs au parlement de Bourgogne.' Mémoire de maîtrise, Université de Dijon 1909

Perroy, Edouard. 'Social Mobility among the French Noblesse in the Later Middle Ages.' *Past and Present* 21 (1962): 25–38

Picot, Georges. *Histoire des Etats généraux.* 4 vols. Paris 1872. Repr. Geneva 1979

Piémond, Eustache. *Mémoires de Eustache Piémond (1572–1608).* Ed. J. Brun-Durand. Valence 1885. Repr. Geneva 1973

Pillorget, René. *Les Mouvements insurrectionnels de Provence entre 1596 et 1715.* Paris 1975

Porchnev, Boris. *Les Soulèvements populaires en France de 1623 à 1648.* Paris 1963

Prudhomme, Auguste. *Inventaire sommaire des archives communales, ville de Grenoble.* 6 vols. Grenoble 1886–1926

Prudhomme, Auguste, and J.J.A. Pilot de Thorey. *Inventaire sommaire des archives antérieures à 1790, Isère, série B.* 4 vols. Grenoble 1864–1909

Ranum, Orest. *Richelieu and the Councillors of Louis XIII. A Study of the Secretaries of State and Superintendents of Finance in the Ministry of Richelieu, 1635–1642.* Oxford 1963

Raveau, Paul. *Agriculture et les classes paysannes: la transformation de la propriété dans le haut Poitou au XVIᵉ siècle.* Paris 1926

Richet, Denis. 'Autour des origines idéologiques lointaines de la Révolution française.' *Annales: ESC* 24 (1969): 1–23
- *La France moderne, l'esprit des institutions.* Paris 1973

Rivoire de la Bâtie, Georges. *Armorial de Dauphiné.* Lyon 1867

Robin, Regine. *La Société française en 1780: Semur-en-Aixois.* Paris 1970
Rochas, R. *Biographie du Dauphiné.* 2 vols. Paris 1856–60
Romans, Joseph. 'Catherine de Médicis en Dauphiné.' *Bulletin de l'Académie delphinale* 26 (Dec. 1882): 156–60, 293–305
Romier, Lucien. *Le Royaume de Catherine de Médicis.* 2 vols. Paris 1925
Rotelli, Ettore. 'La Structure sociale dans l'itinéraire historiographique de Roland Mousnier.' *Revue d'histoire économique et sociale* 50, no. 1 (1973): 145–82
St-Jacob, Pierre de. 'Mutations économiques et sociales dans les campagnes bourguigonnes à la fin du XVIᵉ siècle.' *Etudes rurales* 1 (1961): 34–49
– *Documents relatifs à la communauté villageoise en Bourgogne du milieu de XVIIᵉ siècle à la Révolution.* Paris 1962
Salmon, J.H.M. 'Venality of Office and Popular Sedition in Seventeenth-Century France.' *Past and Present* 37 (1967): 21–43
– *Society in Crisis: France in the Sixteenth Century.* New York 1975
Schalk, Ellery, 'The Appearance and Reality of Nobility in France during the Wars of Religion.' *Journal of Modern History* 48, no. 1 (1976): 19–31
Sclafert, Thérèse. *Le Haut-Dauphiné au moyen âge.* Paris 1926
Slicker Van Bath, B.H. *The Agrarian History of Western Europe.* London 1963
Solé, Jacques. 'Le Dauphiné dans la correspondance du Chancelier Séguier,' *Cahiers d'histoire* 11 (1966): 385–405
Sutherland, N.M. *The French Secretaries of State in the Age of Catherine de Médicis.* London 1962
Tilley, Charles. *The Vendée.* Cambridge, Mass., 1964
Trebillod, Marie-Françoise. 'Etude du registre de l'assemblée de la noblesse en Dauphiné entre 1602 et 1622.' Mémoire de maîtrise, UER Histoire, Université de Grenoble II 1970
Trevor-Roper, H.R. 'The General Crisis of the Seventeenth Century.' *Past and Present* 16 (1959): 31–64
Vaissière, Pierre de. *Gentilhomme campagnard de l'ancienne France.* Paris 1903
Valbonnaise, Jean-Pierre Moret de Bourchenu, Marquis de. *Histoire de Dauphiné et des princes qui ont porté le nom de Dauphin.* 2 vols. Geneva 1722
Valois, Noël. *Inventaire des arrêts du Conseil d'état, règne de Henri IV.* 2 vols. Paris 1866–93
Van Doren, L. Scott. 'Wars, Taxes and Social Protest. The Challenge to Authority in Sixteenth-Century Dauphiné.' PH D diss., Harvard 1970
– 'Revolt and Reaction in Romans, 1579–1580.' *Sixteenth Century Journal* 5, no. 1 (Apr. 1974): 71–100
– 'Civil War Taxation and the Foundations of Fiscal Absolutism.' *Proceedings*

of the Third Annual Meeting of the Western Society for French Historical Studies
(1976): 35–53
– 'War Taxation, Institutional Change and Social Conflict in Provincial France
– The Royal *Taille* in Dauphiné, 1494–1559.' *Proceedings of the American
Philosophical Society* 121, no. 1 (1977): 70–96
Vindry, Fleury. *Les Parlementaires français au xvi˟ siècle*. Paris 1909
Wallerstein, Immanuel. *The Modern World System. Capitalist Agriculture and the
Origins of the European World Economy in the Sixteenth Century*. New York 1974
Weary, William A. 'Royal Policy and Patronage in Renaissance France: The
Monarchy and the House of La Trémoille.' PH D diss., Yale 1972
Weill, Georges-Jacques. *Les Théories sur le pouvoir royal en France pendant les
Guerres de Religion*. Paris 1892
Wolfe, Martin. *The Fiscal System of Renaissance France*. New Haven 1972
Wood, James B. *The Nobility of the Election of Bayeux, 1463–1666. Continuity
through Change*. Princeton 1980
Zeller, Gaston. 'L'Administration monarchique avant les intendants Parlements
et gouverneurs.' *Revue historique* 197 (1947): 180–215

Index